My Road to Radio
and *The Vocal Scene*

My Road to Radio
and *The Vocal Scene*

Memoir of an Opera Commentator

George Jellinek

McFarland & Company, Inc., Publishers
Jefferson, North Carolina, and London

LIBRARY OF CONGRESS CATALOGUING-IN-PUBLICATION DATA

Jellinek, George, 1919–
    My road to radio and the Vocal Scene : memoir of an opera
commentator / George Jellinek.
        p.   cm.
    Includes index.

    ISBN-13: 978-0-7864-2823-6
    (softcover : 50# alkaline paper) ∞

    1. Jellinek, George, 1919–   2. Music critics — United States —
Biography.   3. Radio journalists — United States — Biography.
I. Title.
ML423.J45A3   2007
780.82 — dc22   2006037526
[B]

British Library cataloguing data are available

On the cover: Violins ©2006 PhotoSpin;
George Jellinek *(photo by Mortimer H. Frank)*

Manufactured in the United States of America

McFarland & Company, Inc., Publishers
    Box 611, Jefferson, North Carolina 28640
    www.mcfarlandpub.com

Acknowledgments

My wife Hedy has shared more than 65 years of my life; her influence and this book are inseparable. I also acknowledge the wisdom and affection of Richard Curtis, my literary agent. And I thank my dear friend, the eminent novelist Shirley Hazzard, for her many valuable suggestions.

Portions of my book saw publication in different forms in *The New York Times*, *Opera News*, *Stereo Review*, and *On the Air*.

Contents

1. Prologue

On May 16, 1991, a lovely tribute was organized by Francis Heilbut of the American Landmark Festivals to celebrate the centenary of Richard Tauber, the great Austrian tenor. It was held at the Castle Clinton National Monument at the Battery in downtown New York. The guests of honor were Marta Eggerth and Jarmila Novotná, both operetta queens in their day. Both had known Richard Tauber and Franz Lehár personally, and Jarmila Novotná had been Tauber's partner in the Vienna world premiere of Lehár's *Giuditta* in 1934.

There was a magic quality in Tauber's singing. The voice itself was not conventionally beautiful, but with a combination of solid musicianship and a virtuosic technical mastery, he could produce wondrous effects of melting lyricism. I never saw Tauber on stage, but his name was legendary already in my youth, and he became one of the crucial elements in my budding collection of vocal records. As I was to learn much later from a Viennese gentleman who had been Tauber's personal representative at one time, he was making a great deal of money in his prime years but, living a luxurious life style, he was forever in need of money. Consequently, he did not believe in record royalties. It was cash on the line for Tauber, and he recorded endlessly, often meretricious stuff that he had a way of turning into bestselling gold.

May 16, 1991, was a lovely spring day; the intimate event was attended by New York's Viennese colony and many Tauber aficionados. My wife Hedy, a native of Vienna, and I have been treasuring photographs linking us with Jarmila Novotná and Marta Eggerth, forever glamorous personalities, all in the shadow of the still-towering World Trade Center. I felt very much at home in their company. The art of Richard Tauber was one of the enduring links to my childhood, along with phonographic and cinematic memories of Jarmila and Marta. The common bond was our Central Euro-

1

pean ancestry and the émigré experience. Many of us felt a special closeness to the great tenor who had also been torn from his roots, though famous
enough and fortunate enough to land in England and to survive the war,
recording prodigiously with his vocal gifts almost intact until his untimely
end in 1948.

My own thoughts kept wondering about that "émigré experience." In
1991 I was already in my seventies, four years of my life having been spent
in the U.S. Army. I was thoroughly Americanized in my thinking, with an
American-born and educated child and grandchild. In my frequent visits
to Europe, I was always conscious of my American identity and felt rather
distanced from European politics and mores. At the same time, I was never
alienated from European culture and the music of Hungary and Austria,
absorbed in my early childhood. The operas of Erkel and Kodály, or the
dance elements in the music of Schubert, Brahms, and the Strausses — had
remained firmly anchored in my consciousness. To that extent, I suppose,
I couldn't help clinging to a kind of cultural double identity — a point driven
home to me by the example of Richard Tauber, who may have lived in London and traveled with a British passport but remained identified to his dying
day with a bygone era that virtually ended with World War I and its aftermath.

Four years after that memorable Tauber centenary, I was commissioned
by *Opera News* to write an article entitled "World War II, the Met and the
American Singer." That article rekindled memories of the artists I recalled
from my years as a new American. Music, and particularly opera, seemed
like a lasting link connecting my past and present. Much has happened to
me over my lifespan. Mine was a life that plunged me from benign seren-
ity to a tragedy from which I never really recovered, but it still evolved into
something fulfilling and prideful. It was a life enriched by a devoted and
ever-supportive wife, aided along the way by a few significant mentors, but
essentially brought to fruition by grave challenges overcome by discipline
and endurance. And, what may be briefly summarized as an unconventional
yet truly American success story, it began in Hungary, a troubled land at
the very center of Europe.

2. Childhood

In 1918, at the close of World War I, the Austro-Hungarian monarchy became history. While the victorious Allies were deciding its fate, Hungary, permanently separated from Austria, abruptly became a republic. Its inept provisional government drifted into a communist regime that was soon swept aside, allowing the country to sink into a period of bloody chaos. Humiliated by the treaty of Trianon (at Versailles), which deprived Hungary of substantial territories, the frustrated and vengeful reactionary elements hunted down communists, pacifists, intellectuals, Jews, and other defenseless targets until a new government was formed under the regency of Admiral Nicholas Horthy, on March 1, 1920. Clearly, the safest place to be in those awful days preceding that historic occasion was a cradle where I found myself on December 22, 1919. As I learned much later, my father, Daniel, then 29 years old, was traumatized by those events. The specter of communism, and the subsequent bloody reaction to it, was to haunt him for many years.

Ujpest (New Pest), a town of some 70,000 inhabitants, where I was born, was the northern industrial suburb of Budapest. Incorporated into the capital in 1950, it presented a rather drab assortment of one- and two-story buildings in my youth, not exactly embellished later by a series of mass-produced, Soviet-style residential projects hastily constructed to relieve the postwar housing shortage. To the east, the town bordered on what we used to call the *Kis Duna* (Little Danube), a branch of the great river that merged into its mighty source further north. It was a repository of docks and offices of Danubian shipping commerce and — more important to me personally — the location of a swimming pool of unbelievable simplicity — actually an ingenious contraption of wooden beams and rafters. Looking back, I now assume that the entire *Kis Duna* area was an ecological nightmare, but it was summertime heaven for us kids and, incidentally, many members of Hungary's Olympic champion water polo teams launched their careers in those rather unsanitary waters.

My father was born in a village slightly to the north of Ujpest. He was one of seven children and, having lost his own father in early childhood, had only a limited education. Together with his siblings, he had to assist my grandmother in trying to survive those very difficult times. A serious leg injury exempted him from military service, but he lost two of his brothers in the first world war, two uncles whom I knew only from faded family pictures. All these are submerged in a dimly remembered past. My parents, who were second cousins, married in 1918. By the time I came into this world, my mother, Jolán, who had been working as a bookkeeper for an architectural firm in Ujpest, had given give up her job in order to assist my father in running a garden restaurant at the invisible border line separating Ujpest and Budapest, in the shadow of a railway bridge across the Danube.

My first distinct childhood memory is of walking with my mother toward that restaurant and being accosted by one of my mother's friends: "Well, little Gyuri, would you prefer to have a new brother or a sister?" I was, of course, thoroughly baffled by such a strange question put to a three year old, but the mystery was soon solved by the arrival of my sister Éva (Évi) on November 2, 1923 — a plump, tiny, dark-eyed brunette who later showed some of my father's features, while I, with blue eyes and light complexion, seemed to inherit my mother's characteristics in more ways than one.

My mother was the oldest of seven siblings. How on earth these grandparents of mine — all with modest, lower middle-class means — managed to bring up all those children I'll never know. My grandfather was a grocer in what was in my childhood a very pleasant neighborhood opposite one of Ujpest's public schools. The school was still there in the year 2000, and so was the building that housed my grandfather's store and apartment, but the entire area was in drastic need of whatever the Hungarian term may be for "urban renewal."

My maternal grandfather, Mark, was a kindly and jovial man, neatly groomed and with a becoming white mustache. I was his first grandchild, and he gave me little tasks around the store to make me feel important. Once he took me to a thermal bath in Budapest's famous Margaret Island (not more than 30 or 40 minutes away on the streetcar), a memorable occasion for both of us. I recall spending many days in my grandparents' roomy and friendly house while my parents were working. Two of my mother's sisters were still unmarried in my pre-school years; the younger, Irene, was briefly courted by Károly Kárpáti, a local sports hero (later an Olympic wrestling champion in 1936) and that made me very proud. The older of the sisters, Hermine, was a very talented violinist. Her parents, of modest means, felt it their duty to develop the gifts of such a daughter. Her violin teacher, named Antal Wolf, approached my mother when I was about five, suggesting that he might take me on as a student. My mother wisely countered that I should start elementary school first, but Wolf persisted, no doubt driven by business reasons, but claiming that I was talented. No mother can resist that kind of persuasion, so Antal Wolf began coming to our (actually, my grandfather's) house, introducing me to the mysteries of violin playing while holding me in his lap. He acquainted me with the violin clef, the musical

With my violin at age 6.

notes, the accidentals, until I was able to handle my tiny violin and began to produce recognizable sounds on my two feet, as I was about to enter school.

My grandfather suddenly died while I spent a night in his house. My father awakened me with the sad news as my mother and all her sisters and brothers gathered, filling the house with their disconsolate weeping. Hermine soon married a young man; they took over running the grocery store. Her own violin studies abruptly ended as I was beginning modestly to improve mine, no doubt encouraged by my aunt's example, though suspecting that I could never match Hermine's promising gifts. I continued visiting that old grocery store during my first school years, and eagerly rummaged through my grandfather's illustrated volumes of history, finding horrendous illustrations of the French Revolution with severed heads all over the place, and other atrocities. On the reverse of that the coin, I was reading stories about of a wondrous land across the ocean, where streetcars seemed to run atop the buildings, and skyscrapers were rising beyond the imagination of any Ujpest resident. In another Sunday magazine I also read with enthusiasm about the world champion fight between Jack Dempsey and Gene Tunney. Remote America seemed a land of marvels to me at age 6 or 7. One of my father's sisters had married a young man who had emigrated there, but my parents gently spared me the details of the break-up of that marriage, and of my aunt's sad lot thereafter.

It was our mother who guided our lives; our father was busy in the restaurant, but came home every day for his delicious mid-day meal, fussing over little Éva and treating me, the older bother, with an affectionate but serious formality. There was a gypsy band in our garden restaurant. When the *primás* learned about my violin playing, he became curious, and my father brought me down one afternoon to see if I could learn from them. Gypsy musicians, I soon discovered, never had to practice. They just played, and I was encouraged to try gypsy tunes with them, in my elementary fashion. The *primás* wanted me to stay for dinnertime, displaying me to the customers, but my father summarily dismissed the idea. I returned for short sessions later on. However brief the experience, "playing by ear"—which means finding the exact pitch without the benefit of printed music—is an invaluable asset. I continued cultivating it in later years, as an entertaining antidote to what was as yet a fairly indifferent attitude to my academic training.

3. School Years

My father's garden restaurant was on city property. Early in my elementary school days, the city reclaimed it, to broaden the area that was supporting the overhead railroad bridge, and my father had to move the business elsewhere. This ended my adventure with the gypsy band, although my violin studies continued in a routine and rather predictable fashion. My father opened a tavern nearby, which prospered well enough, but it was a definite downward step for him. Without the restaurant, with its comfortable middle-class atmosphere, the new business attracted dock and factory workers — not a place for small children to visit. My father "diversified" by starting a wholesale wine business, supplying smaller stores, using a nearby cellar as his business center. Later, around 1928, he bought a house near Ujpest's central market place, with a cellar of its own. The wine was delivered by a newly acquired and much-beloved horse named "Csillag" ("Star"), driven by an old family retainer I called "Marci bácsi," a barber by trade, moonlighting for us first as a coachman and, in later years, as an occasional driver. He was notorious for his profane language, for which he constantly apologized, but which I found vastly entertaining and, introducing me to unfamiliar elements in the Hungarian language, eminently instructive.

In retrospect, my four years of elementary school seemed like a series of games, excursions, and little else, yet I must have managed to learn a great deal, for my preparation for the next level was more than adequate. Hungary's educational system in those years consisted of four years of elementary school, followed by eight years of high school, called gymnasium. My mother was the real guide for us in those years. My father was a less immediate presence, always returning home for the midday meal, during which my sister and I were expected to behave decorously and, to use our mother's favorite expression, "honorably." For such a gentle person, she was a surprisingly strict disciplinarian, always concerned about proper behavior, blending a kind of babying boundless love with unexpected bursts of raised tone and occasional spankings to keep both of us in line. She would occasionally remind us that her spanking was an alternative to "telling your father about" our occasional misdeeds, leaving no doubt that we would prefer her chosen alternative. I was a relatively mild and bookish lad in those days, with an unfortunate penchant for involving myself in games that often resulted in personal injuries, which occasioned parental distress and consolation. My sister Éva already had a sharp tongue, and her occasional cheekiness often aroused our mother's swift reaction. Whether or not our father was belatedly involved in these matters is immaterial. He spanked me only once, and for good reason, but my sister never — she was always "daddy's little girl."

My musical studies continued their leisurely pace. Wolf was a rather undemanding teacher. I advanced to the required etudes by Dancla and Viotti, also to certain Mozart sonatas, but practiced relatively little, always veering into some Franz Lehár and Hungarian tunes. Playing by ear was more fun. Wolf had us learn a brief encore piece for the season-ending concert, with parents attending. He called me a "troubadour" because I always asked for selections of limited technical demand, such as Nevin's "Narcissus," Simonetti's "Madrigal," Dřdla's "Souvenir," etc. I had the feeling that Wolf made a good living from collecting money from appreciative parents. Surely, no one was more appreciative than my father, who was determined to shower everything on me that he himself had never enjoyed in his spartan childhood. He attended all these concerts and, in his total lack of objective judgment, regarded me as a violinist of unusual gifts. Nonetheless, I did progress. Wolf even engaged several of his students in chamber music classes — piano trios and string quartets. With my dutiful but rarely enthusiastic attitude, I pursued and even managed to enjoy them.

The gymnasium in Ujpest was named after one of the early kings of Hungary, Kálmán I. He was known in history as "Könyves Kálmán" (Kálmán of the Books) because he was regarded more as a scholar than a warrior in the 12th century, when Hungary was still a semi-civilized, endlessly warring nation. The gymnasium was a very strict institution with high academic standards, and discipline was mercilessly enforced. Those who couldn't keep up intellectually or who did not abide by school discipline were mercilessly flunked out or summarily eliminated. Discipline was no problem for me, but, after the four elementary years requiring virtually no concentration, it took me some time to adjust to a school that really meant business. Within a few months, however, I got the point.

Compared to American standards, the Ujpest gymnasium had an amazing curriculum. From the second year, German was added as an obligatory foreign language. Studies in Latin also began in the second year and never stopped, giving us seven years of Latin, an invaluable asset. In the fifth year, another language was added. In most high schools that would have meant either English or French. Our school belonged to the exceptional few where Italian was taught. Mussolini had become a champion of Hungary's territorial aspirations after 1920; the Italian government created an institution in Rome where young Hungarian scholars were taught to become teachers of Italian language and literature. They were a highly trained group, and taught us well. I fell in love with the Italian language instantly, finding it a very easy companion to my Latin, and my affection for the lovely musical sound of that language has never left me.

Actually, my early life could have easily projected what my later years were to bring. I was interested in history, geography, languages, and Hungarian literature. Basic mathematics and geometry entertained me up to a point, but I had difficulty with advanced algebra; physics baffled me, and chemistry found no response in me. In none of these subjects were my grades poor, but I needed the help of a friend Joe Marton (later a chemistry professor in Göteborg, Sweden, and, later still, an eminent scientist with a prominent American company).

I played soccer for the class team that competed in the inter-school league during our last four years, but soccer soon got me into trouble. One day after school, I was persuaded by some friends not to go home for lunch but to repair to a soccer field for some meaningless kicking. It was a stupid thing to do, knowing how ceremonial my father was about those mid-day meals. When I finally got home, I deservedly paid for my idiocy and, as I recall, my father was quite unsparing. After administering what was coming to me, he characteristically said: "I lost a lot of respect for you," which I thought rather an adult expression to waste on an immature kid. About a week later, my father surprised me with a brand new soccer ball, all my own. No further mention was made of the incident. He never again laid his hand on me and, of course, I learned my lesson. (In those days, excuses like "peer pressure" were not yet known.)

Early in my gymnasium years, I joined the juvenile swimming team of the Ujpest club (UTE) and participated with some success in interscholastic swimming competitions. For water polo, a Hungarian national sport, I had the enthusiasm but not quite the right physique, being a rather slender youth in my early teens. Sports always interested me, especially at the time of the 1932 Olympics in Los Angeles, where Hungarian athletes did remarkably well, and I followed their exploits with rapt attention. It was in 1932 that I lost my paternal grandmother, a remarkable physical specimen, but an old lady of severe manners that discouraged true affection.

She had brought up seven children under straitened circumstances, losing two of them in World War I. Two others would have tragic destinies, but my father, his older brother Ernö and his older sister Frida succeeded in life. In her advanced years, my grandmother divided her time between the households of her children Ernö, Frida, and Daniel, but she was always difficult and interfering. When she was with us, I often found my mother weeping. I understood the reason and held it against my grandmother. Eventually, my father and uncle found an attractive home for the elderly in the Buda hills, where my grandmother spent her final years in relative contentment, receiving frequent visits from her devoted children and dutifully obedient grandchildren. She passed away quietly, mentally strong as ever. At her funeral, I observed my father crying for the first time in my life. I was to see this only once more: the day he said goodbye to me, seven years later, perhaps sensing that it would be forever.

4. Hastened Maturity

In 1932, Gyula Gömbös became the prime minister of Hungary, a politician of the far right who, when Hitler came to power in Germany the following year, became well known to us as a Nazi-sympathizer. Hungary, still wounded by the territorial losses caused by World War I, entered a period of ardent jingoism, with much agitation against the neighboring Czechs, Rumanians, and Yugoslavs. The history they taught us at the gymnasium was severely influenced by the country's political climate and, however uninformed most of us students were about the outside world, we did sense that dangerous trends were developing as we followed the aggressive tone and actions of the new Germany.

Along with the government's increasingly pro–Nazi attitudes, there was a Communist scare, as well. The Communist Party had been illegal since 1919, but there were secret adherents among the students, and two of my older schoolmates were expelled for that reason. My father, remembering the fearful years of his youth, though always voting for the liberal democrats, often told me that, while we had reasons to worry about our semi-fascist government, we needed the conservative party (whomever the premier may have been) because "we need Horthy and we need authority and security." My father's anti–Communist attitude remained with me all my life, especially as my political experience widened and enabled me to learn about the oppression and paranoia that lay beneath the veneer of the idealistic Marxist dogmas. It was nonetheless a shock to learn that one of my closest friends, János Nyerges, was a secret Communist. Both of us being avid readers and frequenters of antique bookstores, he once guided me to a Budapest underground shop specializing in Marxist literature. He trusted me to keep this particular episode secret, and we remained friends for a long time thereafter, but he soon became convinced that, ideologically and politically we were, and continued to remain, poles apart.

Politics, actually, played little part in my teen-age life. At 15, my mother persuaded me (forced me, actually) to enroll in a dancing school jointly organized by the gymnasium and its all-girl affiliated lyceum where, eventually, my little sister Évi also entered. I considered dancing a silly pastime at that point in my life. (I matured later on, but my basic attitude toward social dancing didn't change all that much.) In my studies, I explored my German and Italian classes with rapt attention. My German teacher, a youngish man named Dr. Elemér Rácz, was delighted to discover my interest in the poems of Goethe, Schiller, and Heine, and encouraged my poetic translations into Hungarian. Some of these were published in the school newspaper and, frankly, they were pretty good. At the same time, I remained convinced that such translations, even the best of them, could hardly hope to capture the style and spirit of the originals. It takes a true poet, as well as a master of both languages, to create a reasonable facsimile — a daunting task.

My musical studies gained a new dimension when I joined the gymnasium orchestra which performed at various patriotic and holiday events, playing the ubiquitous *Rákóczi March* and other Hungarian specialties by Liszt, Erkel, Kodály, Weiner, and minor Hungarian composers. On a memorable occasion, we performed the second-act Germont-Violetta duet from Verdi's *La traviata*. A talented local soprano sang Violetta, while the baritone was a "Könyves Kálmán" graduate named Andor Havas who, having completed his vocal studies in Italy, had recently returned home. Sitting in an exalted position next to the concertmaster, I drank it all in — a startling experience made even more memorable because we participated in a bilingual performance. Ever since, whenever I hear that music, my mind returns to the opening lines of the Act II duet, as we then played it:

> GERMONT: "Madamigella Valery?"
> VIOLETTA: "*Én vagyok.*"
> GERMONT: "D'Alfredo il padre in me vedete...."

We all had a great success. Our conductor, a former student at my gymnasium named Tamás Bródy, went on to an important career as an operetta conductor, and his name may be found on several Qualiton recordings. Soon after that momentous event, I went to my violin teacher Wolf and asked him to assign "something operatic" for the season-closing concert. He came up with a Fantasia on themes from *Rigoletto*, arranged for violin and piano by August Wilhelmj. I had known some of the melodies, but not the entire opera. I loved the piece and played it at the concert with great success — or so it seemed to my beaming parents in the audience.

Opera was a relatively new experience for me, but I had been exposed to operetta much earlier. On a summer vacation, our mother took us to Kolozsvár (the largest city in Transylvania, now generally known by its Rumanian name *Cluj*, but never to a Hungarian native). There we attended an open-air performance of Lehár's *Frasquita*, a novelty then, barely a decade old. I didn't know how to pronounce the title, but soon learned that I could pick out the opening melody on the piano of the famous "Serenade," made immediately popular by Richard Tauber, and also in a violin transcription by Fritz Kreisler. After *Frasquita,* the road led to Lehár's *Gypsy Love* at the Municipal Operetta Theater of Budapest, and to other operettas, culminating in the same composer's *The Land of Smiles*, which had been introduced at the Royal Hungarian Opera House. My fondness for Lehár's music, no secret to my radio audience, is traceable to those early experiences. But opera was still a fairly closed book to me until about 1935, my 16th year.

However, I soon began collecting operatic records, beginning with Caruso's "Di quella pira," a single-faced acoustical disc acquired at an antique shop for what seems like twenty-five cents in today's currency. One thing led to another, and I accumulated a decent collection of the great singers — Caruso, Gigli, Ruffo, Pinza — listening to them in awe, and expanding my knowledge of operatic music in the process. One of my schoolmates, Miklós Vermes, a cello student and fellow member of the school orchestra, also became bitten by the opera bug. Italian opera, in particular, affected us deeply, no doubt due to our increased familiarity with the language.

By then, we had discovered great Italian poetry in school, read parts of Dante's *Inferno*, the sonnets of Petrarca, and carefully selected stories from Boccaccio's *Decameron*. (The salacious bits from the same book my friend George Braun and I discovered in the library in which another friend held an administrative position.) I also discovered some great poetry by Giacomo Leopardi and struggled through the eloquent but rather difficult odes of Giosuè Carducci, the 1906 Nobel Prize winner. My growing knowledge of opera and my continued love of the Italian language formed a wonderful synergy that was to last for a lifetime.

Our teachers at the gymnasium ranged from mediocre to outstanding. There were some eccentrics among them, and a few mean ones. One teacher left a lasting impression on me. His name was Dezső Piroska and he taught Latin and Hungarian literature. Strangely enough, "Piroska" also means "Red Riding Hood" in Hungarian, but there was nothing childish about this man. He was strict, showed only an occasional sense of humor, tolerated no nonsense from us but, with his profound knowledge of both of his specialties, he inspired unanimous admiration. Being the malicious teenagers that we were, once we spent some time digging up ancient references in Hungarian lore and addressed him in class with impossible inquiries while pretending benign innocence, hoping to catch him in something he didn't know. It was to no avail — the man's knowledge in his subject was limitless. At the end of World War II, three of my former classmates and I (three of us in the U.S. and one in West Germany) combined our resources and sent $200 to one of my surviving cousins to surprise Prof. Piroska with a television set — a great luxury in communist Hungary, around 1950. And when I first returned to Hungary in 1965, I presented him with my freshly published first book, *Callas, Portrait of a Prima Donna,* with the following dedication: "To my beloved teacher Dezső Piroska who awakened in me the love of literature." The old man didn't speak any English, but I know that he treasured that memento from a onetime student whose life had taken an unexpected and distant path but who still fondly remembered his old teacher so many years later. I corresponded with "Uncle Dezső" until his death some three years later.

My academic and musical studies continued uneventfully through the middle thirties, but storms were gathering not only over Hungary's politics but over my seemingly placid home life, as well. My father grew impatient with his reasonably prosperous but otherwise limiting tavern and set his sights higher, hoping to open an upscale inn and restaurant in the center of Ujpest, across the street from the City Hall. He was encouraged to do so by the mayor himself, Aladár Semsey, a politically well-connected man of military bearing, universally popular across the party lines. Space was secured and construction soon began, as my father started to spend more and more time at the city's prominent (in a modest Ujpest-sense of the word) Circle Café (*Kör Kávéház*). He enjoyed the company of frequent card-playing partners, generally businessmen like himself, although one of them was a friendly gentleman named Jenö Hivessy, whose son George was a classmate, a good friend of mine and one of the foursome who years later surprised Prof. Piroska with that television set. (There were lots of Georges in my generation.) Hivessy was a high government official who never discussed his business, but we knew that his business concerned "national security," which in Hungarian terms meant something like the FBI in the United States, guarding against communist infiltration. Hivessy was to play a very important part in my life a few years later. For now, I should add that he was among those old friends of my father who encouraged him to pursue his new and auspicious venture.

No one, least of all my father, could foresee the objections of the Reverend Gyula Mády, a Protestant minister and, as we soon discovered, a rabid anti–Semite. He cited an old city ordinance according to which alcoholic beverages were to be banished within a certain distance from houses of worship. Mayor Semsey made sure that the Catholic Church — which was even closer to my father's future restaurant — would raise no objections. Construction progressed, the place opened pending an appeal to overcome Mády's objections. My father's legal expenses mounted, his tavern in the outskirts was closed but, as we later learned, Mády was related to the high-placed *ispán* (county head), Laszlo Endre, a notorious fascist. The year was 1937, Hungary was advancing in its Hitlerian path, and my father's cherished plans went up in smoke. (László Endre was hanged by the new Hungarian government in 1945.)

My father fell into a deep depression, which, in his case, meant great outbursts of temper, and all of us at home suffered. But my father was not a man for small decisions. He was ready to sell the house in which we lived, determined to buy the Corvin Buffet on Andrássy Street (Budapest's principal boulevard, a block away from the opera house). His brother Ernö offered to help, as did a wealthy wine merchant named Joseph Grünfeld, my father's old boss who had helped him establish himself in business around 1920. Negotiations with the buffet's aging owner proceeded, and the deal was set before the year ended. I had a few months left in my final gymnasium year. My father rented a spacious apartment near Andrássy *ut*, and the family moved as soon as the school year ended for me and my sister Évi. She was then 14 years old and, according to the customs of that era (with which my father concurred and, as was her habit, our mother would raise no objections), "she did not need a career, she will be married in due course." I, on the other hand, could commute to the school on a bike, as I was preparing for the final exams, and so I did. To concentrate on those exams, I discontinued my violin studies, after performing my final concert for the Wolf School, the violin solo from Hubay's opera *The Violin Maker of Cremona*, virtually unaccompanied, with its tricky Kreisler-like double stops. I graduated from the gymnasium with excellent grades in my favorite subjects and acceptably passable ones in others where I didn't deserve any better. My family left Ujpest and we moved to the big city.

5. The Royal Hungarian Opera House

I reached my 18th birthday in December 1937, and many things changed for me as we became residents of Budapest. My father's exciting new adventure, the Corvin Buffet, opened after months of delay because, typically for my father, who was always "thinking big," it had to be vastly renovated and fully modernized. The contractor was behind schedule (later in life I was to learn that he must have belonged to an international fraternity of sorts, because most contractors I ever came in contact with followed the same pattern with cost overruns and other undesirable results). In any case, the restaurant did open, and it was successful from the outset. Our family routine changed vastly. We had breakfast at home. Our apartment was spacious enough to have a room for my maternal grandmother, so my mother spent much time with her, but we rarely ate our midday meals at home. I assisted my father in many ways with purchasing for the business, setting up a storeroom, and getting acquainted with the customers. Sometimes my sister Évi and I had dinner at home; my father usually dined at our restaurant, usually in the company of newly acquired friends (frequently actors and comedians whose companionship greatly amused him). Soon after I began working, my father told me that I was getting too old to live on my allowance, so he turned over the tobacco and cigarette concession to me with the proviso that I was to utilize its profits to clothe myself. (He said that, but didn't really mean it, since "surprising" me with a new pair of gloves, a new necktie, even a pair of shoes continued to be a regular affair, with the pretense, always, of forgetting our new "arrangement.") His generosity toward me never faltered, and it was probably augmented by the belief that I was "too modest in my desires," and the only things that I wanted to acquire were books and records.

As I reached eighteen, however, my future had to be discussed. I was enjoying myself at the Corvin too much, especially in the night-life of what was regarded as one of the city's theater districts. I worked fairly long hours but, being the boss's son, that wasn't bad at all, and an exciting new experience to boot. During my gymnasium years, when my future plans first came up for discussion, I told my father that I would like to be a teacher. Remembering his childhood poverty and his unfinished schooling,

Top: My family in 1934. *Left to right:* my mother Jolán, my sister Éva (Évi), me, and my father Daniel. *Bottom:* The family I left behind in 1939. *Left to right:* sister Éva (Évi), father Daniel, and mother Jolán.

he became quite emotional and told me what a wonderful profession teaching was but, realistically speaking, "you couldn't make a decent living at it because teachers were notoriously underpaid." When the subject came up again in 1937, he insisted that "your grades are good, my connections are pretty good, choose whatever university you wish to attend." The usual possibilities were considered — medical, legal, and the like — and I professed no interest in any of them. He brought up economics — I laughed it off thinking how little that science could possibly mean in a tiny country like Hungary. Some weeks later, my father told me that in Lausanne, Switzerland, there was a school of hotel and restaurant management on a university level. I was attracted to the idea, so we decided that I would take a year off, learning as much about the business as I could, and start my studies in Switzerland in due course. That pleased both of us.

The Corvin was open from 7 A.M. to 1 A.M., and fairly soon my work schedule was altered so that I could take over from my father's night shift once or twice a week. Needless to say, the business was open 7 days a week. I worked hard, but life wasn't all work. In fact, I had a lot of fun. My father had been driving cars since 1932. In my last Ujpest year I meekly suggested that I should also learn to drive. "You will learn to drive when you can afford to buy your own car," was the stern answer. A year later everything changed. My father took me to the Népliget, the largest Budapest park in the city's outskirts, and began introducing me to the intricacies of the automobile. Within a few minutes, he lost his patience and took me to a nearby bench, where he sat down to rest awhile. Driving calmly back toward the city, he told me that temperamentally he wasn't cut out for the job, and he didn't want to scream at me for my mistakes. (The "driving lesson" had lasted maybe 40 minutes....) He subsequently enrolled me in a professional driving school, which I completed on schedule and, to gain more confidence, I began driving around in the inner city at the safe period around 5–6 A.M. for a couple of weeks before I ventured into going to the market and doing other business-related tasks. My close friend Miklós, now a freshman law student, accompanied me on those exploratory mornings because I needed company and he found my fumblings and insecurities entertaining.

Miklós's father had perished in World War I; his widowed mother, a piano teacher and a gentle soul, wore black throughout most of my gymnasium years. Then she married a genial lawyer who adopted Miklós and treated him as his own. By the time my family moved to the capital, Miklós was an established man about town. Though we were entirely different personalities, we somehow complemented each other. He was far more outgoing, loved to socialize, and enjoyed a lot more freedom from parental authority than I did. At one time he was in love with a banker's daughter named Klári who was celebrating a birthday with many guests, a rather formal affair that found my friend in his element. He insisted that I go with him, and I gave in for his sake. My father, knowing that such dancing soirées were not "my thing," wanted to know the location of the event, and I told him. During the course of the evening, while I was half-heartedly dancing with one of Klári's lovely friends, I sighted my father among the group of outside onlookers. We exchanged glances; my father greeted me with a smile and disappeared without a trace. It was obvious to me that he wanted to be convinced that I wasn't participating at some underground political rally. In that respect, he never changed, nor did he ever waver when it came to looking out for my safety and happiness.

It was opera that really cemented my friendship with Miklós. His cello studies ended when my violin lessons did, and we became operatic regulars, watching all the performances from the gallery, and learning opera with the enthusiasm of recent converts. Miklós was not a record fanatic like myself, but he spent many hours in our home as I proudly displayed my new acquisitions. It was around that time that I discovered the voice of Jussi Björling, the new tenor sensation, already making news in Vienna. Gigli's recording of "Che gelida manina" was a special favorite of ours. Since I owned that aria by Gigli, I felt I was privileged to be treated to the last word on the subject. But one day, while visiting my Ujpest friends, in a music store I heard a sensational rendition of that aria *not by Gigli!* That did it, and I began adding that young Swedish tenor (age 26 at that time) to my recorded list of favorites.

With a backward glance of many decades I cannot describe the Royal Hungarian Opera as an institution of the very front rank, but it was probably, next to the Staatsoper of Vienna, the leading lyric theater of Central Europe. It had a long season (September to June), after which leading opera singers were heard in outdoor performances at various Budapest locales. The theater's repertoire, with opera alternating with ballet, was remarkable. The annual program for my last (1939-1940) season, which I have treasured for the past 60-plus years, showed more than 64 operas, including 16 works by Hungarian composers (Erkel, Liszt, Hubay, Bartók, Kodály, Lehár, Dohnányi, and lesser lights) and 15 ballets. It was customary, for example, to pair *Cavalleria rusticana* with a ballet based on *Shéhérazade,* Bartók's *Bluebeard's Castle* with a terrific short ballet called *Carnival of Pest,* based on Liszt's Hungarian Rhapsodies, and *Gianni Schicchi* with the Dohnányi ballet *Pierrette's Veil.* The house was of normal size by European standards, capacity about 1200, with excellent acoustics. There were several first-class stage directors and designers, with an absolute genius among them, named Gustáv Oláh. With exceptions made for guest singers from various European cities, all performances were given in Hungarian.

The conducting staff was headed by Sergio Failoni, an outstanding

Italian who married one of the house's leading ballerinas, and became somehow Hungarianized. The young János Ferencsik was already showing signs of future greatness. Among the "correpetitors" (assistant conductors) there was the name of young György (later Sir Georg) Solti. Wagner's *Ring Cycle* was given every year, usually with some guest artists, because the Wagner casts, especially tenors, were a chancy lot. Max Hirzel, Set Svanholm, and Maria Müller were frequent guests when Wagner's operas needed more strength. Among the internationally famous Hungarian singers, Maria Németh, Rosette Anday, and Kálmán Pataky, all members of the Vienna Staatsoper, were frequent and welcome guests, while the baritone Sándor (Alexander) Svéd enjoyed membership in both houses. The great Danish tenor Helge Roswaenge, once married to a Hungarian soprano (collectors know that they recorded one duet together), visited Hungary every year. The first time I ever heard Alfredo's Act II cabaletta ("O mio rimorso") sung on stage (Roswaenge did the role in German), I thought it was an "insert aria" from a rare Verdi opera, just to show off Roswaenge's stunning high C!

Today's Erkel Theater, a more spacious venue, is an alternate outlet for the current Hungarian State Opera. In my time, it was known as the Municipal Theater, to be rented out for special attractions, with the Royal Opera having preference. That is where I heard Pertile in *Otello* and *Un ballo in maschera*, surrounded by the best talent Hungary could offer. There, too, I heard Jan Kiepura, still in his thirties, very handsome and a great film star, as Rodolfo and Don José. Gigli sang there once as Turiddu, followed by a concert of songs and arias, and he was sensational. On one evening, there was the double bill of *Cavalleria rusticana* and *Pagliacci*. Turiddu and Canio in one night was not enough for Roswaenge. He began *Pagliacci* by singing Tonio's Prologue (probably transposed up a tone, but no one noticed during the deafening applause.) The ensemble of the Rome Opera House came for two gala evenings, with Antonino Votto conducting. Francesco Merli sang Radames and Manrico; Gina Cigna was the Aida, and Franca Somigli the Leonora.

Naturally, all the standard operas were featured in the main house, but also such rarities as D'Albert's *Tiefland* (which became one of my favorites), Purcell's *Dido and Aeneas* (preceded by a ballet), and two great Russian operas conducted by the émigré Issay Dobrowen: *Khovanshchina* and *Prince Igor*, both stunning experiences for me with their exotic colors and splendid stagings. Among my most memorable souvenirs was the only Hungarian appearance of Lawrence Tibbett as Rigoletto. He was already known to me from his films, but as Rigoletto he was simply overwhelming. Pataky was supposed to be the Duke of Mantua, but he canceled and was replaced by a second-rater, which made Tibbett's characterization even more extraordinary. By then, Miklós and I were able to catch complete operas on the radio from Milan and Rome, where baritones like Mario Basiola and Carlo Tagliabue were frequently heard, but the golden sound of Tibbett surpassed them all. And all this, and more, happened in a relatively short time (1937–1939), as I was eagerly expanding my operatic knowledge, backed up by a gradually expanding record collection. After each performance, Miklós and I dropped in at the Corvin for a bite, to my father's delight. Initially he was concerned that all that opera would turn me into a "one-sided" person without any social life. But when I occasionally borrowed his car and made him sure that nothing musical was involved, he reacted with an obviously knowing and contented paternal reassurance.

I discovered Verdi's *Don Carlos* in 1937, and that opera left a very deep impression on me. I vaguely remember reading about the original five-act version, but only the four-act incarnation was known to us, and never as *"Don Carlo."* The Hungarian cast was the best Budapest could offer, with the great Mihály Székely as an unforgettable King Philip, Ella Némethy as Eboli, Anna Báthy as Elisabetta, and my great favorite, Imre Palló as Posa. (Székely eventually joined the Met after the war; Báthy sang at the Salzburg Festivals under Toscanini, and Némethy, a world-class mezzo, was known in many European theaters.) The opera was given 4 to 5 times each season, and I never missed one. It has been my favorite opera ever since, and not only because of its undisputed greatness. I own probably 10 complete versions, and its music symbolically connects my early life with one that followed the period when Verdi's monumental music first registered on my still idealistic young mind. One particular performance stands out in my memory because of its weirdness. It was truly international. The great Greek mezzo Elena Nikolaidi took the part of Eboli, singing in German. The tenor was a new sensation from Vienna, named Todor Mazaroff, who sang the title role in the only language he knew, his native Bulgarian. The rest of the cast, naturally, sang in the language of the audience: Hungarian. Verdi, who originally heard the opera in French, wouldn't have been shocked, and I, as always, was deeply moved and entranced by it all.

Baritone Imre Palló was my great favorite, and here I'd like to elaborate. Many years ago (1972, to be exact), the Hungaroton label released an LP tribute to Palló, who was then 81 years old. I requested the disc for review in the magazine *Stereo Review* with which I had been associated for decades. Among other things, this is what I wrote:

> I was too young to witness his spectacular rise: his creation of the title role in *Háry János* at the 1926 world premiere of that Kodály opera, his celebrated Falstaff when that Verdi opera entered the Budapest repertoire. But

as the strange and incurable fascination of opera began to cast its spell over me and my knowledge of the repertoire deepened, I found more often than not that Imre Palló was the link. He was the first Rigoletto I ever saw, the first Germont, Renato, and Di Luna. I discovered Rossini's playful Figaro through him, and my impressionable student heart was inflamed by his visionary Rodrigo in Verdi's *Don Carlos*. I discovered all sorts of oddities, such as Respighi's *La fiamma*, and this baritone idol of mine was there every time.... First impressions being overwhelmingly important, the aural sensation of his voice remained with me long after my departure from Europe as a youth. In time, I would discover singers with larger and more resonant voices, possessing techniques even more refined than his (not many), or more impressive stage presence (even fewer), but I always retained an indelible memory of Palló's dashing figure and dependable artistry.

Many years later, but not long after this article, Imre Palló entered my life unexpectedly and unforgettably. But, as my Hungarian operatic experiences were approaching their final months, I thought it fitting to end this chapter with a remembrance of this national cultural icon.

6. Farewell to Europe

The year 1938 changed my life forever. On the surface, things were looking up. The Corvin Buffet was doing extremely well; my father's hazardous business venture exceeded all expectations, and he was able to repay all his debts. And he did it in a manner that contributed to my education and character development. Every time he made a partial payment to Joseph Grünfeld, his old mentor, he told me that owing other people was an humiliating experience at his age (he was 48 at the time), and I should avoid that kind of humiliation in my future life. My father never forgot his difficult beginnings and, as if he could have envisioned my own future, he never failed to remind me that I was lucky to grow up when I did, never knowing material needs, let alone poverty. At the same time, he never failed to emphasize that worldly goods are transitory in life; what you own today may be lost tomorrow. Paying off his debts was essential to him, and he casually mentioned that even his generally helpful brother Ernö frequently lectured him about his great risk-taking with the "Corvin Adventure." Otherwise, Ernö and my father were very close despite differences in their personalities. The details of their business relationship was not known to me, but when my father retired from his wine wholesaling activities, he turned over his entire stock to Ernö, and his brother became Corvin's principal supplier of wine.

My uncle Ernö was a very stern and rather dogmatic man. Once in my early school years, when he overheard me complaining about periodic headaches, his answer was: "Children should have no headaches." (Actually, I was suffering frequent migraine attacks, went through World War II with them and, after the war, was treated at the Montefiore Headache Clinic, whose founder accepted me as a private patient and treated me with a then revolutionary medication called "Sansert. " I was thoroughly cured of my seemingly unusual migraine in my middle forties, and my headaches miraculously disappeared thereafter.) Uncle Ernö had two sons. One was Imre, a medical student in 1938, later an internist, who never seemed close to his father, nor to the rest of the family. By contrast, his younger son, Paul (Pali), and I were like brothers from our teens. He was a year older, a university student by 1938, well built, dark-skinned, bespectacled, and looking like a young professor, but full of mischief. He and I rooted for rival soccer teams, and had bitter arguments when our teams opposed each other, but all was forgotten thereafter. We spent unforgettable summers together at the villa my father had bought in 1935 near Fonyód on the lake Balaton, swimming, sailing, and doing all sorts of crazy things, usually with cousin Pali as the ringleader. Living close to the Buda hills, he adored skiing, but in the summer he swam almost as well as I did. He became a very good friend of Miklós as well, and we formed a well-knit threesome, though Pali, a fairly good pianist, never really warmed to opera. Being sons of a Viennese mother, both brothers were bilingual. Their mother, my aunt Melanie, totally excluded from her husband's business life, formed a little independent business of her own, details of which later escaped me. She spoke a Viennese-inflected and grammatically incorrect Hungarian all her life but what else can you do with a language that is unlike any other?

On the surface, then, my life was serene and I felt fulfilled as my father's apprentice, confidant (up to a point), and potential heir to a flourishing business. I fell in love with a cute and flirtatious girl named Emmy who frequently dined at the Corvin with her parents. On one occasion, after having received encouraging glances, I asked one of our waiters to smuggle a little note to her, asking for a date. Another note was returned to me through the same channel, and we began sedately dating. She was a voice student, pupil of one of the opera's principal baritones, Andor Lendvai, and I took her to her classes whenever my father's car became available to me. I introduced her to my sister, and the two girls took to each other, and one afternoon Évi surprised me by inviting Emmy to our apartment to meet my mother.

The world, however, kept intruding on our daily lives. After the death of Hungary's unlamented Prime Minister Gömbös, the succeeding governments kept strengthening their ties with the German-Italian Axis; anti–Jewish laws were enacted and gradually worsened. Friends and relatives were losing their jobs and began emigrating to whatever country would accept them. I was attending a *Carmen* performance at the Municipal Theater in March, the day Hitler annexed Austria with a devastating effect on Hungarian Jews. A young and recently unemployed teacher approached my father one evening and suggested that he might "teach me some English," just in case. Naturally, he was engaged and I began learning some of the basics and even read a few English novels with him. Relying mainly on the government-controlled Hungarian press, I wasn't perceptive enough to realize the international implications of the "Anschluss," but my father certainly understood the situation. When the Munich pact was signed between Hitler and Chamberlain, most people hailed the supposedly peaceful news, but my father became convinced that war could break out any day. Even under the most threatening internal conditions, he seemed more fearful of the war than he was of the Nazi threat. Convinced that I, of military age, had no future in Hungary, he began investigating the emigration possibilities and soon learned that England and the United States were impossible destinations under the severe limitations of the immigrant "quota system." The decision was made that I should go to Cuba and, being an obedient son and accustomed to accepting the soundness of my father's judgment, I did my best to prepare myself mentally for a new life of adventure, independence, and uncertainty. Unfortunately, I was then qualified only for the last of the three.

My English lessons stopped and my father engaged a pianist named Paul Barna, who was making a living on cruise ships between Spain and Morocco, to teach me as much Spanish as he could, given the little time available to us. Leaving nothing to chance, he was already making financial arrangements (illegal in Hungary) through a friend in Switzerland to have a considerable amount of American dollars ready for me when I would arrive in Havana.

My father then tried to persuade his brother Ernö to let Pali join me. "These two boys are very close and they would be there for each other, making both their lives easier," so went my father's wise and logical argument, but Uncle Ernö disagreed. "You exaggerate everything, including your efforts to save your son." I suppose Ernö had a point, but all my father wanted to do was to save my life, which he did. My cousin Pali got his doctorate in 1943, was sent to a labor battalion and perished somewhere on the Russian front.

So there I was, at age 19, in the spring of 1939, preparing to leave a home that had given me all the love and security that are so easy to accept and so foolhardy to take for granted. I went to the Royal Hungarian Opera House for the last time. The opera was Delibes's *Lakmé,* with a lovely and talented young soprano named Ilonka Szabó. (She was to die as the German army, withdrawing from Hungary in 1945, blew up all the historical Danube bridges separating Buda and Pest, destroying all living beings along with the structures.) I remember enjoying Miss Szabó's singing, but neither I nor my sister who accompanied me could concentrate on the opera....

A few weeks earlier, my father had the idea to have his sister Frida in

Belgrade invite me for a week's visit. "At least Yugoslavia is another country," he said. "It will serve as a transition." I spent a few pleasant days with my aunt and her husband, who was a highly educated and amiable man. He was in the lumber business, and he took me out to the countryside as he was calling on his customers. They even took me to the Belgrade Opera, enabling me to hear *Un ballo in maschera* in Serbian. It was not quite on the Budapest level, but an unusual experience nonetheless. Still, the visit didn't work out. I got restless and homesick and, after four days or so, thanked my relatives for their hospitality, got on the train, and returned to Budapest, unannounced. My father greeted me with a mixture of bafflement and anguish. "You got homesick? What will you do in April?"

In April, the inevitable parting had to come. With the help of my father's old-time friend Dr. Hivessy, I got my passport without any difficulty. He literally took me by the hand and, cutting through the ministerial red tape, explained to various bureaucrats that I was going abroad on a study trip. Thanks to this extraordinary connection, the subject of my military obligation didn't even come up. Then I went to Ujpest to say goodbye to my former schoolmates, George Hivessy, Joe Marton, and George Braun. My grandmother was also given the "study trip" story. (The old lady was to die peacefully several weeks later, thus avoiding a sordid fate in Auschwitz.)

I spent the early hours of my last day in Budapest with my mother and sister. My mother was a gentle, loving, and sentimental woman who wielded a strong enough hand in my upbringing, but by the time I reached 19, I realized her vulnerability and was very protective of her. My father was living, understandably, in an extremely tense state in those days, and his notorious temper went frequently out of control. Besides — and this had been known to me for some time — he had a roving eye, and the Corvin at night offered many temptations.

Saying goodbye to my 15-year-old sister was a different story. When we were younger, that four-year difference in our ages meant a lot. She had her friends — and I knew them all — and I had mine; we moved in different circles and I had been a decent but not particularly attentive older brother. Growing up, we grew closer. My parents gave me a season's subscription to the opera on my last birthday, and I presented Évi with the same gift so we could attend some performances together. Leaving her, I realized that she was growing into maturity and I wouldn't be there for her to lean on. Our farewell was quite emotional, with some older-brother pomposities on my part, reminding her of her "responsibilities" toward our parents and, above all, asking her to do what she could to bridge the void caused by my absence. I only hope that, amidst all my preachings, somehow I also found the opportunity to tell her how much I was going to miss her.

My father took me to the railroad station, controlling his emotions, telling me how important adult decisions were, how I had to rely on myself now that he would not be there to guide me. "But don't worry," he said. "You have a good judgment about things in general and, what is important, people seem to like you wherever you go. In any case, whatever decisions you'll make, I'll be behind you." I wonder what decisions he was thinking about. My mind was full of doubts about my ability to make my way from one city to another, let alone starting a new life in a new country, on another continent, among strange people. What would become of me without his strength, his foresight, his resolute and protective hand? The horrible thought that I might never see him again briefly crossed my mind, but I refused to entertain it. After all, Hungary was an independent nation and, despite all the menacing outward signs, Europe was still at peace in April 1939.

I remember nothing more until our final goodbye. "Remember, my son, *one year*. That's all. Here, or in America, we'll be together. Just hold out for one year." Having said this, his voice broke briefly, as he was fighting back his tears. And then, this man, who had sternly guided me through my early life and now was saving me for a later one, looked around, searching for one more thing he could do for me. And he took his gold pocket watch with its rather flamboyant Egyptian chain pendant and quickly, wordlessly pressed it into my hands as I entered the train. My tears did not stop until I reached Vienna. We never saw each other again, and I had to become a parent myself before I could fully realize what must have passed through my father's mind, not only at that moment but through all the months between his decision to let me go and my actual departure.

Today that gold watch hangs, suspended, in a glass enclosure, near my record-playing equipment. The hands are stopped at 6:40. In all likelihood, it was P.M., because I don't remember ever rewinding it since the watch passed into my hands at the railroad station in Budapest in April 1939, the last day of my "early life."

7. At Sea

A few months before Austria was absorbed into the Third Reich, a soccer match was played in Vienna between Austria and Hungary, traditional
rivals in the sport, that used to meet regularly every year, in alternating
capitals. I enrolled in a 3-day bus tour, joining 20 or 25 soccer fans, all
older than I and all previously unknown to me. My former schoolmate
János Nyerges was a student at Vienna's Commercial Academy, so the trip
presented me with an opportunity to spend some time with him. But the
big match was supposed to be the central point of the whole adventure. That
wasn't quite the way it all turned out because I missed the big event altogether. It must have been the excitement of being on my own, surrounded
by somewhat older men, and enjoying my "independence," that made me
follow the gang to a nightclub called Schiefe Laterne (Crooked Lantern),
where we stayed until the wee hours, drinking wine, listening to Viennese
songs and American jazz, and having a good time. A bit hung over the following day, I met Nyerges, took walks around one of Vienna's beautiful
parks, admired the Staatsoper for the first time and learned that Puccini's
Turandot had been the performance (with Maria Németh and Jan Kiepura
in the lead roles) the night before. Chances are that it was a sold-out affair,
at least that is the way I consoled myself for having chosen a night of revelry in preference to the higher arts. On the ride home to Budapest (about
4 hours), my companions provided enough material so that I could inform
my father about the details of the game I had neglected to watch. Hungary
lost it, by the way — a fact that left my father rather unconcerned, not being
much of a soccer fan.

That was less than 2 years before my return to Vienna in April 1939.
In my mind, I could barely recognize that callow youngster in the suddenly
homeless refugee who now arrived at the Vienna train station. There were
only a few hours before meeting the train for Hamburg, and I spent those

hours talking to fellow passengers. They were virtually all refugees like myself, with a few Hungarians among the many Austrian Jews lucky enough to escape a life that was forever shattered by the German annexation and its brutal aftermath.

I don't remember the length of the train ride to Hamburg, with a relatively pleasant brief holdover in Würzburg, a picturesque town full of ancient houses that called to mind the streets from Wagner's *Die Meistersinger von Nürnberg*. I found it almost incomprehensible to reconcile those cozy and *bürgerlich* Würzburg impressions with the rigidity and menace the new Germany symbolized for me.

Hamburg in earlier years must have been a vital and lively harbor city, but it seemed cold to me now, exuding a characteristic German neatness and orderliness that couldn't conceal an ominous aura. Anti-Semitic posters were everywhere, with relatively few people on the streets and, though I had my passport with me all the time, in that police-state atmosphere I was glad to have followed someone's good advice in displaying a miniature Hungarian flag in my buttonhole. I am sure that the Hamburg of today presents tourists with an entirely different profile, but in 1939 I was certainly no tourist. Nor did I ever wish to re-visit Hamburg again.

The last entry in my Hungarian passport tersely states: "Hamburg, Hafen, ausgereist am 27. Apr. 1939." The ship was *Iberia*, a prideful property of the Hamburg-America line once known as Hapag. A handful of Hungarians provided a small contrast to the predominantly German and Austrian contingent that was greeted in a properly courteous manner. In all fairness, I must admit that the entire all–German crew, from the captain down, behaved with the utmost correctness throughout the entire extremely long voyage. Leaving the harbor must have been a wrenching experience for all the German-Jewish exiles; it meant nearly nothing to me. Not only was Germany not my home; it was a country that I had never planned to visit when thoughts of traveling abroad occasionally had crossed my youthful mind.

Soon after we cleared the harbor, I experienced a strange and troublesome feeling that shadowed my natural curiosity on discovering so much water around me. Hungary is, of course, a landlocked country, but our Lake Balaton, the largest lake in Europe outside Russia, is affectionately called "the Hungarian ocean," and it is famous for its sometimes violent and deadly storms. There were no storm clouds above us, and the water seemed relatively calm. Since my stomach continued churning, I asked one of the crew whether I was experiencing seasickness. He laughingly reminded me that we were still navigating the river Elbe, several miles before we would reach the open sea. That information gave me the shivers and, soon enough, I discovered the real difference as the miserable feeling of seasickness took hold of me. I don't think that my exposure to the North Sea was in any way as cataclysmic as the stories I used to read about in romantic novels or, for that matter, in Wagner's *The Flying Dutchman,* but it took little time to discover that the sea and I were not created for each other. A few evenings later, it was announced that, in honor of the Hungarian passengers, the captain was treating us to a "Hungarian dinner." It was a thoughtful gesture indeed, but the German chef's idea of Hungarian cooking revealed little resemblance to what I was brought up on. Besides, we had trouble keeping the plates steady before us with all that maritime turmoil. Eating on the ship became reduced to the essentials needed to keep myself alive. On one particular occasion — following the advice of a passenger whose knowledge of the sea probably equaled mine — I was urged to seek "a bit of fresh air" on the open deck. That was a huge mistake. The ship was shaking and, as I was trying to balance myself at the stern, looking down at the giant waves with disgust, I was suddenly plunged forward, tumbling down at a headlong pace. Nowhere was I in danger but, once I was able to steady myself against the railing, I had a distinct suicidal feeling: why not end it all right there, instead of worrying about that uncertain future of mine? It was only a passing moment, but one that I have never forgotten. I consoled myself by realizing that not even that miserable voyage would last forever. Little did I know that the ocean and I would be reacquainted within two years....

The *Iberia* stopped at Cherbourg to pick up a few more passengers without actually landing at the docks. Those of us who were still unconvinced that war was already imminent now gained added proof. Within the next day or so, we reached Lisbon, and the weary passengers were given four hours for sightseeing — a remarkably novel experience for me because I found that city entirely different from anything seen in Central Europe. Lisbon had a Mediterranean aura, somewhat exotic, colorful and, as the last European outpost, it filled me with a wistful feeling, realizing that I was leaving not only my home but an entire continent behind me. Somewhere between Cherbourg and Lisbon, an elderly gentleman died of a heart attack, and was buried at sea in the evening, with at least a hundred passengers attending a funeral according to Jewish rites. That, too, was an unforgettable experience and, again, the German crew behaved with perfect decorum.

After Lisbon, the ocean also began to behave itself. The sun came out long enough for me to try out the ship's small swimming pool, which, under the circumstances, turned out to be a very pleasant way of passing the time. Soon I began to notice that several passengers were keeping diaries. At first

I thought it to be a silly pursuit, but soon I was tempted to follow their example. Juvenile cynicism aside, seasickness aside, this voyage was a unique experience for me, worthy and perhaps essential to commemorate it in a lasting form. In doing so, I was less interested in capturing my reactions to the teeming world of an ocean liner or to the newly experienced beautiful nights at sea than in expressing my introspective thoughts.

I began writing on May 11, after 14 days at sea, somehow aware that I was leaving behind a sheltered childhood and not too much of a youth. I was approaching a new continent with unforeseen but radical changes, with my life literally "at sea," and I felt that the thoughts of a 19-year-old voyager would be worth taking down, primarily for my own satisfaction and, perhaps, for later evaluation. The excerpts which follow, originally written in the kind of literate Hungarian I have long forgotten, but which would have pleased my old teacher Piroska, are rendered here, more than six decades later, in English, for the first time.

> What ties me to Hungary is a succession of memories allied with the persons dear to me, images to which I am inseparably linked. And yet I can imagine myself reasonably settled in a new environment, reunited with my family. It isn't hard to accept one's fate when there is no other way. And there isn't.... I was never an adventurous soul. Did I ever think that my life, after such placid beginnings, would continue on a different part of the globe? I never regarded myself as a restless spirit dissatisfied with the state of the world. On the contrary, I felt that I could be easily reconciled with whatever situation I would be thrown into by inconsistent fate. In short, I am basically a passive person. And yet, I am experiencing a heretofore unfamiliar feeling that fills me with an almost joyful anticipation: I am about to become *active* for the first time in my life! Thanks to my parents, I had a good education and no wish of mine ever went unfulfilled. That, I suppose, is a parental obligation that no child could ever directly reciprocate, except, by doing everything he can in the interest of his own children. I was always considered an "obedient" kid. There are families where a giant chasm separates fathers and sons; in other situations, there could be an intimate, almost "buddy" kind of relationship. Ours fell somewhere in between. My great love and respect for my father has always been somewhat tempered with a touch of fear and a sense of inadequacy on my part. I did not inherit his remarkable strength and self-confidence. I knew how he suffered as he had to let me go, but he went through with it. It is my obligation now to behave likewise.... For me, at least, our relationship was ideal. I feel his confidence in me, his trust, which he clearly expressed before our final parting, and I know that I will not let him down.
>
> And my mother? My own nature is an amalgam of both of my parents. I inherited my father's nervous disposition and his occasionally extravagant trust in humanity, and we usually looked at the world at large with a similar view. My passivity and quiet behavior is a maternal inheritance. She is a sensitive, tender soul who found it difficult to avoid falling into

baby talk, much to my annoyance as I was growing up. I often felt guilty for not responding to her with the same kind of gentility, much as I tried. She is incapable of hurting anyone, she trusts everyone, feels sorry for anyone and expects the rest of the world to respond in kind. Like perhaps all mothers, she regarded her son as someone very special, and never hesitated to say so, openly.

Thinking about my sister Évi, I feel that I am leaving her with many things undone. I remember having been too critical of her on many occasions, and impatient when I felt she wasn't mature enough, whereas chances are that it was I who was too serious and she was only appropriately childish. Will I have an opportunity to make amends? This journey seems like a first step toward making amends. My previous life has been too smooth and effortless; I must learn about the *real* life out there, a life where I can accomplish something out of my own strength, even if I must give up a lot in the bargain.

On the subsequent pages of my journal, I recalled my short-lived romance with Emmy and my profound friendship with my friend Miklós, who took my departure very hard. With my imminent departure hanging over us, Emmy and I parted tearfully, but lovingly — the world in which we lived left us with no common future to contemplate.... Then I reflected on the nature of friendship in general, and realized, with a measure of self-satisfaction, that I was leaving Hungary with no one harboring hostility, rancor, not even irritation toward me. I had many friends, and we influenced each other in many ways, but Miklós was special. We had contrasting personalities, but over the years — with shared secrets and shared memories, heated arguments, discussions on music and especially opera, long evenings spent in serious discussions on the Danube bank — we became inseparable.

> Yes, it is very painful to leave all this behind: the Danube, that beautiful city with its exciting night life, a wonderful and loving family, the sweet memories of romantic car rides with Emmy, and a devoted friend. It is painful to start a new life facing an unknown future, but I must confront that uncertainty.

I concluded my shipboard journey recalling three lines from a Schiller ballad about mythological characters but metaphorical events that resound with eternal truths:

> Noch Keinen sah ich fröhlich enden
> Auf den, mit immer vollen Händen,
> Die Götter ihre Gaben streun.

Briefly translated, and shorn of Schiller's terse eloquence: "Heaven never endows human beings with a full life undisturbed by travails."

As the *Iberia* entered the Caribbean waters with their welcome sunshine and minimal aquatic disturbances, I avidly gleaned my book of Spanish grammar, assisted by my trusty pocket Hungarian-Spanish dictionary. The immense agitation great discoverers must have felt on sighting land couldn't have been further away from my confused young mind as we approached Havana harbor.

8. Havana (1939–1941)

La Habana, as I soon learned, was the true name of the city that was to become my home for the next two years. But — as I was to discover shortly thereafter — in the Spanish language the consonants "b" and "v" are pronounced interchangeably. Therefore, I will continue referring to the city as "Havana."

My initial impressions were, of course, endlessly fascinating. Old Havana, around the harbor, revealed a medley of houses centuries old, with ornate Baroque churches in disrepair jutting out at unexpected points. Extremely narrow one-way streets framed by sidewalks barely accommodated vehicular traffic. It was all noisy and disorderly by my European standards, but there was an unusual aura to it, later to be identified as "freedom." There were many black people in the streets — approximately 30 percent of the city's population, with another 30 percent of mixed races. The only black person I had met in my 19 years in Hungary was a jazz drummer in the Arizona nightclub, two blocks from the Corvin Buffet. He caused enough sensation to have street kids follow him wherever he went.... Racially, Cuba seemed a totally relaxed city. As for the country's politics, I was to learn a great deal later on, but it should be borne in mind that Fidel Castro was still an unknown schoolboy in 1939....

After reclaiming the enormous trunk my mother had lovingly and tearfully prepared for me, I found temporary quarters with a man named Ott, a Hungarian restaurateur of Swiss origin, whom my father had contacted with the vague idea of taking me on as a junior partner and, eventually, my taking the business over once Ott would repatriate, having had the enviable choice of re-settling in either Switzerland or Hungary. The plan turned out to be unrealistic and it was abandoned almost immediately. As I learned to my grave disappointment, foreigners were not allowed to take jobs in Cuba, so my chances of gainful temporary employment vanished quickly.

But then, who would employ a refugee without any tangible skills and lacking a working knowledge of Spanish?

What to do? I teamed up with another Hungarian refugee and bought a coffee shop in a more modern section of the city on Calle Infanta, adjacent to a movie house that was to provide much of our business. To my very pleasant surprise, with my Latin and Italian studies behind me, I picked up the language with relative ease, though its similarity to Italian caused me to keep mixing the two together, perplexing the suppliers I was doing business with. (More than three decades later, on visiting Madrid for the first time and talking with a hotel concierge, I was told that my otherwise fluent Spanish had an Italian accent. I took that as a great compliment.)

My partnership was short lived because my partner and I disagreed about virtually everything and got on each other's nerves. I soon I bought him out, and, instead of an obnoxious partner, I acquired an honest and personable employee named Emiliano, about my age, who helped me immensely with the language. Emiliano had limited schooling, but he was well read, quoted Cuban poets with enthusiasm, and filled me in on the country's political background, its economic dependency on the United States, and so on. His views were probably colored by the fact that he was an idealistic Marxist, but many of his statements sounded convincing, especially those relating to the prevalent corruption in Cuban society, manifestations of which I was able later to observe firsthand.

Most of the Cubans I got to know on a personal level impressed me with their friendliness and generosity. Emiliano once explained to me that, while the people at large (especially in the rustic areas) were extremely poor, it was easy to survive because the tropical climate would never let you freeze to death and you would always find a friend to treat you to a banana and a cup of coffee, both costing a penny each in those days. The movie house was located immediately to the left of my shop; my neighbor on the right, a handsome ladies' man named Eladio, was selling lottery tickets (and probably doing some bookmaking on the side). We became fast friends, as I did with the black "limpiabote" (shoe shine boy) named Pepe, who did business in front of our shops. One day, I noted an elegantly dressed man involved in a tense political discussion with Pepe, after which he dropped in for a cup of coffee and a Danish. He wanted to know where I came from, and seemed impressed with my unusual background. Afterwards, he left his business card with me, which identified him as an "abogado" (attorney). Pepe later explained that he was actually the secretary of commerce. Democracy indeed! I must not overlook another important neighbor, the policeman on the beat, who was also an aspiring opera singer. Taking advantage of the friendly acoustics of the building's lobby, he was practicing

Fiesco's "Il lacerato spirito" from Verdi's *Simone Boccanegra* one morning, and was surprised and pleased that I knew the piece and enjoyed his singing.

I corresponded with my family uninterruptedly during my Havana stay, and the first few letters were full of bad news. Soon after my departure, my uncle Ernö collapsed and died at the railway station as he was leaving for a business trip. Thus, my father had to face yet another blow, because the two brothers were very close. Then, my friend Miklós, who simply couldn't get over my leaving Hungary "unnecessarily," in his view, expressed his feelings in such a manner that my father showed him the door, never wanting to see him again. I begged my sister in my next letter to intercede because both men wanted the best for me, and I didn't want to be the cause of such a bitter friction. It took several weeks for the two of them to reconcile. (Poor Miklós was to die in the Mauthausen concentration camp during the war.)

I was lucky enough to find a sublet in an apartment rented by a family of German refugees in a modern (if far from elegant) building between Calle Infanta and the famous Hotel Nacional, a pleasant walking distance from my shop. On some evenings, I would stop along the Malecón, a winding boulevard whose extended stone wall girded that part of Havana from the sea. I would look out on the ocean pretending that it was the Danube, with Budapest on "the other side" and, with tears in my eyes and, as the waves were breaking over the rocks in eerie counterpoint, I would ask myself what I was doing in this strange country, and why?

Initially, I found Havana's tropical climate very hard to take but, on the positive side, one of the beaches — not the luxurious one — was reasonably accessible. I remember spending a few hours there, having a professional photograph taken on December 22, 1939, which I sent to my family with the date imprinted, so that they could see in what luxury I was "celebrating" my 20th birthday. Just the same, the climate was hard to take and, after a few months, I realized that, like all the natives, I needed an hour of mid-day *siesta* to make it through the day.

Miraculously, given the impossible schedule of my working day, I managed to spend two free evenings in the two Havana years to get reacquainted with opera. Havana did not have a regular opera schedule, but occasional performances were given at the *Teatro Nacional*, organized by independent impresarios. I attended a fairly high-level *Tosca* with a good Cuban tenor named Francisco Naya as Cavaradossi and the young American baritone Robert Weede (unknown to me then, but not for long thereafter) as Scarpia. Ungallantly, I no longer remember the name of the Tosca. Some months later, at the *Palacio de Bellas Artes* in the exclusive Vedado section of the city, I enjoyed opera's inseparable twins at a price I could barely afford.

Armand Tokatyan and Carlo Morelli sang the male leads in *Cavalleria rusticana*, with the excellent Morelli returning as Tonio with Giovanni Martinelli and Vivian della Chiesa completing the *Pagliacci*. Martinelli, as I recall, disappointed me, considering his world fame, but he was already 55 at the time.

The *Teatro Nacional* was not an independent structure but part of a large building on the Prado, Havana's principal avenue, adjacent to the Capitolio, a very impressive edifice indeed. It was constructed in the 1920s, I was told, under the government of President Menocal — a crook on the grand scale, according to my local informants but, unlike other crooks, he at least left Havana with a number of beautiful public buildings to remember him by. In Cuba 1940 was an election year, after many months of intensive sloganeering (accompanied by catchy Latin-inflected campaign songs which I, a foreign and disinterested outsider, rather enjoyed), Colonel Fulgencio Batista, the elected president, was popular with the electorate, a "man of the people" who had gone from sergeant to colonel with surprising rapidity. The local communists supported him and, of course, so did Emiliano, but he added his own reservation: "He is likely to be less corrupt than his rival." History didn't bear out Emiliano's assessment, but I was lucky enough to leave Cuba before Batista would turn the country into a mafia-infested morass.

Thanks to my frequent visits to the adjacent Cine Infanta, I was learning Spanish and English simultaneously. (American movies had Spanish subtitles, while Spanish-language ones, starring the likes of the wonderful comedian Cantinflas and the balladeer Tito Guizar, needed continually less and less linguistic efforts on my part.) I also became a regular reader of the *Havana Post*, an important and influential English-language daily. There was also an English business school in my building, operated by two Americans who were customers of mine, but I couldn't afford the tuition.

World War II had broken out in Europe in late 1939, and Cuba's refugee contingent observed with mounting fear how the German Wehrmacht swept through Western Europe. My correspondence with the family continued but, the less detailed manner of their letters suggested censorship control, and the events filled me with fear for their welfare. My spirits found considerable uplift in those days with the presence in my life of a lovely Cubana with the highly operatic name of Leonora. She frequently joined me at the Cine Infanta, helping me with my linguistic progress, among other things, and we occasionally spent time at the beach, but she never invited me, a foreigner of uncertain future, to visit her family, which, as things were to turn out, was just as well.

I also became very friendly with two brothers — George and Charles

Turi — whose parents eventually became acquainted with my family back home, no doubt exchanging stories involving our similar fates. Both brothers were lawyers, as was their father back home. They had arrived in Cuba a few months before I did. George, who was artistically gifted, became a photographer's assistant specializing in retouching (off the books, of course), while Charles turned himself into a house-to-house salesman, barely making a living (more-or-less like me). We spent as much time together as our busy schedules allowed, and took special delight in the fact that the three of us, in addition to our common destiny as Hungarian exiles, were also born under the same constellation, all in December — George on December 9, 1913, Charles on December 19, 1916 — three astronomically calculated years between us.

The dramatic change that soon overtook us was worthy of an Italian opera. With the war spreading through the European continent, France having surrendered and the Low Countries occupied, the outflow of emigrants was grinding to a halt. The Turi brothers and I had already registered for U.S. immigration despite the limited possibilities on the Hungarian quota, since we all wanted to get out of Cuba, and had nothing to lose. Now, in late 1940, we learned that the U.S. government would allow Hungarians in all of Latin America to enter the United States if we possessed the required affidavits. George and Charlie soon acquired them from their New York relatives and I told Charlie to procure three steamship tickets, hoping that, selling my shop, I would have the minimum financial resources to guarantee that I wouldn't become a burden to the USA. So it happened. I quickly gave up my sublet and moved my meager furniture to the apartment of an elderly Hungarian couple, Antonio and Ida Wecherka. Tony was a barber who had been neatly coiffing me for months, giving me more haircuts than I probably needed. They were childless and treated me like a son, dismissing my efforts to pay rent for the remaining few months. I went back to the old trunk, extracting some of the apparel my mother had lovingly assembled for me (including a heavy overcoat and a debonair-looking topcoat, neither meant for the Cuban climate), and prepared for departure in early March on an inexpensive Chilean ship, with New York as our destination. Of course, my family was informed by cable about the fortunate turn of events.

As I was giving Emiliano a hearty *abrazo,* he told me that, as the son of a Puerto Rican father, he was also trying to move to the U.S. I said warm farewell to the Wecherkas, promising to stay in touch, which we did for many years thereafter. I cannot say that I was leaving Cuba with a heavy heart, because my life was going nowhere in a country where I never felt at home. I grew very fond of Latin-American music but, as I was to learn, those catchy rhythms would follow me to the USA. In any case, those years were far from wasted. I sensed that such an adventurous experience would be valuable to me later on, to say nothing of my fairly easily won Spanish fluency. Having seen many young American tourists for whom Havana was but a tropical playground, I was hoping that I would also return some day and enjoy a tourist's visit. Circumstances and Fidel Castro denied me that opportunity, but in time I was to see much of the world, certainly all the countries I *wanted* to see. In early March, the Turi brothers and I said farewell to our three girlfriends, and embarked on the Chilean "motonave" *Aconcagua*, bound for "the land of opportunities."

❖ ❖ ❖

The ship *Iberia*, which had brought me to Cuba two years previously, was the last German vessel to land there undisturbed. A few weeks later, the *St. Louis*, also of the Hamburg-America line, entered the harbor, but only a handful of its some nine hundred passengers were allowed to disembark. The ship's very humane captain attempted to reach port in Miami, but the refugees were denied entry and, after several futile attempts, the *St. Louis* was compelled to return to Europe. As detailed in the book "The Uprooted" by Dorit Bader Whiteman, 280 of the desperate passengers found safe haven in Great Britain. The other six hundred or so were given asylum in France, Belgium, and the Netherlands. Within a year, the German army occupied all those countries, and the unfortunate refugees were facing deportation and, in most cases, death.

If I had been among them — and it was only a matter of a few weeks that I wasn't — I would have rushed back to my family in Budapest, and would have perished. Reading about the *St. Louis* affair in Havana, I was perplexed that the United States could act so inhumanely. Only years later did I learn how President Roosevelt had acted to please the reactionary Southern Democrats, thereby preserving party unity before the 1940 presidential elections. Survival — mine, in this instance — can often depend on a roll of the dice.

9. First Year in the USA

Viewed with 21st-century eyes it may seem strange that my two friends and I went to New York by boat. Indeed, there was already an established Pan-American Airlines connection in 1941, but such luxury was beyond our means. As I recall, the sea voyage on the *Aconcagua* took four days and, true to form, I hated it. And yet, there was no comparison between the first two sea adventures of my life. Landing in Havana had seemed like an enormous question mark in the middle of an interrupted youth, while heading for the United States meant a positive step ahead. Thoughts of future uncertainties were dissolved by a conviction that my life was going to have some meaning, and that I was, for better or worse, my own man who would eventually have the benefit of options rather than accepting a thrust-upon and impossibly limited way of life.

Above all, I was not alone. Shipboard intimacy brought the Turi brothers and me even closer together. We spent many hours talking about the families we left behind and worrying about the war, sensing that, sooner or later, Hungary would be drawn into it with possibly tragic consequences. At the same time, the immediate future looked bright with the promise that there would be a place for us in this "land of great opportunities." George and Charlie described their American relatives to me in loving detail. Their aunt Lilly, sister of their father, had married an Austrian officer, Charles Dicker, after World War I, during which he had spent several years as a prisoner of war in Siberia. From what I learned, Charles was a professional musician, making a good living in New York where they had landed among the thousands of fortunate Austrian refugees in 1938, shortly after the Anschluss. Their only daughter, a college student named Hedy, was to celebrate her birthday on March 17, the date of our scheduled arrival, and the whole family was looking forward to greeting the three of us.

We spent a sleepless night on March 16, hoping to catch sight of the

An adopted cousin —me (at left) —joining (left to right) cousins Hedy Dicker, George Turi, and Charles Turi in New York, 1941.

Statue of Liberty. Instead, we docked at an obscure pier at Joralemon Street in Brooklyn on the morning of March 17, which, as I learned, was St. Patrick's Day. The significance of that day, unknown to Hungarians, was duly noted and, unaware of any other event on my social calendar, after clearing customs, I followed my friends into Manhattan where, according to plan, the Dicker family had already sublet an apartment for us not far from their own place on West 144th Street, near Riverside Drive. Charles Dicker and a family friend formed the reception committee at the pier, while Aunt Lilly was busy preparing the 18th birthday party for their daughter Hedy, my future wife.

I was somewhat speechless at that lovely party, as hours were spent exchanging news about the Turi and Dicker families, and terrific Hungarian food was served (at last)! Though the family could not have been warmer and friendlier, I still felt like a stranger. (Some weeks later, Hedy confessed that her initial impression found me "good-looking but dumb.") Her father brought out his violin, played for us, and I was happy to engage him in some fiddle talk, finding little else to converse about.

Realizing that the three of us were very close, it took very little time for the Dickers to accept me as a quasi-family member. Hedy, a pretty and lively brunette, had graduated two years earlier as valedictorian of her high school class, at age 16. She had been offered a scholarship to Wellesley College, which she declined because she couldn't bring herself to part from her parents. Now she was a sophomore at Hunter College, majoring in economics. She loved music, had a fine musical ear and could have also pursued a singing career, but chose a wiser course of future employment.

It was reassuring to learn that one didn't have to be a U.S. citizen to get a job in this country. My first thought was to take advantage of my fairly fluent Spanish and become a translator. Of what? No research was needed to realize that interest in Spanish-Hungarian translators was not acute, and my command of English, with its basic Hungarian accent made even more quaint by a Spanish overlay, was still extremely limited. Charlie and I became shipping clerks in a toy factory, while George quickly found more gainful employment as a photographer and retoucher. I avidly read *The New York Times* and books by Hemingway, Steinbeck, Maugham, and other novelists, and found that I had to rely on a dictionary less and less as time progressed. The four of us, the three boys and cousin Hedy, went to the movies a lot and enjoyed the spectacular offerings of Radio City Music Hall, with the Rockettes and a full symphony orchestra under Hungarian-born Erno Rapée.

A man by the name of Eugene Kálmán, whom I had befriended in Havana and now met again in New York, treated me to lunch at a Chinese restaurant and then took me by taxi down Park Avenue from the 90s to midtown. That part of New York, known to me only from Hollywood movies, now came vividly to life in all its luxurious immensity before my eyes. Later, on visiting new acquaintances in The Bronx and Brooklyn, and meeting childhood friends in Staten Island, I gained a full measure of the gigantic essence of what "New York City" represented. In those early New York days, I was puzzled by the frequent appearance of music that I recognized as coming from Puccini's *Madama Butterfly.* Not much later the puzzle was solved when I heard "The Star Spangled Banner" in its entirety and discovered that Puccini had adapted fragments of it to underline the American characters of Sharpless and Pinkerton and, eventually, to briefly emphasize Butterfly's assumed new American identity. That experience showed me how much I still had to learn about American life.

Very soon after my arrival, I paid a visit to the Metropolitan Opera, the fabled theater I had been reading about ever since my childhood. Finding it in the middle of the city's unromantic garment center was nothing short of depressing to an opera lover accustomed to the regal sites of the Budapest and Vienna houses, to say nothing of the Paris Opera, already known to me from newspaper and magazine sources. A few days later, I discovered that the Plaza Hotel at the edge of Central Park would have been the ideal location for the most famous lyric theater of the world but, obviously, back in 1883 the founders had thought otherwise. In any case, as the Met (not yet known in that abbreviated fashion) was about to close for the summer, I soon discovered the Salmaggi Opera in Brooklyn and Fortune Gallo's San Carlo Opera in Manhattan, where modest but fairly good productions were offered at popular prices. As an "honorary cousin," I took Hedy to the San Carlo once or twice and I am sure I filled her head with an excessive amount of operatic lore.

As summer was approaching, I was offered a job as a waiter in the Catskills to earn some extra money. It wasn't like being the boss's son in Budapest's theatrical district but, being familiar with restaurant life, I took the job and returned to New York in September, with a distinct improvement in my conversational English, as Hedy dutifully noted, and with a newly acquired handbook on Spanish business correspondence, ready to explore the field of international trade. I was soon hired by a very nice gentleman named J. H. Cazes, of Sephardic background, and he seemed pleased with my skills, though at times he commented that my writing style was "too elegant and formal" for everyday business correspondence. This, naturally, was the result of my recently purchased handbook, which I religiously followed. Cazes was export manager for a big manufacturer named American Rattan and Reed Co., and my activities started with consulting the dictionary and discovering that "Rattan" was a Malaysian palm tree used for wickerwork. For a small company employing one person (me), we did a considerable amount of international trade, and I learned a lot about export documents, spending a great deal of time in the U.S. Customs House and with shipping companies.

Unfortunately, Mr. Cazes suddenly died. Faced with an emergency, his widow Estrella (who became a lifelong friend) and her brother, a successful exporter of films named Henry R. Arias, asked me if I could continue carrying on the business under Henry's supervision. Their offer of a "princely" salary of $30 a week was tempting enough for me to say yes, and I did the best I could until December 7, Pearl Harbor Day, followed by the presidential "Greeting" alerting me to my military obligations. In the meantime, at a Saturday matinee on November 29, I attended my first performance at the Metropolitan Opera, witnessing the debut of Jan Peerce (whom I had earlier admired at Radio City Music Hall) as Alfredo in *La traviata* opposite the Violetta of Jarmila Novotná and the Germont of Lawrence Tibbett. It was painful to note the toll the years had taken on that great baritone's resources since his Budapest visit four years earlier.

On December 22, as previously arranged, my parents called me from Hungary to greet me on my 22nd birthday — the last time in my life that I heard their voices. Thinking back to that moment, I find it hard to imagine how I was able to cope with the emotional impact of that brief conversation. Naturally, I said nothing about my impending army service. Mail to Hungary, now an "enemy nation," soon came to an end. The Turi brothers, the Dicker family and I gathered for a New Year's Eve celebration at the house of friends nearby in the Columbia University area but, whatever joviality we could summon for the occasion, it was beclouded by the knowledge that all of us were about to say goodbye to the world at peace.

As I began to prepare myself mentally for another radical change in my young life, I realized that I was about to face loneliness again. Compared to the truly tragic separation from my Hungarian family, that in itself was not all that depressing. From a career point of view, I was still in the middle of nowhere. Going into the service was happening to young men everywhere in America, and this being 1942, I could count myself lucky that I was here and not in war-torn Hungary. As I was viewing my newly jolted life through an optimistic lens, I suddenly realized that the only true loss I was facing at that moment was the separation from Hedy. There was no need pretending that we were "cousins." I was in love with her, and time was too short to keep that knowledge to myself. I took her to a nearby French pastry shop for a late afternoon coffee, unburdened my feelings, and received, joyously, similar sentiments from her. As luck would have it, her father walked in a few moments later. Suspecting nothing, he told his little schoolgirl daughter that he was about to get some pastry, and all three of us should go "home" to continue our conversation.

Words failed us at that awkward moment. Hedy followed her father home and I went down a few blocks and told George and Charlie about us.

Acting like "big brothers," they demanded assurance that my intentions were honorable. The happy-go-lucky Charlie quickly embraced me, but George remained guarded for some time thereafter. At the first opportunity, Hedy and I told her parents what was happening. Charles Dicker accepted the new situation with a philosophical bemusement that barely concealed an internal paternal shock. My future mother-in-law, the daughter of a physician, faced the news that her adored little daughter would want to tie herself to a prospective army buck private with understandable trepidation.

On Valentine's Day, we celebrated our engagement in the smallest possible circle of friends. With an even smaller ceremony, the U.S. Army welcomed me to its ranks two weeks later.

10. The U.S. Army —
Stateside

I reported to Fort Dix, New Jersey, a giant induction center, on February 23, 1942. Like all the new recruits, I was properly outfitted in olive-drab uniforms, medically examined, found physically fit, and got a preliminary sense of army life. We were marched to and fro, learned about the meaning of the various trumpet calls, and discovered the unpleasant task of KP duty. I also learned that "bitching" was the soldier's only outlet to defy (quietly and uselessly) superior authority. We were given various aptitude tests to determine if we had any usable skills. One of these tests had to do with the Morse code, which meant a succession of dots and dashes assaulting your earphones in unpredictable sequences. Our job was to identify their similarities or differences. Having a musical ear is crucial here, and I did very well. In today's age of electronics and cyber optics, the Morse code is regarded as something on the level of the Wright Brothers, but in World War II, it was still an essential means of communication.

On Sundays we were allowed visitors, and Hedy came to see me the first available Sunday, accompanied by one of my ex–Cuban friends, Steve Halmi, who quite seriously accused me of "stealing" Hedy from him, as he had been entertaining similar ideas before I beat him to the punch. As March 17, Hedy's 19th birthday, was approaching, with uncharacteristic bravado, I decided to steal away from my tent into the village of Hights-town, N.J., a local train stop to Trenton and New York. The family was horrified by my "lawlessness," anticipating a court martial, imprisonment, and whatnot. I wasn't all that calm myself but, sizing up the situation, I thought that my chances of getting away for one Sunday were reasonably good. Having thus lawlessly celebrated the anniversary of my first American day, in the evening, I took the train and the bus and tried to sneak back into camp. Sure enough, I was caught by the sentry who was about to file his report when I summoned the courage to talk to him, soldier to soldier:

> "Let me get you straight. I sneaked away on a Sunday so I could visit my fiancée in New York. I came back within the same day, and you are about to report that I was caught sneaking *into* the camp."

"Get lost, soldier!" End of story.

Within a day or so, along with a large number of inductees, I was shipped out to Keesler Field, Biloxi, Mississippi, to complete my basic training. It was a bleak-looking place but, fortunately, within 15 days I was already on my way to Scott Field, Illinois, to enroll at the Air Corps Radio School. The Army works in mysterious ways but, apparently, the good results of my Morse code tests were instrumental in getting me there. (In 1942, the Air Force was not yet an independent branch; the Air Corps was part of the U.S. Army.)

Belleville, Ill., where Scott Field was located, is only a few miles away from St. Louis, Mo. As luck would have it, a Viennese couple, friends of Hedy's parents, had settled in St. Louis in 1938 and invited her to be their guest for a few weeks. I was making excellent progress in school insofar as the operational requirements were concerned, and handled the technical elements adequately. I spent the entire summer of 1942 at Scott Field, with Sundays in St. Louis, where Hedy's friends, Leo and Blanche Rosenbaum, treated both of us royally. I must have had a special effect on barbers because Leo, a barber himself like my dear Cuban friend Antonio, took special charge of my "G.I. haircut," trimming it every Sunday with great care. Blanche was a seamstress with a nice private income, so the two of them lived modestly but well. One Sunday, Hedy and I attended the St. Louis Opera at the Park, where I discovered Gershwin's long-neglected youthful operetta, *Song of the Flame.*

St. Louis can be brutally hot in the summer and I remember taking what should have been a cool and romantic boat ride for Hedy and me down the Mississippi, but it was spoiled by one of my worst migraine attacks. Just the same, Hedy's presence was a godsend. She decided to stay with her friends until I finished my school but, as that day was nearing, we both got panicky thinking that overseas service would soon follow. In view of our unwillingness to part, we decided to get married in St. Louis. Since non-essential wartime travel on such a short notice was not possible, Hedy's parents could not attend our wedding, but we did ask their advance consent. They had, of course, little choice in the matter. I contacted a justice of the peace by phone and the brief ceremony went off without a hitch on a beastly hot day on July 29. With marriage certificate in hand, we presented ourselves to Leo and Blanche. She was heartbroken because Hedy was married in a simple blue dress instead of the wedding gown Blanche would have

happily created for her. Our
wedding night was spent at the
Belleville Hotel, after which I
duly reported for reveille at
6:00 A.M.!

I remember sending a let-
ter to my in-laws after the fact,
reassuring them that we were
not only very happy but also a
very *mature* couple at age 41
(our combined ages). After my
graduation (with excellent
grades) from the Radio School,
I was transferred to the Lemoore
Air Base in Southern California. Hedy went home to collect
her things, dropped out of
Hunter College temporarily,
and took a very long train ride
from New York to Fresno,
where I was waiting for her as
she began a fairly long existence
as a camp-following army wife.

Our wedding photograph, taken in Belleville, Illinois, 1942.

What then followed turned out to be an adventurous and very valuable process of Americanization for both of us. We learned more about this
country than many young people who had the privilege of being native sons
and daughters. My own westward path — via a railroad car in which a huge
block of ice in the middle of the aisle served as an "air conditioner" — crossed
the vast cornfields of Kansas and a brief slice of Oklahoma and Texas, where
I learned about the Texas Panhandle. Then came a very large stretch of New
Mexico, a brief and extremely hot layover in El Paso (Texas again, briefly),
and an even hotter and seemingly interminable stop at Yuma, Arizona. Finally, we arrived at Bakersfield, California, our transfer point to the Lemoore
Army Base, a tiny but important spot where I was to spend four weeks. After
picking up Hedy in Fresno, taking advantage of the Army's generous attitude toward married servicemen, we rented a nice room in the town of
Hanford, a short bus ride from Lemoore.

I no longer remember what my army duties were at subsequent army
posts while waiting for my long-delayed citizenship papers to catch up with
me, but Hedy found immediate employment wherever we set up temporary lodgings. Very gifted artistically (a paternal heritage), she worked as a

window designer, administrative assistant, and heaven knows what else in Sacramento, Stockton, and eventually in South San Francisco. At that time, I was stationed at what used to be the Tanforan Race Track, hastily converted into army barracks. (Now, it is a giant shopping mall just north of the San Francisco International Airport.) In Sacramento, we were lucky enough to attend a guest performance of the San Francisco Opera (*Carmen*, with Irra Petina, Raoul Jobin, and Ezio Pinza); in San Francisco, we heard the Symphony under Pierre Monteux, and concerts of Mischa Elman, Joseph Szigeti, and Paul Robeson. These were, of course, weekend treats, but they stand out in my memory in clearer detail than the routine, occasionally trying, but never truly unpleasant army duties. Hedy's wonderful presence, a violinist's daughter and a budding opera lover, often made me feel like a civilian. Unforgettable, too, are my recollections of traveling to and fro between the various towns and camps. Hitchhiking in those days was the norm; all a soldier had to do is stand still and point toward a general direction; the locals considered it a privilege to pick you up and entertain you with local lore and gossip. Of course, you had to get up early enough to get to your unit for reveille at 6:00 A.M.; there was a limit to the army's accommodating attitude!

We greeted the year 1943 in Northern California. Occasionally, and miraculously, I was getting some mail from my parents through their friends in Spain, and we, too, managed to get a photo to them, taken in the Capitol Park of Sacramento. As I was to learn many years later, that was the very last message they ever got from their son.

In April 1943 I was transferred to the Reno Army Air Base as a radio operator in a unit already organized for overseas service. Reno was a very small town then, picturesque in a Wild West manner, at the foot of giant mountains. I bought an old Chevrolet two-seater for $150 to facilitate travel to and from the base. One day, while I was occupied in serious field exercises, my intrepid wife decided to get her driver's license. Making up in charm what she lacked in experience, she somehow conned her gallant examiner into giving her a license. As she proudly displayed it to our landlord (at 440 Hill Street — a small house still unchanged when we revisited it 40 years later!), the old-timer explained to us that his own license dated back some 20 years, and renewing it seemed like a needless effort. Nevada was a rather open-minded state, even then.

We enjoyed Reno immensely, but life at the base was much less happy. By then, I knew enough about Army red tape to realize that, as a non citizen, I became an "odd man out" within the unit. A guardian angel in the shape of a well-meaning sergeant from New York (we became friends because we had that in common) called my attention to a brand new army appeal for transfer to the ASTP (Army Specialized Training Program) for servicemen with foreign language skills, earmarked for occupation duty. Yes, there was indeed a war going on while I was marking time in the States; the U.S. Army was advancing in North Africa, soon to invade Italy, and our government was already looking forward to an occupied Western Europe. I applied for the ASTP program, was accepted immediately, and received orders to report to the University of Utah at Salt Lake City to await my next assignment. That seemed to signal the end of my career with the Signal Corps, the Morse code, and the world of radio. Who could tell about the future?

We sold our trusty old jalopy, which was ready to give up the ghost anyway. Hedy and I covered the vast expanse between Reno and Salt Lake City separately, but, seasoned troopers that we were, we quickly readjusted to our new surroundings. The university was located on a mountain overlooking a city with wide thoroughfares laid out with almost geometric precision. Salt Lake City was a monument to orderliness. The army detachment was basically a replacement center for ASTP enrollees and, to my delighted surprise, the Army actually gave me an option to choose between various colleges back East, all ASTP participants. With this in mind and realizing that our remarkable western tour had come to an end, Hedy packed up her belongings and returned to her parents. As for me, I chose Lafayette College in Easton, Pa., only a 2-hour train ride from New York.

At Lafayette, we lived the life of college students, subject to army discipline, but free on most weekends. Five of us New Yorkers formed a little group; one of us, named Eddie Erdman, had a car that we used for weekend transportation, sharing the expenses, of course. Our assembly point was the Cinema Giglio on Canal Street, where we separated on Saturday afternoons, to be reunited on Sunday afternoons for the return trip to Easton. Unfortunately, Eddie Erdman died serving with the 84th Division during the war, but another fellow traveler, Sid Krumholz, became a lifelong friend and my longtime CPA later on, once civilian life enabled me to earn an income complicated enough to require an accountant.

Our courses at Lafayette covered the geography, history, and the political landscape of Central Europe. Of special interest to me was a more objective view of the Austro-Hungarian Empire before World War I than I had been allowed to learn in my earlier rather jingoistic Hungarian studies. We had a choice of three languages — French, German, and Italian — and, since my conversational German was still quite fluent, I happily chose Italian. My previous studies proved helpful enough for me to be appointed as a kind of assistant instructor for our professor. He was an unusual man, the Reverend Francis C. Capozzi, who once invited the whole class to his home for dinner and, over spaghetti and wine, informed us that, after having been initially trained for the priesthood, he fell in love with a lovely lady — a great cook, by the way — and that event determined his future as an Episcopal minister.

As we expressed concern over the huge amount of spaghetti on the table, the Rev. Capozzi shared with us an Italian saying (probably from the Scriptures), according to which "nothing that *enters* the mouth can ever cause as much harm as our mouth is capable of uttering." I wish I could remember the original quote because, like just about anything else, it sounds better in Italian. Incidentally, one of my fellow Italian students was a brilliant young man named Frank Church, later to become United States senator from Idaho. We maintained contact after the war and I was happy to make a modest contribution to Frank's election campaign many years later.

Even before that memorable spaghetti dinner (December 3, 1943, as a souvenir postcard bearing a blessing from Rev. Capozzi attests), a very important event occurred. My stay at Lafayette was extended enough to allow my personal records to break through the red tape, making it possible for me to get my citizenship at last. A sergeant from the camp administration packed three of us, caught in the same honorable bind, and delivered us to the Eastern District Court of Philadelphia on September 20. The judge in session was just delighted to interrupt court proceedings, delivered a brief but touching speech about us servicemen who chose to become citizens of this country, and swore us in to enthusiastic applause from all those present. Brief formalities having been completed, I became a United States citizen two and a half years after landing on these shores. (One of my fellow compatriots was called Hans Bach when he entered the court, and walked out as John Brooks. When his new name was called, it took some time for him to realize that it was *his* name.)

But all good things must come to an end. While most of my colleagues completed the 90 days of ASTP training, some of us were yanked out of Easton and transferred to the U.S. Army Intelligence School at Camp Ritchie, Maryland. The characteristic suddenness of the transfer was mitigated by granting us a two-week furlough to end on January 1, 1944, which I happily spent with Hedy and her family, except for the evening of December 27, when we treated ourselves to Mozart's *Le nozze di Figaro* with Steber, Sayão, Stevens, and Pinza at the Met, Leinsdorf conducting. By then, cousin Charlie was in North Africa with the Fifth Army, while cousin George was an artillery man at Fort Sill, Oklahoma, soon to be shipped overseas. (Apparently, both had received speedier citizenship treatments than I did.)

Of course, citizenship meant that, as an American soldier, I would be obligated to bear arms against the country of my birth. For me, it came down to choosing between the country that rejected me and the one that offered me a chance for a new and better life. It was not a difficult choice.

11. Camp Ritchie
and Fort Benning:
Two Important Landmarks

As the year 1944 started, I was beginning to feel guilty about staying behind while thousands of young men of my age were being shipped overseas every day. Arriving at the Military Intelligence Training Center at Camp Ritchie, Maryland, quickly removed my anxieties. The camp was all business; it was efficiently run and dedicated to the single purpose of preparing its military students to be readily dispatched for overseas service. We were trained for alternate duties as either intelligence interpreters or prisoner interrogators. The former specialty involved studies of aerial photographs of enemy terrain, recognition of different types of aircraft, and detailed studies of maps of every nature. As interrogators, we were trained by former graduates of the school; the classes were conducted in German, and we would alternate playing roles as either German captives or American interrogators. As Germans, we acted reclusive and antagonistic, refusing to disclose anything; as Americans, we were supposed to be shrewd enough to obtain data by whatever possible means excluding violence and mindful of the Geneva Convention. We went on frequent overnight bivouacs to work under nighttime and adverse winter conditions — it *was* January. The camp was located near the Maryland-Pennsylvania border, and these overnight exercises occasionally took us to the vicinity of Antietam, where famous battles were fought during the Civil War.

As I recall, it was a very intensive three-month course, with only a few free weekends. Transportation to New York was problematic, involving local trains either to Baltimore or Gettysburg, then the express to New York. Either way, it was lengthy and exhausting. Hedy was already working on her bachelor's degree at Hunter College, but, since she had more disposable time, she could visit me on a few (very few) weekends. On those occasions, I rented a room from an elderly couple in Blue Ridge, Md., accessible to the camp and, being a lover of nature and enjoying the wintry landscape, Hedy made the most of the hours when my duties kept me away from her.

I remember that mine was Class Number 16 at Ritchie, and everything went well for me. I enjoyed the challenge of those interrogation dynamics, regarded the tough Antietam bivouacs as positive elements in my Americanization process and, though interpretation of aerial maps was not exactly my forte, I did well enough with it. On graduation, we were informed that those who had reached a certain level of academic excellence could apply for admission to the Army Infantry School at Fort Benning, Georgia. I asked myself, what could I lose? Overseas service was imminent in any case and, should I be lucky enough to gain admission and complete the course, going abroad as an officer was likely to be more advantageous than continuing in my present status.

As I recall, about 15 graduates applied and, after being rather scrupulously interviewed by the camp commandant, Brigadier General Charles Y. Banfill, I was among the ten who were chosen. The general made our situation very clear to us. We were now in the military intelligence branch of the U.S. Army, but there was no officer's school for that branch. Being in the Intelligence Corps implied no special privileges at Fort Benning. We would become infantry officers if we managed the 13-week course. Those who would flunk out would be returned to Ritchie and immediately assigned to an overseas unit as noncommissioned officers. The general further stressed that Fort Benning was a very tough school, and that he doubted that all of us chosen at Ritchie would "make it." None of that sounded too encouraging but, as I was already amazed having gotten this far in the army, I refused to be disheartened. After a week's furlough happily spent with Hedy in New York, my nine comrades and I took the train and I added the state of Georgia to my constantly growing exploration of the United States of America.

General Banfill was absolutely right: the Infantry School was very tough in every way — physically, scholastically, and psychologically. The pressures were enormous, the tempo exhausting, and the humiliations severe and calculated to determine just how much we could endure. According to the graduation program I retained among my souvenirs, 107 of my class completed the course, roughly half of those who originally entered. The high casualty rate was the result of injuries, physical disabilities, personal problems, or just plain unwillingness to put up with all that torture. Perhaps the most difficult trial was the shortage of drinking water. We would fill our canteens every morning, but by noon the water was too hot to be potable. Our instructors in the field, on the other hand, had their lunches delivered by truck, along with an abundant supply of ice-cold water, which they ostentatiously displayed while the rest of us cursed and suffered.

Our training company had four lieutenant platoon leaders, ranging from good to excellent in both teaching ability and popularity. Our company commander was Captain William V. Ogle, a blond, well-built athlete of a man. After a lecture, which frequently contained seemingly unreasonable requests, he would ask this question: "Isn't that fair?" The answer invariably was a resounding "Yes, Sir!" The motto we candidates often repeated among us was "Collaborate and graduate!" We had also learned that it was unwise in class to ask questions to which our instructing officers may not have had ready answers.

Major General Walker, the commandant of Fort Benning, who as far as I could remember remained invisible to us, was a veteran of the Italian campaign, where he must have discovered the omnipresence of mud. It seems that many of the field exercises required crawling through endless amounts of mud, leaving us unbelievably filthy at the end of a tiring day. It was the height of summer (June, July and August) and dehydration presented another serious problem. Passing out on the field was too common an event to be humiliating, and the medics were always there to help. On the one occasion when I fainted and moments later came to, I found Capt. Ogle's concerned face looking at me accusingly, saying "You probably didn't take your salt pills this morning, Candidate!" Of course I did, but my faint answer still was: "I guess not, Sir." Cooperate and graduate!

Complaining — "bitching" is the word in military parlance — is a soldier's prerogative but, to be fair, there was much to admire about the school's organization and efficiency. Our instructor for bayonet training was a tough retired sergeant who was the actual author of the army manual. We even practiced hand-to-hand fighting under supervision. I was paired with Charlie Jelavich, a lanky Californian at least five inches taller than I, and our "rough" and pseudo-realistic combat must have been a grotesque sight. On one occasion, we were taught the elements in dispersing the platoon under our command. Our instructor exclaimed, "Suppose an enemy plane would suddenly appear over your head?" At that precise moment, a plane appeared, literally out of nowhere, in perfect coordination with our instructor's uttering that phrase, and quickly disappeared from sight. I couldn't help feeling at that moment that an army so well trained simply could not lose wars.

Two unrelated events stand out in my memory from the earliest phases of the course. One morning, as we were lining up for the usual formation, several of us, myself included, received demerits for "improper" (meaning untidy) haircuts. When that same procedure was repeated, I made a bee-line for the company barbershop and soon re-emerged as bald as a billiard ball. I was not about to flunk out for that kind of nonsense! The other event occurred on June 6, 1944, when Capt. Ogle announced that our army had landed in Normandy, and the "second front" was on.... Our reaction was extraordinarily joyful.

Flunking out for whatever reason was a frequent occurrence. After an ominous early morning call, certain candidates would not join the rest of us for the daily exercises. Then they would simply disappear, leaving behind an empty bunk and a bunch of shocked observers. Borderline cases were judged by a board of senior officers at the end of the first and second months of the 13-week course. Since I was, at 24, the second oldest man in my platoon, competing against a band of young gladiators, some fresh out of college, my chances of surviving were borderline, at best.

The first month went by without any mishap, so I continued with my athletics, marksmanship, weapons training, obstacle courses, and crawling around in the naturally pink Georgia clay or the artificial mud. Much of it was probably fun for those in better physical shape, but for me it was nothing short of a miracle of survival. To top it all, I was the only foreign-born candidate in the group, the only one with an accent. Candidates were frequently called upon to act as teachers explaining various arcane military subjects to the rest of the group. Out in the open air, surrounded by many regional varieties of American English, my Hungarian-inflected harangues delivered from an elevated platform must have sounded exotic! And, without fail, there would always be a wise guy in the last row who would interrupt my talk by raising his arm and calling out: "We can't hear you back here, Candidate!" Regardless of my increasing self-confidence, I still considered my situation a "borderline case" in my own judgment.

As we reached the halfway mark, my company was granted our only weekend pass, and Hedy joined me for the first time in her life below the Mason-Dixon line. We rented a room in a house owned by two lovely old sisters in nearby Columbus; the ladies couldn't be friendlier and they seemed rather thrilled by their "Yankee" visitors. Hedy was shocked to see me still almost bald but, as she looked around in various Columbus venues, she realized how many of us Benning soldiers looked like that. Needless to say, those two days with her lifted my spirits.

But, sure enough, I was called before the examining board at the end of the second month. My background as a "new American" generated some sympathetic interest, and my command of languages seemed impressive, but the officers rightly noted certain deficiencies in "leadership qualities." The presiding colonel observed: "The problem with you, candidate, is that your voice is too soft and you don't seem to project authority. But I have a solution for that. Meantime, we are going to pass you conditionally, and keep an eye on you for the rest of the course."

The colonel's solution was for me to enter the woods after sundown and strengthen my voice by issuing loud commands to imaginary troops. Night after night, I walked among the trees that darkly towered over me, piercing the nocturnal calm with my ferocious shouts.

There were many leadership tests, as the colonel predicted. I remember a crucial overnight exercise in which the candidates, working in pairs, were dropped at various points and expected to find their way to home base with the aid of a compass. We all had been trained for such events, but not at night, and for a guy like me, who had spent his previous life in big cities, that was quite a challenge. Through the benign placement of my name in the alphabet (between Jelavich and Johnson), I was teamed with one of the best among us, an Oregon country boy named Elmer C. Johnson, who moved with the speed of a gazelle and the confidence of an Indian scout. Following him like a faithful poodle, I not only reached my destination but, undeservedly, even shared my buddy's outstanding mark for completing the course in record time. (Elmer and I went our different ways after Benning; I met up with Charles Jelavich, now an emeritus professor at Indiana University, several times decades later, and we are still friends.)

I graduated on September 26, 1944, a big event for all of us except, apparently, for 1st Sgt. C. J. Maliszewski, whose parting words to us were: "Enjoy your day, guys, but don't look for me at the ceremony. I'll be damned if I'll have to salute such a sorry lot as you are." That sounded rather insulting to us, except that we were sure that he talked like that to every graduating class before and after us. I returned by train from Atlanta to New York in my smartly cut officer's uniform, still somewhat unbelieving, excited, and happy. I still regard those hard-won lieutenant's bars as one of my proudest achievements. It may have seemed somehow out of character, but Fort Benning gave me a new sense of self-awareness. I was a more ambitious person than I had thought myself to be. The Infantry School certainly hardened me, though — and there was no way I could then foresee it — that "soft voice" that bothered my examining colonel would later caused me no harm in my broadcast career.

After spending only a day with the family in New York, I returned to Camp Ritchie immediately. I did learn that cousin Charlie was already with the Fifth Army in Italy (no longer an enemy since the country had surrendered in September 1943). Cousin George was with the invading force of the First Army in France. At Ritchie, as I had expected, my stateside days were ending. Hedy came to spend a weekend with me in the little hamlet

A "shavetail" before embarking for World War II, 1944.

of Cascade, adjacent to the camp. Then we parted with the understanding that the day of my departure abroad was a military secret not to be disclosed. We arranged a safe and innocent way to get around that severe ban: we would correspond in Hungarian and, when suddenly she would receive a perfectly innocuous letter from me in English, that would mean that I was on my way to an undisclosed destination.

When I contacted the National Personnel Records Center in St. Louis, requesting transcripts of my Army records in preparation for this book, I was informed that the sources in question "were destroyed by fire on July 12, 1973." I therefore do not remember the exact date of my departure from

New York harbor, but it was in November 1944. It was a crowded troop ship that took me back to Europe after an absence of more than five years. I must have spent a great deal of time meditating on how much had happened to me in the intervening years, and how that clueless youngster of yore had turned into a married man, nearly 25, and a U.S. Army officer, to boot.

A few miles out, on the open sea, an announcement was made by loudspeaker that our destination was Southampton, England.

12. England, France — And Some Opera

By the fall of 1944, with American troops advancing from the west and south, and Russians approaching from the east, the retreating Germans were losing their grip on their subjugated satellites. Taking advantage of its geographic position, Romania suddenly changed sides and accepted the Russian rule. Admiral Horthy's Hungary, with its succession of weak prime ministers totally under the Nazi thumb, was anxious to follow the Romanian example. But Horthy miscalculated by announcing an armistice with the Russians on his own on October 15. Within a few hours, he was deposed and taken prisoner by the Germans. In his place, Ferenc Szálasi, a former major and the leader of the loudest and bloodiest Hungarian Nazis, the "Arrow Cross" party, took power. Under the cover of German tanks, Szálasi was declared "Leader of the Nation," while Regent Horthy was deported to Austria, along with the officers and body guards who remained loyal to him. Suddenly, Hungary came under the rule of "types who might have been recruited from the lunatic asylum of the underworld" (*Hungary* by Paul Ignotus, Praeger, 1972). The notorious Eichmann was already on the scene, and the murderous rounding up of the Hungarian Jews was underway. My parents vanished, with hundreds of thousands of those victims, while my sister Évi went into hiding with false papers.

The troop ship transporting me to Europe while these gruesome events, unknown to me at that time, were happening was a good-size French vessel, but I just wasn't interested enough to inquire about its history. The crossing was smooth enough (something of an oxymoron in my case) and, benefiting from my experience, I moved away from my bunk only for breakfast — the most reliable of all army meals — or for satisfying the calls of nature. Otherwise, I remained stretched out, spending my time reading those wonderful pocket-size editions of novels, plays, and other reading material the armed services provided precisely for my kind of eager-to-learn American. We also listened to the Armed Services Radio, enjoying nostalgic tunes like "I'll Be Seeing You," "The Last Time I Saw Paris," "The White Cliffs of Dover," and "Blues in the Night" by Arlen and Mercer which, even to this day, call that long-ago voyage to my mind. Eating virtually nothing after breakfast but cookies, doughnuts, and Hershey bars seemed to be a rather astute solution to avoid sickness insofar as this particular seafarer was concerned. Still, as I was mentally congratulating myself on my cleverness, I reaffirmed my resolution that this would be my penultimate sea exposure; if I would be lucky enough to make the way back, that trip would be my last. (I was to keep that pledge for 40 years!)

Southampton turned out to be merely a point of transit, because within hours after our arrival, we were on our way by train to a giant replacement depot for U.S. servicemen at Birmingham. Everything was blacked out: air raid sirens resounded all the time, but I don't remember any real Luftwaffe strikes during my brief stay there. Our camp was outside the city, but I vividly remember one evening when I was lucky enough to attend a concert with the City of Birmingham Symphony Orchestra conducted by (not yet Sir) Malcolm Sargent. The featured work was Mendelssohn's Violin Concerto (with Henry Holst, the excellent soloist). It was sheer heaven for me after not having heard music on that level for such a long time. *God Save the King* was played *after* the concert, not before (a great idea!), after which the audience filed out in solemn silence into the darkness of the night. It was my first experience with the admirable discipline of British people in wartime, and there were more to follow in the days ahead.

Days indeed, because personal orders came to me very shortly to be transferred to London, pending further assignments. The Grosvenor House near Hyde Park had been taken over by the U.S. Army for the duration, and it couldn't have been more spacious and comfortable. With two officers per room, we were free to explore London, except for special events clearly posted on various billboards. London's underground system was always full, with double-decker bunks alongside the tracks for Londoners to stay during the night. (The V-1 and V-2 rockets were already flying and hitting their random targets.) Here I found another example for admiring the remarkable orderliness and discipline of the British people under extreme stress.

I attended an English-language performance of Puccini's *La Bohème* at the Sadler's Wells Theatre, with the excellent James Johnston as Rodolfo. As I learned later, Johnston was an Irishman and, since I wasn't saving programs in those days, I don't remember the rest of the cast or the conductor. I also managed to catch a revival of Noel Coward's *Private Lives* with no doubt celebrity performers who were at that time unknown to me. During the day, I made contact with the Geigers, friends of Hedy's family from Vienna, who had fond memories of my wife as a little girl. Their son, Hans, a violinist like his father, was somewhere in France with the British Army; their son-in-law, Otto, was serving in the Near East. Their daughter Gretl, Hedy's friend since they were 5 and 10 respectively, is still in close contact with us after all these years. Hans Geiger eventually became a member of the London Symphony Orchestra and toured with them worldwide until his untimely death several years later. I also looked up a few old friends, and was welcomed everywhere like a conquering hero. My flexible schedule allowed me to attend one concert each by the London Philharmonic and London Symphony Orchestras, full of amazement that the city could sustain two such world-class ensembles in wartime.

My London stay came to a sudden end when orders were delivered to me at the Grosvenor House to report at a military airport to depart for Paris on the evening of December 14. This being my first flight ever, I was quite excited about it, though alarmed when I found the airport enveloped in impenetrable fog. Surely my flight would be canceled, or so I innocently thought. Quite the contrary. Two other officers and I were ushered into a small Army plane in which mailbags served in lieu of seats. Our plane took off, ostensibly for a brief hop across the channel but, evidently, our pilot decided not to risk the flight after all, and some minutes later returned the plane to our point of origin. Shaken up by the experience, I and my two fellow passengers spent the night at the airport, to be awakened by the radio and the morning edition of *The Stars and Stripes*, our excellent Army newspaper, with the blazing headline "Glenn Miller's Plane Missing Over The English Channel!" The wreckage was never found, and the disappearance of that gifted and beloved bandleader has remained a mystery to this day.

It was a cold and miserable morning that found our depressed threesome airborne again. Thinking back on my brief time in England, I realized thankfully that, the V-1 and V-2 rockets with their shattering impacts notwithstanding, I was leaving the country with only one great disappointment: the inexplicable British preference for warm beer. And now, here I was, great world traveler, warrior and adventurer, on my way to Paris.

The morning continued rainy and bleak, and yet the "City of Lights" looked beautiful as our army truck sped through the Champs Élysées, allowing us brief glimpses of historical and eternally awe-inspiring churches, palaces, and bridges. Our destination was Le Vesinet, once a fashionable suburb, partly taken over by the U.S. Army. Somewhat befuddled but quite hungry by that time, I was treated to a modest Army lunch, properly billeted, and, as usual, awaited further orders.

Paris had been liberated in late August 1944, but the German counter-offensive, which began in the Ardennes on December 16, precisely coincided with our arrival. Some 30 German divisions under General Rundstedt attacked the Allies in the so-called Battle of the Bulge, causing our forces some 75,000 casualties. But, by the end of January, the Allies had retaken all their lost positions. The Battle of the Bulge was Hitler's last hurrah.

Nowadays, it takes some 15 minutes by the Metro to reach central Paris from Le Vesinet — the time was somewhat longer on the wartime suburban train that took us to the Gare St. Lazare. I spent an incredible week at my "work place" during the day, allowing me to explore Paris at night. The city was blacked out, but the Parisians were more leisurely than the Londoners in observing regulations. With the battle raging not far away, we heard rumors about German infiltrators allegedly dressed in American uniform, speaking perfect English, ready to inflict serious damage to our forces. As a security measure, we learned that any American soldier could be accosted by our MPs to check his legitimacy. One way to do that, I was told, was to quiz the accostee to name, say, the starting pitchers for the Boston Red Sox. Thanks a lot, I thought. I never ceased to read the sports pages, even in *The Stars and Stripes*, but my knowledge of baseball was still minimal. Strangely enough, one evening in a Paris bar, I joined a dozen or so GIs surrounding Mel Ott, the great home run hitter for the New York Giants, evidently sent to Paris by the USO. As he regaled us with tales I listened to with rapt attention, not always knowing what his stories were all about.

Other evenings found me more in my element. On my first visit to the Paris Opéra, the fabulous Palais Garnier, I enjoyed Verdi's *Otello* "en français" with the superb cast of José Luccioni, Geori Boué, and José Beckmans, conducted by Louis Fourestier (all these names are known to record collectors). I went back to a *Boris Godounov* a few evenings later, with the outstanding Henry Etcheverry in the title role. It was a night of bitter cold, and I remember envying the cast in their colorful furs and dolmans, while we in the unheated auditorium sat around with chattering teeth, numb with cold. I hated myself for doing so, but left after the second act to return to the warmer environs of Le Vesinet.

My last Paris operatic evening took me to the Opéra Comique for *La traviata,* and I was lucky to get a side seat on the balcony. The performance was good enough, but I was shocked to discover several changes in the music, particularly in the second act where Violetta's "Amami, Alfredo" was turned into a duet with the tenor, robbing the scene of its poignancy. Many years later, I learned that all those changes were Verdi's own, expressly written for French-language performances given at various Paris theaters between 1856 and 1886.

Operatic diversions came to a sudden halt by an order from Seventh Army Headquarters, sending me, along with three noncoms, to the city of Le Mans, famous to this day for international car races. Our army had apparently liberated a camp full of Allied prisoners. The French, British, and American soldiers had already been returned to their various units by the time we got there; our job was to identify and process the remainder: several hundred Italians and Yugoslavs, even a few dozen Russians. There was a group of Red Cross workers to facilitate communication between the liberated prisoners and their loved ones at home, but the situation wasn't that simple. The Italians were a volatile and undisciplined lot; the war was over for them, America was now "their friend," why couldn't we just let them loose so they could return to their homes? My knowledge of Italian came in handy; we briefly interrogated them all, found them OK and properly vouched for by their comrades. We made up a list with as much information as we could get, and turned them over to Seventh Army Headquarters for further disposition.

By contrast, the Yugoslavs were extremely disciplined, always lining up in an orderly manner, saluting left and right, but always distrustful and reluctant to provide information, even to the Red Cross. They were Serbs and Croats, Titoists and *chetniks,* fiercely anti-communist adherents of Mihailovich, agreeing on one issue alone: they were on the side of the Allies. We managed to communicate with them in German, and placated them with the promise of repatriation. But many of them refused to sign anything for the Red Cross, preferring anonymity to being identified with one Yugoslav group or the other. Already in 1945, the germs of the atrocities that eventually led to the dismemberment of that violent and fragile country were evident. We had no trouble with the small Russian group, which included a couple of fearsome-looking Asiatics. A Russian officer-captive volunteered to translate for us. When I asked him what his duties had been in the Russian army, he said: "I was an expert." That had to do. Our mission completed, with not a single German agent found, we returned to Le Vesinet, but not for long.

At least I knew where I belonged. I was part of the XV Corps, Seventh Army, under the command of Lt. Gen. Alexander M. Patch, and I was to head a team of military intelligence interpreters, all of us reporting at Metz, more or less immediately. (Metz, capital of the region of Lorraine, close to the German border, had been taken by the Allies only a few weeks earlier.) Rundstedt and the Battle of the Bulge were now ancient history, the German army was retreating fast, and we were after them. Arriving at Metz, I found many shops open, so I bought a bottle of perfume and a couple of silk stockings for Hedy to celebrate her college graduation. We had been writing each other almost daily, and my wonderful tiny microfilm V-mail messages were reaching her with regularity, while her letters, addressed to my APO number, came occasionally bunched up, thereby increasing my joy of reading each single item. A substantial portion of my army salary went to her (that was common practice in those days), since we needed relatively little money for what we were doing.

In Metz I finally met the rest of my team: Staff Sergeant Martin Becker, a smart and well-educated Carlton College (Minn.) graduate, Sgt. Grigout, and Cpls. Edward Rauner and Willy Juchem. Grigout, a French native, soon opted out to join a unit where his fluent French was better appreciated. Becker's French seemed equally fluent, while Rauner and Juchem were native Germans. Our team at that point was not isolated; we were part of an M.I. pool, pursuing similar tasks: following the infantry, reconnoitering occupied villages, interrogating and frequently arresting suspects, and lining up willing (sometimes all too willing) informants. We were still in French territory, spending considerable time in villages like Sarralbe and St. Avold, frequently going on nightly raids, following leads from informants. Alsace-Lorraine was once a disputed territory, and we had reasons to presume that many residents might have been German sympathizers.

We were ordered to enforce curfew after sundown, mainly for the protection of the locals against trigger-happy GIs. One evening I regretfully arrested an old Frenchman gaily biking homebound. "Mon vélo!" he yelled out pleadingly. I reassured him that we wouldn't take his bike away; in fact, both he and his bike would be retired for a night's rest.

As our advance was unbelievably fast, I was commanded to appear at an intelligence seminar in nearby Nancy, where we were told that within days we would reach Germany proper, and we should anticipate a more hostile welcome. We were also given the all-important book called "Automatic Arrest Categories," listing names of SS members, known war criminals, and pre–1933 members of the Nazi party. These were to be arrested on sight and turned over to the MPs for the purpose of immediate internment. That immensely worthy and well-documented tool was to simplify our work in the days ahead.

Slowly we were exchanging positions with the arriving Free French forces. I was asked to act as a liaison in one instance, and my French counterpart was shocked to discover that I was uncivilized enough not to be able to discuss matters with him in French. Luckily, Sgt. Becker was there to "moderate," but it was an unpleasant enough episode to becloud my last days in French territory.

13. The End of the Third Reich

In March 1945, the U.S. Army advanced through German territory at a headlong pace, and our team (M.I.I. 426-G) followed the tanks and the infantry, spending every night in a different location. We were getting our orders from XV Corps Headquarters, sometimes from Col. Welch, the G-2 chief, and more frequently from his deputy, a major who was always good to me and whose name I was unable to locate through army records. We and other teams within the corps intelligence pool did raids at a frantic pace, generally using scare tactics by rushing into buildings, brandishing carbines, and doing business the only way Germans understood war. We managed to arrest some people listed among the official suspects; others were revealed to us by informants. We had been instructed to consult local priests and ministers, which we did very respectfully — some readily cooperated, others acted confused and not particularly forthcoming. In one memorable instance, we entered a house in our usual rambunctious way, and the man whom we were about to arrest pleaded in this manner: "I am not the man you want, it is my brother who is the Nazi!" He pointed out his brother's house, and we duly accommodated him. The tiny village of Blieskastel near Saarbrücken was our first, and not too important, German point of entry. There we received orders to report as soon as possible at the City Hall of Mannheim, about 100 miles to the west, for further briefings. My team followed orders, just to discover that the bridges on the Neckar River had all been destroyed a few nights before by our Air Force. We had to leave our jeep behind in Cpl. Juchem's care, as Becker, Grigout, Rauner, and I proceeded to row across in a small boat, causing some merriment at City Hall. After receiving further instructions, we rowed back and continued on our prescribed journey. The city of Mannheim lay in ruins, with abandoned

German vehicles and dead horses littering the streets. I saved a photograph showing the Nazi poster "Niemand kann den Sieg uns rauben weil wir an den Führer glauben!" ("No one can rob us of our victory because we trust our Führer!") It was a grotesque sign of useless defiance amidst all that devastation, and we could hardly wait to leave that once beautiful city behind.

Pressing northeast, we passed through Darmstadt and Aschaffenburg and established temporary domicile in the very pleasant town of Bad Brückenau, where we set up our own center of operations in a spacious three-story house. As usual by then, the men of the house, if any, were serving with the German army; the women were reasonably friendly, especially after I informed them that we would share our food rations with them if they would do the cooking for us. Willy Juchem was charged with keeping us supplied with rations. Willy was very good at that, also with keeping our jeep in good running order, and with mechanical things in general. Matters involving military intelligence work were outside his ken. We did plenty of that at Bad Brückenau, arresting — without resistance — several rather surprised and indignant individuals, usually echoing the phrase that had become all too familiar to our ears: "*Ich war gezwungen....*" ("I was forced to do whatever you are accusing me of doing.") Men of my generation are not likely to forget where they were on April 12, 1945, the day President Franklin D. Roosevelt died, a mere three weeks before the German surrender. We were at Bad Brückenau, shocked in disbelief.

In John Toland's book, "The Last 100 Days," (Random House, New York, 1965) I found the following (p. 237): "In the meeting at Lúneville, Eisenhower mentioned that the West Wall was still standing in front of Patch's Seventh Army, while Patton had made a breakthrough, and then asked Patch if Patton could attack across the northern section of the Seventh Army zone. Patch readily agreed. 'We are all in the same army,' he said."

Naturally, soldiers at my level couldn't have known about such discussions. But it made eminent sense in retrospect why my little unit was suddenly ordered to drive about 200 miles south to join up with the 3rd Infantry Division of Gen. Patton's Third Army as it was ready to attack Nürnberg in mid–April. We drove past the lovely town of Würzburg, which I had once admired in 1939, and joined up with the 3rd Infantry at the outskirts of Nürnberg, not always knowing whether we were in safe or still in German-held territory. Finally, we received orders to report at a local high school gym for a briefing by the Division CG, Major General John W. O'Daniel, in the wee hours of April 20. The general entered, flashing that morning's issue of *The Stars and Stripes* with the headline Nürnberg Taken By Patton's Third Army. He then jovially said, "Let's get going, guys. We can't make liars out of the press!"

In Darmstadt, Germany, 1943.

Encountering sporadic resistance, the city was taken that afternoon. By the end of the day, Hans Sachs's beloved Nürnberg looked worse than Mannheim, as our artillery had demolished the buildings the Air Force might have overlooked. It was a horrendous sight, but Wagner's opera only fleetingly crossed my mind as I was musing that the Nürnberg of 1945 was

Hitler's city, just receiving what it had asked for. My team remained attached to the Third Division as we moved toward Dachau and Munich, in that order. Munich had been scorched, though not as badly as Nürnberg, but some of its splendid historical public buildings had sustained direct hits, among them the Bavarian State Opera.

The capture of Dachau (April 29) inflamed the entire area. General Patton made the entire town of Dachau march through the camp to witness the horrors. Then, after having supervised the needed medical care for the surviving inmates, but leaving the dead bodies in place, Patton requested a delegation from the U.S. Congress to fly in and inspect those otherwise unbelievable sights. Meanwhile, in Munich, enraged GIs were beating up whatever Germans they saw in uniform (mailmen and policemen), believing them to be either camp guards or soldiers. Although our GIs were allowed to visit the camp after a few days, I chose to relieve a colleague on duty so that he might visit the dreaded camp. A news photographer later showed me a photograph of bodies lying in a heap. They were all prison guards killed by the attacking U.S. forces.

My team finally caught up with units of the Seventh Army (or it was the other way around, I no longer remember) in the very pleasant resort town of Bad Aibling, near Rosenheim in southern Bavaria, not too far from what used to be the Austrian border. There I received my promotion to first lieutenant, but my always benevolent major of the XV Corps told me: "You'll have to go to Heidelberg to buy your silver bars." (That great university town had surrendered to us without a fight, wisely to avoid destruction. Subsequently, Heidelberg became the location of the Seventh Army Post Exchange, among other good things.) I immediately requested, and was granted, promotions for my teammates, now T/Sgt Becker and Sgts. Juchem and Rauner.

Our entire function had changed as the war reached its final stages. There was no need for prisoner interrogations, because the dejected and undernourished German soldiers were surrendering in huge numbers. Our informants meanwhile had multiplied, making arrests relatively easy. Counter-intelligence personnel began to join our ranks. They were, as a rule, a cocky lot, usually noncoms, but wearing no special insignias enabled them to act like officers. With our workload temporarily eased, we began to spend our Sundays exploring the countryside.

In one memorable instance, we decided to visit Willy Juchem's mother in Idar-Oberstein, a town quite a distance away in what was then the French-occupied zone. I left T/Sgt Becker in charge, and Ed Rauner joined us on that (totally unauthorized) jaunt. It was a surreal experience: a German mother welcoming her American elder son, with her younger son (a recently discharged, or AWOL, German army man) sharing the family table, to which part of our rations had contributed. The wine was local, very good, and plentiful. Idar-Oberstein was the center of Germany's industry of semi-precious stones. Since just about every older man we met seemed to have been one of Willy's uncles, we spent our valuable dollars to good advantage. I left with a giant topaz and two smaller stones of aquamarine to be brought home eventually for Hedy — and all to be stolen many years later during a house burglary in good old New York.

After Hitler's suicide was announced on May 1, the surrenders multiplied, causing our troops a multitude of problems in terms of managing the sick and the wounded, and handling the sheer number of captives involved. Word was received from high above that we would have to discharge all except SS personnel as soon as possible. My team was assigned to an army battalion nearby, whose commanding officer asked us to help them out ASAP. Surveying the situation, I asked for some administrative and medical assistance and a row of tables. Setting the tables up in the manner of a Detroit assembly line, we had the forlorn captives lined up to be deloused, inoculated, interrogated, and summarily discharged (after signing a hastily improvised statement testifying to the truth of their personal data). Hundreds were thus processed within a matter of hours. The battalion commander reported the affair to corps headquarters, praising my methods, and within a few days I was awarded a Certificate Of Merit "for a high degree of devotion to duty," signed by Lt. General Wade H. Haislip, commanding general of the XV Corps.

There was no longer such a thing as a functioning German army, but the "Automatic Arrest" principles remained in force, and our counter-intelligence agents (including my team) continued looking for SS elements, reported war criminals, and the like. A wonderful letter from Hedy reassured me that my sister Évi was alive, and that cousin George had been hospitalized in Germany with severe frostbite and, after receiving a medical discharge, was on his way home. His brother, Charlie, was sending very optimistic news home from what was, by then, a totally pacified Italy.

Locating Charlie's unit was reasonably easy through the Seventh Army resources in Augsburg, their new headquarters. I had recently visited there on official business, which, nevertheless, allowed me to take pictures of Augsburg's historical sights associated with Martin Luther. Charlie's Fifth Army unit was located somewhere near the Brenner Pass, not too far from Bad Aibling, the pleasant town we were soon to depart from. Wasting no time and accompanied by Martin Becker, I set out the next Sunday, driving southward on a scenic road past Kufstein, then on secondary roads toward the Brenner region. There, at an army checkpoint, I was told by a

Fifth Army lieutenant that, as I had no valid pass, he had no jurisdiction to allow me into the Fifth Army zone. It was late evening by then and, after hearing my emotional plea (in which Charlie became my "brother"), my highly sympathetic counterpart suggested that Martin and I spend the night at the checkpoint, while he would give our names to the officer who was to relieve him at midnight. "You look for him in the wee hours, and he'll let you pass. Then you'll be on your own."

With Charlie (right) at the Brenner Pass, 1945.

So it happened. We found Charlie's company commander in the village of Vipiteno, a few miles south of the Brenner railroad station. Not surprisingly, Charlie, a natural *charmeur*, was the most popular member of the group. He was also an amateur pianist who knew hundreds of melodies by heart and played them not always accurately, but usually with clever improvisations of his own. Our encounter was very joyful, and Charlie treated my companion, Martin Becker, like an old family friend. Our immediate plan was to have Martin take a picture of us at the very railroad station where Hitler and Mussolini had held a historic meeting not long before. But we found the station in a heap of ruins, not an alluring sight for the folks at home, so Martin caught us leaning on my jeep at a wonderfully happy moment, all smiles. But our joyful meeting had to be brief because we had to hurry back to Germany. Getting out of the Fifth Army zone was much easier than getting into it. Little did we know that Charlie, an old Army veteran by then, rich in point credits, would spend his remaining military months as a member of the American mission in Russian-occupied Hungary!

Words reached us at Bad Aibling that the new headquarters of the XV Corps was now located in the vicinity of Salzburg, and my team was expected to set up shop in the town itself as soon as possible. That, of course, meant immediately. We proceeded through Rosenheim, partly on the Autobahn, partly on secondary roads and, as we passed through villages toward the end of our journey, we observed a far more relaxed attitude on the part of the local residents. It took a while to realize that we were now in what used to be Austria. Eagerness to provide directions and the ready smiles accompanying them, sometimes followed by a desire to convince us that we were talking with "Hitler's first victims," fell on the occupants of our jeep with a hollow ring. We knew that these very same people had extended a far more joyful reception to Hitler in 1938, lustily shouting "Ein Volk, ein Reich, ein Führer!" Thus unimpressed, we reached Salzburg a few days before V-E Day was solemnly announced on May 7, 1945.

14. Salzburg, and
My Moment in History

Before the complete surrender of the German Army, rumors were flying about hard-line Nazis hiding out in the Bavarian caves, planning last-ditch counter attacks of some kind. It was absurd; the war was over and German units were surrendering all over the place. My team, joined by a few additional counter-intelligence personnel, was quartered elegantly on the bank of the river Salzach, with a beautiful view of Salzburg, the very scenic and mercifully undamaged city of Mozart's birth. The house belonged to an officer, somewhere in captivity, I suppose. The family, after reassuring us that they were Austrians, not Germans, was pleased to have Americans as occupiers, and not the dreaded Russians. They gave us their best rooms, cooked for us and we, in turn, shared our generous food rations with them. Our workstation was the "Gerichtsgebäude" (Court House) across the river. There we were interrogating political prisoners, most of whom had surrendered a few days before our arrival. Among them were such Nazi bigwigs as the repulsive Julius Streicher, the notorious agitator, and Fritz Sauckel, the boss of slave labor throughout the Reich — both were eventually executed in Nürnberg, along with other major war criminals. At the end of my first working day, contemplating the peaceful Salzach and the city of Mozart it surrounds, I couldn't help feeling immensely grateful that I could celebrate the arrival of peace in such surroundings.

On May 9 I was summoned by Col. Welch, the G-2 chief of the XV Corps. He informed me that a certain Hungarian high official, claiming to be the national leader of Hungary, and his very large entourage, had surrendered to one of our regimental commanders. "Go to the village of Mattsee, some 20 miles from Salzburg," ordered the colonel. "Find out who this guy is and report back to me as soon as possible!" My heart began pounding, because I sensed that the "guy" in question had to be Ferenc Szálasi, the leader of Hungary's Hitlerite party who had recently arrested Regent Horthy on Hitler's orders and seized power. I took Sgt. Becker with me, and we took off immediately.

When we arrived at Mattsee, we found the entire village brimming with Hungarian soldiers. We were directed to the "Gasthof Seewirt," a spacious hotel where U.S. officers were waiting for us and guided us toward a special dining room to meet the inn's mysterious guest. I entered, followed by several U.S. officers, and recognized Szálasi from his pictures. His wife was standing beside him. Before I could open my mouth, an insignificant-looking solemn German bureaucrat (later identified as Kurt Haller, Hitler's delegate to keep an eye on Szálasi) tried to introduce his principal to me in German. I wordlessly but roughly pushed him aside and, first looking at Szálasi, turned around and addressed myself to the American officers: "Gentlemen, let *me* make the introduction. You are not facing a head of state but a murderous thug who seized power from Hungary's legitimate government, causing the death of thousands of victims. I urge you to regard him as a war criminal." Then I turned to Szálasi and said a few choice words in Hungarian, calculated to scare him out of his wits. By that time, emotions completely took hold of me. The place was in an uproar, and my U.S. superiors advised me to collect myself. A fellow lieutenant, probably in charge of public relations, openly accused me of behavior unfit for an officer and hinted that a report would be made of my "improper" behavior. After a few more words of explanation to the other U.S. officers, amplifying the basic facts of Szálasi's miserable past, they thanked me for my participation and suggested that I should go out to the fresh air and calm down.

In the courtyard, I was approached by a Hungarian colonel named István Mészáros who was totally unaware of the events inside, but who had been told that I was a native Hungarian. After lamenting to me about how his nation was caught in a tragic fate "entirely due to the German affiliation," he asked me if I could say a few words to his confused and depressed troops. "It would cheer them up to be talked to in Hungarian by an officer in American uniform," he said. I stood on top of my jeep and the colonel gathered perhaps a hundred soldiers around me, all eagerly listening. In my brief talk, I told the soldiers that the war was over, the American army had no intention of further detaining them, and, unless we had special reasons to hold certain individuals, most of the others would soon be properly released and free to go. "You'll find the way," I remember telling them. "Hungary isn't far away."

After my little speech, I was accosted by a Hungarian civilian who must have escaped from some German detention camp and who assured me that he was already on his way to Hungary. He wanted to know if I had any relatives there and offered to contact them. I gave him my sister's name and address, but later I learned that he did a lot more. He contacted a Budapest newspaper with his own version of Szálasi's capture, in which I played a somewhat exaggerated role. Several versions of that story and other variants continued to reappear in the Hungarian press in later years; the last such appearance known to me was in the March 27, 1996, issue of *Magyar Nemzet*.

My mission completed, Martin Becker and I returned to Salzburg, and I was ready to submit my report to Col. Welch when a phone call requested my immediate presence. "The old man wants to see you personally," said his deputy, sounding somewhat ominous. That caused me worry about the fate of my recently acquired silver bars. When we entered the Colonel's office, he said, "I hear, Lieutenant, that you had an adventurous visit at Mattsee, and I want to hear *your* account of it." Obviously, the report of that busybody PR officer had already reached him. I proceeded to give Col. Welch a terse but essential background of Hungary's recent history, and Szálasi's part in it. The Colonel listened with great interest. Here is a summation of our brief dialogue:

> "Tell me, did you hit the son of a bitch?"
> "No, Sir."
> "Never laid a hand on him?"
> "No, Sir, not for a moment. But I wasn't polite, either."
> "OK, George. That's all."

He even called me by my first name. That was the end of the story, only a postscript is needed.

At this point, major events were taking place, about which neither Col. Welch nor I had any knowledge. Szálasi was a very stupid man who, in his delusional mind, had believed that, as a chief of state, he would meet with an American general to discuss Hungary's future. After all, he had never fought Americans and only wanted to keep the country free of the Russians. Besides, part of his military entourage included the honorary guard entrusted with the safekeeping of the 1000-year-old Crown of St. Stephen and other sacred relics, symbols of the nation's government. He knew where the iron crate containing those priceless treasures was hidden. Of course, in due course, the chief of the honor guard disclosed their location to the commanding general of the American Seventh Army. After months of complicated diplomatic maneuvers on two continents, the Hungarian national treasures were transferred to Fort Knox, where they remained for more than 20 years during the Cold War. They were returned to the Hungarian government only in 1978 under the Carter administration.

Szálasi was transferred to Augsburg soon after the Mattsee episode. There he continued spinning his delusionary dreams for a few more months. He and other war criminals were delivered to the new Hungarian government in early 1946. Szálasi was soon tried, found guilty of all charges, and hanged on March 12, 1946. To this day, I feel a certain amount of satisfaction, even elation, knowing that I was able to make a modest contribution to that event.

Our Salzburg stay was short after that exciting Mattsee adventure. The U.S. military government took over the Court House and my team's further activities were strictly counter-intelligence by nature. So, after a fond farewell to Mozart's Salzburg (contaminated briefly by the likes of Julius Streicher), we took to our jeep and moved to temporary but very agreeable quarters in Ludwigsburg near Stuttgart, with the principal mission to round up members of the Gestapo. Very little resistance was encountered, particularly since we received unexpectedly benevolent help from professional German police officers. Obviously, there was no love lost between the "Staatliche Kriminalpolizei" (the State Criminal Police) and the "Geheime Staatspolizei" (The GeStaPo), and the former group knew how to ignore the latter's frequent protestations of "innocence." At Ludwigsburg, I ran into an MI colleague, Lt. Roselinsky, a New Yorker, who showed up in a small Mercedes he must have "liberated" from a German officer. (I was not above such "liberating" activities myself, though I preferred Luger pistols for which actually I had no use, but sold a few of them to "behind the line" GI officers for good money). In any case, Roselinsky and I made a Sunday excursion to Marbach, the birthplace of Friedrich Schiller. I took pictures of the Neckar river and the Schiller Museum (which was closed for the duration), where I would have loved to browse through material pertaining to such opera-related works as *Wilhelm Tell*, *Die Räuber*, and, especially, *Don Carlos*.

Mail service improved a great deal after VE Day both ways. Hedy was enrolled in her master's course at Columbia University; her father was doing defense work as an architectural draftsman (his initial specialty before he had switched to music, his real love). Cousin George established himself as a photographer, and his brother Charles became attached to the American Military Mission in Budapest. There he located my sister Évi, but also fell in love with another Éva, a Hungarian girl and his future wife. Everything seemed to be in order, except that I was still in Europe, long enough but quite short of the "point credits" that would make my return home a possibility.

With the Japanese surrender in September 1945, a new hope dawned on the horizon. Hungary had been occupied by the Russian forces since February and, keeping in mind the existence of a modest American presence with a military mission manned partly by Hungarian-speaking military soldiers like Charlie, I felt that I might have a chance to apply for a "compassionate" leave. I submitted such a request at SHAEF (General Eisenhower's Headquarters) in Hoechst, near Frankfurt. It was rejected with a note that the United States had no military authority to consider such a request. My attempt was probably ill timed at such an early date. Soon I was already established at Schwarzenborn, not far from Frankfurt, so I felt encouraged to try again, later. Schwarzenborn, in any case, turned out to be my last European station, and it deserves a separate chapter.

15. Back to Hungary

The Schwarzenborn internment camp was probably a Nazi legacy. By October 1945 it had been transformed into a gathering place for holding discharged German soldiers, Nazi politicians, SS men, and other suspected persons captured by U.S. troops under our government's "automatic arrest" directives. The camp was located outside the tiny village of Hauptschwenda, in the province of Hessen, north of Frankfurt. There two other intelligence teams joined mine, led by Lieutenants Weik and Peters, both Ritchie graduates. The camp was already full of detainees, hundreds of them, all guarded by our MPs. The task of our teams was to study individual dossiers, interrogate the prisoners one by one, and make recommendations regarding their future. The options were (1) further detention, (2) transfer to a higher echelon for further investigation, and (3) recommendation for release upon determination that the individual represented no danger to our security. Our initial impression was that we were facing an enormous task, but there was no hurry; our "clients" were not going anywhere.

Hauptschwenda was a dot on the map, perhaps a mile or so from the camp, and we took over its spacious hotel for our headquarters. The hotel seemed quite large for a village of only a few houses but, as we soon learned, Hauptschwenda, surrounded by forests, was a favorite hunting area in peaceful times. The setting was quite bucolic and, as usual, we were amply supplied with food, shared with an all-too-eager personnel under Willy Juchem's capable supervision. We kept a fairly normal schedule, on duty seven days a week, with a skeleton crew alternating on Sundays.

I traveled quite a bit during those days, to Heidelberg on business, also to reasonably undamaged Darmstadt, Wetzlar (home of the Leica factory), and Giessen — all nearby and easily approachable via the Autobahn. On these short travels, I was pleased to see posters about symphonic concerts featuring music by Mendelssohn. That made me think that an entire generation of Germans were now allowed to discover the music of that genius, also that of Mahler, Offenbach, and Meyerbeer — all taboo during the Hitler era. I suppose they even became re-acquainted with the poems of Heine in recitals offering musical settings by such respectable Aryans as Schumann, Brahms, and Liszt. I didn't have time to attend any of those concerts, but when I heard of an open-air performance in Frankfurt of Gluck's *Orpheus und Eurydice,* I couldn't resist the opportunity.

It was a remarkable event. Frankfurt, nowadays a blooming metropolis, was totally bombed out in 1945, and the opera was given, literally, in the craters created by recent British or American raids. Whoever the stage designer was, he or she used exceptional ingenuity in placing that archaic story into an aptly realistic setting, abetted by simple but dignified costuming. Naturally, it was a German-language performance with an outstanding baritone Orpheus, who was unknown to me at the time. Not too many years later, I was happy to recognize him as Hermann Uhde, the Met's memorable Telramund, Wozzeck, and Grand Inquisitor.

At the camp, matters ran a businesslike course. My fellow officers and I studied the prisoners' records and first selected individual cases of special interest. To facilitate our task, we also considered files where incriminating data seemed either insufficient or nonexistent. When I consulted corps headquarters about them, I was told that in such situations I should not hesitate to recommend release. "Don't worry about guilty parties escaping," my superior said. "They usually go back to their home town and, if they have something to hide, the informants will turn them in." That sounded wise, and we acted accordingly. Other cases were far more complicated, especially one of great personal interest to me, the case of Ferenc Rajniss, a onetime member of the Hungarian Parliament, also an editor of a pro–Nazi newspaper and even, briefly, a member of the Szálasi cabinet. A physically attractive man in his forties, he came into the interrogation room, greeted me in excellent English, and explained that he had attended Columbia University for a year as part of his university studies. I reacted coolly and immediately turned the conversation into Hungarian, telling him that, while I was unaware of his American connection, his history was quite familiar to me. I named the Hungarian newspaper he once edited and, quite stunned, he then proceeded to explain to me that he regarded the Nazi movement and his "slight" involvement in it "on an intellectual level." Not wishing to get my temper up, I kept the rest of the conversation short, and sent him back to his barracks. In my subsequent report to my superiors, I provided chapter and verse on Rajniss, and my connection with him ended there, except that I retained his photo identification card as a souvenir. I later learned with some satisfaction that he was delivered to the new Hungarian government, and was executed by a firing squad in early 1946.

The camp was divided into rows of barracks, several of which formed larger units under the administrative supervision of a senior inmate demo-cratically elected by his fellow detainees. All this was organized with tradi-tional German efficiency, and once a week these "department heads" were expected to report to me and my fellow officers with whatever complaints and suggestions they might have regarding discipline, hygiene, and med-ical welfare. One of these barracks chiefs was Prince August Wilhelm, the son of the Kaiser, who — according to his dossier — was an "Alter Kämpfer," a name denoting Nazis who had joined the party in 1928, long before Hitler came to power. "AuWi," as he was called behind his back by fellow inmates, was then a man around 60, dressed with a certain shabby elegance, courtly and soft spoken in manner. The first time he gave us his report, he did so in flawless English, prompting Sgt. Bienstock of our staff to address him as follows:

> "Prince, I must compliment you on your command of English."
> "Thank you, Sergeant. But please remember that I am a grandnephew of an Englishwoman ... Queen Victoria! *Touché!*

Bienstock, a native of Frankfurt, was an excellent interrogator. It was his good fortune to examine the former Bürgermeister of Frankfurt, and to dazzle him with his intimate knowledge of the city where he had spent his early childhood some two decades before the interrogation in question. The courtly prince, incidentally, remained in detention for the rest of my stay and beyond. His further fate was unknown to me. We had nothing "crim-inal" on him, but the glory of that early Nazi membership cost him dearly.

One quiet evening, my colleagues had an idea that we should go hunt-ing in a nearby forest, taking a local citizen as our guide. Never being inter-ested in the sport, I joined the little group, taking my regulation carbine, without ever intending to use it. As night was descending, suddenly a majes-tic stag appeared on the moonlit horizon, in a clearing not too far away. As I stood by, weapon firmly on shoulder and dazzled by the view, Lt. Peters fired a single tracer bullet, and the beautiful animal collapsed with the grace of a ballet dancer. We gathered our victim and pitilessly delivered him to the kitchen. Thanksgiving Day was nearing, and more than a dozen of us ended up enjoying a cozy Thanksgiving venison dinner with wine, and a few more venison dinners thereafter.

The days at Schwarzenborn were otherwise passing more or less uneventfully, as I was getting frequent news from Hedy, now about to get her master's degree at Columbia University. She kept me informed about my sister Évi's situation, which appeared not too bad, considering Hun-gary's deplorable state under the occupying Russian army. As a new year was approaching and my return home seemed closer, I decided to re-apply to SHAEF for that "compassionate leave" to Hungary. This time I felt that a more personal approach was needed. At SHAEF Headquarters, I managed to make contact with a sympathetic captain who helped me rephrase my original application, making it more urgent and personal. In about 10 days, miraculously, my leave was granted. It called for 15 days effective the date of my reporting to the American mission in Budapest, subject to approval by the Russian authorities.

Christmas went by quietly in our snow-filled, sylvan, Christmassy surroundings. But New Year's Eve was greeted at Schwarzenborn by a barrage of gunfire, as rifles, carbines, and pistols fired into the air, scaring the orderly villagers of Hauptschwenda, unacquainted with this kind of gung-ho GI exuberance, to death. My team at the inn celebrated in a more disciplined manner, though not quite soberly — armistice being the cause of it as much as the day of the calendar.

Within a few days, I was on my way, driven to Frankfurt by Sgt. Willy. There I mounted a train, with my cherished furlough in hand, *en route* to Vienna, then a city partitioned by the three occupying armies, the United States, Great Britain, and Russia. The train ride was slow but smooth. In dreary Vienna, I no longer remember the U.S. Army authority where I reported, but I was assigned to the Hotel Regina, near the city's many attractive parks. Duffle bag unpacked, I went to sleep in the lap of relative luxury. Next morning, at breakfast, I was told that others had tried to get into Hungary on official business, but had encountered all sorts of difficulties with the Russians. But, with that wonderful open-end furlough in my packet, I refused to be disheartened. I was in Vienna, after all; the Staatsoper must have reopened by then, I thought.

It was open all right — open to all the elements. The center of the "Opernring," the very heart of Vienna, had been totally destroyed by Allied bombs; the famous Staatsoper would remain closed for seven more years. But the opera company was functioning at two locations, the Volksoper (within walking distance from the Hotel Regina) and the Theater an der Wien, where Beethoven's *Fidelio* was premiered in 1805. This is Vienna, I thought gratefully, and things are almost normal. That same evening, I went to the Theater an der Wien with a Navy lieutenant who was also on his way to Budapest on some official business. *Hoffmanns Erzählungen* ("The Tales of Hoffmann") was on the bill, with Julius Patzak in the title role. Two evenings later, by which time my Navy colleague had received his Hungarian entry and flown away, I went to the Volksoper and heard an exciting double bill "auf Deutsch" of *Cavalleria rusticana* and *Pagliacci,* with the great Hungarian soprano Maria Németh as Santuzza. With that, my personal little Vienna Opera Festival came to an end. The Russians took pity on me, and in early January of the new and peaceful year of 1946, I was on my way to Budapest, a city from which I departed in April 1939, leaving a serene childhood behind and heading toward an uncertain future.

There were only a handful of passengers on the small army plane that flew us to Budapest, only an hour away. We followed the path of the Danube, as I remembered it from my school maps, but the aerial view, with its vastly increased dimension, was thrilling. On arrival, a waiting army truck soon delivered us to the commission headquarters at one of the many hotels on the Pest side of the Danube. The American presence was very small in that Russian-occupied country so, understandably, all American visitors were cordially received. I never had the pleasure of meeting Col. George Kovach, the senior U.S. officer, but his deputy smilingly greeted me, saying, "I am delighted that you are finally here, lieutenant. Your sister has been driving us crazy." (Évi had been told that I was on my way by cousin Charlie, now back in New York and enjoying civilian status.) I presented my furlough, made the rounds, and was assured that a military jeep would be at my disposal on request, restricted to the Budapest area.

My sister showed up soon thereafter, and we had a tearfully ecstatic reunion. She was 16 when we had last seen each other; now she was a 22-year-old young woman. She lived in a pleasant one-room apartment crammed with whatever pieces of furniture she had been able to rescue or reclaim from our parents' home. We walked there as I observed, and photographed, the Danube with its destroyed bridges eerily submerged in the water. At her place, Évi treated me to "aranygaluska," a highly caloric pas-

Reunion with my sister Évi in Hungary, 1946.

try we both loved since our childhood. Our talk about our parents was filled
with infinite mourning because we knew that, even if some survivors would
occasionally filter back literally from the dead, our parents would never
return. Much of the night was spent in a tragic accounting of who was still
alive and who was not. All of my mother's six siblings were gone except her
younger brother László, his wife and older son Endre (Bandi); the younger
one (Pista) had emigrated to Palestine, signed up with the British army, and
perished there. Our aunt Melanie (Ernö's widow) survived, as did her older
son Imre, a physician now, enrolled in military hospital duties. Most of my
former schoolmates had disappeared, but Joe Marton was reported to have
been rescued by a Swedish humanitarian agency, as was Margit Róna, our
mother's close friend. Her husband was killed, their two children, Miklós
and Ágnes, survived. The Róna family were our neighbors at Lake Balaton,
and close family friends. The Balaton villa, Évi explained, was still ours, the
property having been jointly owned by our father and uncle Ernö. Évi and
I, with cousin Imre, were now the surviving owners, but with the Russians
around, we didn't know how long personal properties would continue to be
respected. Our long yearned-for reunion was filled with too much sadness;
the memories we shared were too tragic to be called bittersweet, but at least
the two of us were together in loving closeness and consolation.

The following day I picked up a jeep and we drove to Ujpest, where
I found my uncle László and his wife in pitiful condition. Their modest
apartment had to accommodate a couple, perfect strangers, under orders by
the authorities, due to an acute housing shortage. László had already known
of my arrival because, miraculously, a young Hungarian soldier, who had
been part of the group I had addressed at Matsee during the Szálasi
encounter, recognized me and remembered me from childhood. I told both
my uncle and my sister not to talk about Szálasi and me to anyone. I had
no time for reporters or any other curious and inquisitive people. We left
Ujpest and communicated with Melanie and Imre on the Buda side of the
city by phone because, with all bridges destroyed, the Russian authorities
limited all traffic to "official business," and I was taking no chances. Now
that she was free to talk, my sister described in horrid detail the abysmal
behavior of the marauding Russian army during the siege, how they drunk-
enly raped and brutalized their way through the city until some semblance
of order was established, weeks later.

My sister was able to gather up a few childhood friends for pastry and
coffee in the late afternoon. My old friend George Braun had Magyarized
his name in the interim and became Besnyő. After a few moments of conversation he wanted to compliment me on the way I had retained my
idiomatic command of Hungarian, but I felt almost offended, declaring that

my Hungarian was as good as theirs. That was greeted by general hilarity and, of course, they were right. The English language has a way of neutralizing vowel sounds; what sounded perfectly idiomatic to my ears was found "accented" to the natives. An absence of six years can do that; for the rest of my life, I was destined to speak various languages well, but that trace of an accent would never leave me. Our cousin Bandi was with us, and he cautioned me not to speak Hungarian to any strangers. The American uniform will work wonders, he said. "There are long lines everywhere, and you can easily ignore them; if you talk Hungarian, people will not leave you alone." It was good advice and, in any case, my sister just loved to see me in uniform, especially as we would occasionally encounter GIs in the city and exchange salutes.

I went to the American Consulate one morning, alone, and the throng respectfully allowed me to enter ahead of the line. The consul had only a temporary rank, but he was fully in charge. He received me cordially, but explained to me that diplomatically Hungary's situation was still unsettled, and pre-war conditions still applied regarding visa restrictions. When I asked if I could arrange to have a *pro forma* marriage for my sister with an American citizen back home, he said that such a question should not be addressed to a consul — leaving me corrected but disappointed. Évi didn't have immediate financial needs; she had a job of sorts, but everybody I met during my stay looked poor by normal standards, in shabby and frequently ill-matched clothing. Having foreseen her plight, I was able to leave a moderate sum in dollars with her — in those days that meant a lot.

On the brighter side, I took her to what once was the Royal Hungarian Opera House, now the Hungarian State Opera. The building itself stood solid and unscathed, the interiors somewhat faded, but full of sentimental memories for both of us. Wartime conditions still prevailed, and the house was not open every night. We caught an interesting balletic double bill: Liszt's *Carnival of Pest* (based on the Hungarian Rhapsody No. 9) and Gershwin's *Rhapsody in Blue*, rechristened choreographically as "American Rhapsody." The former was known to me from the old days, and it seemed nicely refurbished; the latter sounded reassuringly idiomatic.

Before leaving Budapest, we went to the best local photographer and sent our joint photo to Hedy in New York. I also promised my sister that I would do everything in my power to facilitate her joining us in the United States. She knew that I would soon become a civilian but, with all the better prospects before us, our parting was still very sad. The years we faced would turn out to be immensely complicated in the political sense. We maintained contact by mail, later by phone, but it took ten years and a revolution before we could be together again.

16. Homecoming

I flew back the way I came — to Vienna with an army plane — but this time I was too gloomy to trace the downward flow of the Danube from the skies. My meeting with Évi after all those years naturally lifted my spirits, but the finality of my parents' death overpowered all other emotions. My sister represented the present: peace, survival, and a promise of a brighter future for both of us. But we both were orphaned; something irreplaceable and invaluable was erased from our lives with brutal finality. The majestic Danube reminded me of the spectral sight of those destroyed bridges ... the city was also dead to me now, inhabited by sorrowful survivors and the ghosts of those relatives and friends who vanished forever — my cousin Paul who could have shared my exile and perhaps survived among the fortunate American soldiers, and my unforgettable friend Miklós. Évi and I actually visited Miklós's widowed mother one afternoon, and when she met me she broke into uncontrollable sobbing.

Before I knew it, the plane reached Vienna. There, instead of an interminable and cold train ride to Frankfurt, I made connection with an army cargo plane and was smoothly delivered to that bleak city within hours. Returning to Germany, of course, brought no remedy to my desolate moods, but in ways I no longer remember, surely involving some military hitchhiking, I managed to reach the vicinity of Hauptschwenda within a few hours. My buddies welcomed me, not realizing that I had been gone for two weeks. Nothing seemed to have changed around the camp, except that several prisoners had been released and no new arrivals were being reported. The combat part of the war was, by then, old history. Our army's main concern now was military government, which meant finding responsible people without a Nazi taint to fill administrative positions. It was not easy, as our American newspapers had duly reported, but that wasn't really what I and my colleagues had been trained for. The good news, however, was that my point credits were approaching the desirable numbers for homecoming. My colleague, Lt. Peters, was already planning his departure for mid–February.

It was already possible for my sister to write me at my APO number, but our correspondence was not long lasting because, miraculously, my point credits reached the appropriate figure by late February, and the day of my long-awaited departure became imminent. How lucky I was that I had been able to return to Budapest when I did — the timing couldn't have worked out better. My interest in the duties around the camp was waning at a steady pace. On the late evenings I was listening to U.S. Army radio programs that featured Tommy Dorsey, Duke Ellington, the late Glenn Miller, some country tunes — all nostalgic stuff. One of the programs used Eleanor Steber's "Out of My Dreams" from *Oklahoma* as a theme song, and every tuneful moment of her wistful song turned into audible homesickness for me.

In early March, the Army relieved me of my Schwarzenborn duties in preparation for the homeward journey. Along with a number of officers I was sent to Hanau, not far away, to organize what was to be known as the 693rd Field Artillery Battalion, unit exclusively created to prepare our return in the manner of an organized Army unit. Within a few days, I was told that I would become a battery commander in charge of 110 men. All this may sound simple, but it meant working several days and nights in a "regular army" way, in sharp contrast with the flexibility of a small team dedicated to a highly specialized duty. Incidentally, no field artillery work was involved, just army formations, calisthenics, lectures and such, but an army unit had to have a designation of some kind. In Hanau I came under a different APO number and, given the quick change and the brevity of time, I could no longer hope that any of Hedy's letters would reach me. On March 7, I sent a cable informing her that I would be transferred to Antwerp awaiting embarkation. I received no further correspondence from home. (I am able to reconstruct this timeline based on my last three letters from Germany, which miraculously survived. All of my other letters, which Hedy had meticulously saved, were terminally misplaced in 1975 by the transport company that arranged our last residential move from Long Island to Westchester County.)

Our stay at Hanau was dull but not unpleasant routine, once the battery was properly organized. To my surprise, the regimental commander approached me one evening, holding out the possibility that, should I be willing to postpone my return home, he could have me transferred to his already established cadre, tempting me with the captaincy that would go with such a transfer. I respectfully declined the offer. The colonel was a pleasant and sociable guy in the daytime; at evening meals he presided over the dinner, usually monopolizing the conversation with his ideas about the "unavoidable" war with the Soviet Union. However depressing it sounded at the time, it confirmed my decision that I should hold on to my commission in the Army Reserve, just in case. (I remained a reservist for a year thereafter.) In my last letter from Hanau, I wrote to Hedy, among other things: "I know no one who is basically as home-oriented as I am and so repelled by the idea of wandering around the world. And yet, I was doing just that in the past seven years. Perhaps now I will succeed in creating the settled and relaxed kind of life with you that I was always dreaming about."

It took our crowded and unheated troop train two and a half days to cover the seemingly simple 400 mile journey from Hanau to Antwerp. Several crucial bridges, destroyed in wartime sieges, compelled delays and reroutings; transportation in Western Europe was still a long way from normalcy. Once settled at "Camp Top Hat" near Antwerp, there was no point in bitching about the lack of comfort and the usual bureaucratic nonsense that goes with army life. The camp lay close enough to the harbor to hear the horns of departing ships — each sound caressed my ears with the magic of a symphony.

The wait at "Camp Top Hat" was longer than expected, and the exact day of my departure is no longer known to me. My last letter to Hedy was dated March 10; we embarked some two weeks later. The SS *Marine Raven* was one of those "Victory" ships constructed for the troops, a small vessel estimated to make the transatlantic journey in about 14 very long days. Our accommodations, however, were almost luxurious compared to my experience of nearly two years earlier: four double bunks, meaning eight officers per room. The company was collegial — we were, truthfully, all in the same boat, all tired of Europe, all eager to come home. The sea was reasonable as we departed in early April. All went well until the ship's captain announced that all personnel had to participate in daily "evacuation exercises" because there was a fear of loose mines left over from the hostilities. All officers were taking supervisory turns and, sure enough, as soon as the ocean started to misbehave, my stomach responded accordingly. My cabin mates affectionately called me "Old Salt," which I thought was appropriate enough. With my considerable maritime experience behind me, I ate very little, ventured into the "fresh air" only sparingly, and spent my time mainly reading and thinking.

There was a great deal to think about. Above all, I was grateful to be alive and to have made a contribution to a just war. Though still separated from my sister, in my misguided optimism I was convinced that we would be together fairly soon. Above all, I was returning to a kind of wife destiny must have selected for me, a loving mate, all heart, a brilliant intellect, the daughter of a musician, herself gifted with a wonderful musical ear and a God-given artistic talent. And she even spoke excellent Hungarian! In short, I felt near to Schiller's ideal of a man on whom "*mit immer vollen Händen die Götter ihre Gaben streun.*" This came from a stanza that became my life's motto ever since I first set it down in another ocean voyage, on the way to Havana back in 1939.

Yes, I had a lot to be thankful for, but my future loomed ahead in fuzzy colors within an indistinct shape. I had spent less than a year as an American civilian. In my four and a half years of Army service I became thoroughly Americanized and very much matured. I gained a lot more self-confidence and abandoned my inborn "continental" reticence. I surmounted obstacles and handled responsibility and even authority with a facility that once was contrary to my basic nature. But, in full knowledge of all these positive elements, I had the feeling that I was still one of those new Americans who "had just come off the boat." I was in my 27th year, with an interrupted schooling and without any firmly formed ideas of what direction my future would take. These uncertainties haunted me for the rest of my voyage. When the unique outline of New York appeared on the horizon, the ship's captain announced that it was too late in the evening to dock at our assigned pier — the ship would drop anchor overnight further up on the Hudson. This time, unlike back in 1939, we did pass by the Statue of Liberty, enjoying and reciprocating the welcoming happy sounds from the shore. The simple, unglamorous SS *Marine Raven* brought me home.

In the morning, we moved into New York's Pier 94, greeted by the joyful sound of awaiting multitudes — Hedy among them, accompanied by her beaming cousin George Turi. When my name was called over the microphone, I rushed down the gangplank like the kid I imagine I used to be, if indeed I ever was.... After endless hugs and kisses, the following brief dialogue ensued:

GEORGE: How thin you are!
HEDY: How fat you are!

Ulysses and Penelope we were not, but my Penelope was right. All that German cooking in Hauptschwenda added at least eight pounds to my weight. I would have never made Fort Benning with that paunchy shape!

Shortly thereafter, we were moved to Camp Kilmer, New Jersey, where on May 10, 1946, I became a civilian again.

17. Civilian Life
and Musical Beginnings

The Claremont Inn, once a New York historical landmark, was a lovely garden restaurant near Riverside Church. For reasons best known to local authorities, it was torn down decades ago, but it was there that Hedy and I celebrated our fifth wedding anniversary on July 29, 1947. On the photograph taken to commemorate the occasion, she looks very pretty, smiling and elegant; I looked youthful enough, but rather morose, reflecting perhaps my anxieties of the moment. I had promised Hedy to take her to Havana, a place I longed to re-visit as an "American tourist," and share that experience with her. But, even after collecting the decent sum the Army owed me for accumulated leave, our finances did not, in my judgment, encourage such extravagance. Hedy was already working as an economist at the Federal Reserve Bank, a very promising beginning even though, in those days, young women were earning considerably less than young men equally qualified for the same position. While I felt confident that in due time that Havana trip would materialize (thanks to Fidel Castro, it never did), I also felt guilty enough to promise her right on that anniversary occasion that we would exchange Havana for a more modest vacation in Montreal. That did happen, and we had a wonderful time.

Earlier, immediately after my discharge, we had briefly moved into Hedy's parents' apartment on Riverside Drive and began searching for one of our own, fairly nearby. Circumstances then required that you had to buy an apartment with the existing furniture — normally an illegal procedure, but made unavoidable by the post-war housing shortage. We did find a suitable place on the corner of Riverside Drive and 136th Street, easily accessible to both the subway system and to the Fifth Avenue bus that provided a much slower but more pleasant transportation to the city. I found employ-

Our fifth wedding anniversary, July 29, 1947, celebrated at the Claremont Inn.

ment soon enough in the export-import trade, so with our two incomes we made a decent living, at least for the time being. Our close family and friends formed a rather large circle. The Turi cousins, as always, felt like brothers to me. George, after working with various studios as a portrait photographer, established a place of his own on West 72nd Street. He worked very hard and chased women with as much energy as his line of work permitted, though he seemed to show surprising (for him) loyalty to his girlfriend Peggy. Charlie had already brought Éva, (later Ava), his Hungarian war bride, home. All three of us began thinking about starting families of our own. So did several army buddies of mine, with whom I quickly established contact, among them Sidney Krumholz, my friend from Lafayette College, and Joe Kestler, a former Camp Ritchie colleague. The Army had sent us on separate ways in Europe, but Joe's wife Ann and Hedy became very close friends while exchanging news "from the front" and commiserating over their parallel solitudes. That was the age of the baby boomers: worldwide statistics were soaring skyward.

I had to make an essential decision, and fast. There was the G.I. Bill of Rights, assuring generous government educational assistance for servicemen. Researching the subject, I learned that my European schooling plus six months of ASTP studies at Lafayette College would give me the equivalency of two college years. That looked very good on paper, but we were contemplating having a child in the full knowledge that Hedy would not be granted a maternity leave. Besides, what were my own plans and desires with that interrupted education of mine? A frank soul searching made me recognize a shocking lack of interest in various possibilities. The legal and medical professions never attracted me. Hedy was a terrific economist and, in future years, I was able to learn more about that subject than I had ever hoped to learn. History I always loved and I became fascinated by political science during my courses at Lafayette, though not enough to consider it as my life's work. I inherited my father's high regard for the teaching profession, but my own nervous and impatient nature did not suggest the makings of a good teacher. None of the sciences held any allure for me. The long list of negatives narrowed down to one subject, music. But my violin studies and limited background in theory and harmony were not sufficient for a higher academic pursuit of music at that time. I was confident that I would eventually amount to something in the field, but a career in music had to be put on hold. Thus, I regretfully decided to forgo the wonderful opportunities offered by the G.I. Bill and to continue in the export trade that would assure me a livelihood, hoping that I would build my future slowly, one step at a time.

Cousin George, who had enjoyed his bachelorhood with a passion, eventually married his Peggy. His brother Charlie, who was establishing himself very modestly as a jobber in gold jewelry (becoming, within a few years, a very successful manufacturer) and his wife Ava were already expecting their first child. All the boomers were obviously booming, and, without any further soul searching, Hedy and I agreed that our time had also come.

While in many ways the future augured well for the American postwar generation, the news from Hungary had turned depressing. Stalin and his Hungarian henchmen began to take over the nation. Several liberal parties were disbanded and, under the rule of Mátyás Rákosi, Hungary — like Nazi Germany a few years before — was gradually becoming a one-party state. My sister's letters revealed increasing signs of censorship, making one thing clear: as the daughter of a family of means, she was regarded as a "class alien," not allowed to hold jobs in keeping with her education. That she had been orphaned by the holocaust and had barely survived failed to penetrate the communist ideologues.

During her pregnancy, I told Hedy of my determination to have only one child. Coming to terms with the loss of my parents was trying enough. Now, with the "Iron Curtain" descending, it seemed that I would never be reunited with my only sister. Siblings would therefore mean little in a family context as long as the people involved were fated to live lives separated by an ocean. Hedy, an only child herself, shared my distrust of the familiar clichés about the alleged disadvantages of that "predicament," and we happily resolved that we would concentrate an undivided love on that only child of ours.

Her name was Nancy and she was born on August 4, 1948. Soon thereafter, we sold our Manhattan apartment in the same manner we had bought it, furniture and all, and moved into a modest house in Hollis, Long Island. With a reasonable deposit and a wonderful 3.5 percent interest on a 20-year mortgage, thanks to the G.I. Bill, we were now the owners of what was to become our home for the next 16 years. A nicely furnished nursery for Nancy and a double bed for ourselves were all we could initially afford, but within a few years, we had all the essential furnishings, even a television set by 1952. Regretfully leaving a position with the Federal Reserve Bank, which would have led her to an outstanding career with that institution in a world

Baby boomer Nancy with her mother and me, 1948 (photograph George Turi).

more concerned with the rights of women, she welcomed full-time mothering of a child who was to bring joy and pride into our lives in the years to come.

But, as Schiller had wisely postulated in more poetic terms long time ago, there is "no such a thing as a free lunch"—life exacts a toll for one's good fortunes. My father-in-law suffered a heart attack that removed him from full-time activities for a number of years. Our new home in Long Island made it possible for my in-laws, not too willingly, to move in with us. We had an extra bathroom installed on the ground floor for them, and we all enjoyed a cozy living room. Hedy and I had a fair-enough sized bedroom, Nancy was ensconced in her nursery, and a very small guest room was serving both as my study and as the repository of my growing library of books and 78-rpm records. Cousin George and his family were moving to Garden City, Charlie with his wife and (by then) two boys set up their home in Forest Hills and, later, in Woodmere—so our close family circle became contented residents of Long Island. At home, of course, living arrangements were far from ideal, but our little daughter certainly benefited from the enormous amount of affection two generations showered on her. She showed a distinct artistic talent already as a baby—crayons were virtual extensions of her little hands and, as her grandfather gradually recovered to resume work at home as an illustrator and colorist for an art supply firm, Nancy kept him company and tried to imitate what he was doing.

I did a lot of reading in those days in musical literature and, browsing in discount book stores, I began acquiring a modest library of biographies of Wagner, Verdi, Mozart, Berlioz, Puccini, and several volumes in the English *Master Musicians* series. My endless search for vocal recordings soon led me to the Merit Music Shop on Manhattan's 46th Street. Its owner was a very unusual man named Jack Meltzer, then in his late forties. He was not a musician but a fount of knowledge about recordings popular and classical, vocal and orchestral, Dixieland and big band, and singers ranging from Al Jolson to Lauritz Melchior. As a longtime manager of the Liberty Music Shop on Madison Avenue prior to establishing his own shop, he was widely known in the recording industry. Jack's memory for dates and numbers in general was phenomenal. (Rumor had it that he was an inveterate high-stakes poker player—a subject I never pursued with him because that part of his life was not my concern.) You could hand Jack a Victor catalogue of any vintage, pick a disc number at random, and he would identify the selections on both sides, the artists involved and, probably, the year of the issue.

I spent several lunch hours at the Merit Music Shop, buying records, browsing around, enjoying Jack's reminiscences about his past years in the record business, and absorbing a lot. Back in his days at Liberty Music, during the busy holiday season, he told me that he would position himself behind the sales staff and, as customers were piling in asking for this symphony or that concerto, or the latest Crosby or Sinatra records, he would instantly shout out the respective list numbers so the sales help wouldn't have to waste useless time looking up catalogues.

This was a very important period in the recording industry. Long-play records had come on the scene, a revolutionary development even to such a veteran as Jack. Also, that was the time in postwar economy when a new generation of home owners were buying table radios, toasters, blenders, irons, etc. Jack had a specialist for that phase of the business, but handled everything else himself, with his older brother Harry as a bookkeeper and administrative assistant. (Having an older brother in a subsidiary position was not a good arrangement, and they argued a lot.) Jack and I, kindred souls, became good friends, and one day he offered me a job because he felt that my knowledge and enthusiasm would benefit his growing business. As he was willing to match my present earnings and promised that I would "grow with the business," after discussing the matter with Hedy, I decided to accept Jack's offer. Leaving the export trade forever behind, in 1950 I entered the music business, thus embarking on my "one step at a time" master plan.

Aside from the lively movement caused by the LP revolution, Merit Music Shop on West 46th Street was one of New York's principal sources of "out of print" recordings. Jack regularly bought collections amassed by earlier generations of vocal fanciers and bequeathed for unappreciative younger ones, usually at very low prices. We would store those old recordings, arranged in their proper numerical order, in the back room, ready for prospective customers. Many of these discs were never sold but, as long as they were properly filed, Jack (and I myself, soon enough) could easily locate the desirable items and sell them at a good profit. I learned fast, enjoyed every moment of it, and my own vocal collection expanded whenever Jack felt that he had enough duplicates of an old record by Caruso, Ruffo, Ponselle, De Luca, or others to spare a copy for me.

A number of younger men connected with the record business who later went on to prominent positions started very modestly, as I did, in those days. The late Marvin Saines, initially a salesman for London Records, eventually became a highly successful retailer before transforming himself into a top executive with Columbia Records. The late Willy Lerner once sold the burgeoning Westminster label to retailers before opening his own Music Masters store on East 44th Street — a haven for "pirated" recordings. The Vanguard label was born in those years; its young owners, the brothers Seymour and Maynard Solomon, began their worldwide activities around that time, as did the fast-growing Vox Records owned by Hungarian-born George Mendelssohn. Within a brief period, Jack entrusted me with buying all LPs for the store, and I became friendly with all these "recording pioneers."

One day, a customer named Ernest Fischel, a man of some means and an avid collector of vocal records, asked me if I would consider writing liner notes for his newly formed Eterna Records, a label dedicated to out-of-print vocal recordings appearing for the first time in the LP format. I was tempted to seize the opportunity, yet apprehensive since I had never written anything for publication in any form. Hedy, however, encouraged me to give it a try. Needless to say, while Eterna, a small operation, had only a limited budget, whatever side income I could manage would certainly help with the household. And so, without any writing experience *in English*, my literary career began with those Eterna liner notes. Fischel continued the label with my annotations (immeasurably helped by Hedy's expert editorial assistance) for several years until his sudden death, which also signaled Eterna's expiration.

I had the pleasure of entertaining several famous men of music during my stay at Merit Music Shop. Vladimir Horowitz came in one day, asking for records by the great *bel canto* baritone Mattia Battistini. Under the guidance of his eagle-eyed and somewhat forbidding-looking wife Wanda, he immediately disappeared into an audition booth, removed from all human contact except myself. I suggested a few items, we listened together and discussed Battistini's legato phrasing which, Horowitz said, was the kind all pianists should imitate. Always soft spoken, courteous and quite fastidious, he made his choices, let Mrs. Horowitz pay for them, and they departed as quietly as they had entered. Lawrence Tibbett turned up one day and asked to hear part of a new LP recording of Gershwin's *Porgy and Bess* with Lawrence Winters and Camilla Williams. He liked what he heard, but said, "With all due respect, *my* Porgy was even better." (He was right, of course. Tibbett's 1935 recording of the opera's excerpts with Helen Jepson remains, from the singing point of view, peerless.) The veteran baritone, in the twilight of his career, was delighted to learn that I had witnessed his Budapest *Rigoletto,* and talked briefly but nostalgically of his European tour of 1937.

Francis Robinson, the Met's assistant manager, had been a friend of Jack Meltzer for many years and indebted to him for small favors and occasional discographic information. I was to inherit their friendship and continued to remain in frequent contact with Francis until his death in 1980. Back in the 1950s, long before I became recognized as a "member of the media," I had also been a grateful recipient of occasional press passes from

Francis Robinson. In those days, when Nancy was still a baby, we hardly attended musical events, but later, with built-in babysitters (grandparents) and slowly improving finances, our visits to the Metropolitan and the New York City Opera and various concerts became more frequent. Our radio, of course, was permanently tuned to WQXR.

A bright-eyed, smiling teenager walked in one day, full of questions and eagerness to learn about new LP releases. He told me how he adored the art of John McCormack, the great Irish tenor, and soon I learned that he was an aspiring singer himself, the son of a tenor. Jack became involved in our conversation and, putting two and two together, it was revealed that the young man's late father, Joseph White, a prolific Irish tenor and Victor recording artist, had been a friend of Jack's in the old days. That youngster and I later reconnected and continued friendly contact throughout various phases of my musical life. And so I watched Robert White develop from a child prodigy on the Arthur Godfrey TV Show into a Juilliard classmate of Martina Arroyo and, eventually, a concert singer and recording artist of worldwide fame. He was to record a huge variety of songs once made famous by his idol John McCormack. Alice Tully and Princess Grace of Monaco (Grace Kelly) were among Robert's many friends and admirers. Robert (always "Bobby" to me) has appeared as my guest on *The Vocal Scene* several times, but whenever our paths cross, and they often do, we never fail to remember the circumstances of our first meeting half a century ago. Robert White has been a professor of voice at Juilliard for many years now.

Irving Kolodin, the noted author and influential music critic of *Saturday Review*, was a regular visitor at the store, and I frequently discussed current musical events with him. When my longtime singing idol, the great baritone Titta Ruffo, died in July 1953, I offered to submit a concise appreciation of Ruffo's art for Kolodin's consideration. (He was 11 years my senior and, though we were to become closely associated in future years, he remained "Mr. Kolodin" to me for a long time.) On his encouragement, I did a modest piece and received no reaction from him for a while. A few weeks later, with Kolodin on a trip somewhere, I received a call from Roland Gelatt, his assistant editor, that went like this: "George, the writer who was supposed to deliver the lead article for our forthcoming issue cannot finish on deadline. I have your Ruffo piece here, ready to go. Could you expand it, doubled in size, and deliver it to me in a week?" And so, "Ruffo in Retrospect," with my byline, saw the light in the August 29, 1953, issue of *Saturday Review*. That lead article turned out to be my first published work and, among other wonderful things, it was to come to the attention of the late artist's son, Dr. Ruffo Titta in Rome, and led to a lifelong friendship between us. Kolodin continued to assign freelance projects to me (articles and reviews), an association that expanded when *Saturday Review,* under his editorship, assumed publication of the Metropolitan Opera program booklet.

Before the year ended, (on December 14, 1953), my first article for *Opera News* appeared under the title "Puccini, Master of Monotone." The late Mary Ellis Peltz, a courtly lady who was then the magazine's editor, sent me a very appreciative note, encouraging me to submit more material in the future. I have been doing articles and reviews for *Opera News*, under a number of outstanding editors, ever since, an association that has lasted more than 50 years.

In retrospect, I find it surprising and perhaps amazing that I (with a most beneficial uxorial help) was able to accomplish what I did after 1953 without the benefit of any formal and academic courses in writing and even in English. Naturally, with increased experience, gradually coming to terms with the syntax, my task grew easier. Spelling was never a problem — a gift I attribute to my early foreign language studies, beginning with Latin, and to the mental discipline that goes with that experience. Difficulties of natives with spelling their own language springs, I am afraid, from the weakness of English and American schools in that area.

Even before the folding of Eterna Records, I had connected with the editorial department of RCA Victor and had become one of the company's several regular annotators. As LPs began exploding all over the worldwide markets, my freelance activities prospered. With loving babysitters attending to Nancy, Hedy was able to resume her business career, beginning as one of the editors on a financial periodical published by Prentice Hall. After completing nursery at a very good private school (St. Gabriel's, across the street from our house), Nancy enrolled at first grade at that very school with a partial scholarship. We bought a used Frazer car (only my generation remembers that make!) from a family friend and, with two modest incomes, we were feeling quite content.

To keep my writing activities going, I spent many hours at the Music Library, doing fascinating research, and saw to it that my own music library should grow at a steady rate. I worked very hard, but spent Wednesdays (my day off from work) driving Nancy around, spending what in later years became known as "quality time" together, and taking the delights of fatherhood very seriously. Meantime, in Hungary, the extremist aspects of political life seemed to have relaxed somewhat. My sister Évi married a young man in the diplomatic service and, while the marriage was not long lasting, knowing her to be in more-or-less settled condition eased my concern.

But, after six years in record retailing, at age 35, I knew that I had to make a career move. I was immensely grateful to Jack for so much that I had learned from him during those six years. While I never ceased to be amazed by his virtuosic memory, he kept telling me: "You can do the same thing, George. Just concentrate on the numbers until they remain fixed in your mind." This, of course, sounds absurd. But how else can I explain that even now, at past 80 in age, when catalogue numbers have become immaterial to me, I am able to dial at least several dozen telephone numbers of family, friends, and business associates, without any external assistance?

An opportunity suddenly materialized when I became aware of an opening at SESAC, Inc., a music rights organization, for an administrative assistant at an attractive salary. Jack understood my reasons for a career move, and we remained friends even after he discontinued retailing and retired to Florida. In 1972, in the fourth year of *The Vocal Scene*, I invited him to join me for a taped interview of reminiscences of his early years in music. What should have been an interesting program turned out otherwise. Jack appeared intimidated before the microphone; he sounded labored, all the personal traits and all the "old New York" flavor evaporated from his speech, and he failed to respond to my various cues with any of the colorful anecdotes with which he had entertained me during our long association. Jack Meltzer died in Palm Beach, Florida, a few years later, but I will always remember him with a smile of fondness and gratitude.

And I joined SESAC, Inc., in the summer of 1955, a step that turned out to be a major leap in my upward climb.

18. Copyrights, Country Music — and Callas

SESAC, Inc., was established in 1930 as "Society of European Stage Authors and Composers, Inc." by its founder, Paul C. Heinecke. Mr. Heinecke was still alive when I joined the organization in 1955, a quiet, distinguished-looking elder statesman-type gentleman, but the organization's dominant force was his wife Ruth. She was a vigorous and strong-minded person who could turn on the charm when it suited her purposes, but that surface sheen barely concealed the tough core that lay beneath. When the organization was founded in 1930, it was protecting the American interests of several old European music houses like Eulenburg and Lienau (one of the publishers of Sibelius's works). In the subsequent quarter century, SESAC had acquired the performance rights of more than a hundred American firms, as well as affiliates from Poland and Israel. Though never achieving the mighty strength of the giant ASCAP and BMI, it still created a notable presence in the copyright protection field — with its catalog particularly strong in the areas of choral, band, and gospel music.

Some time after my joining the firm I discovered that Mrs. Heinecke had strongly believed that European natives were "reliable and hard workers" and, without being aware of it, I became the beneficiary of that bias in the sense that she "suggested" to Robert Stone, the executive who interviewed me, that I would be the best choice among the various applicants. Stone was then the director of program services, and I was hired as his assistant.

Program services was a multi-faceted department at SESAC. We maintained contact with the publisher affiliates, urged them to promote their works and, if commercial recordings resulted as a result of their efforts, it was SESAC that licensed their music to record companies and collected royalties on their behalf. In the case of publishers of serious music, SESAC became instrumental in promoting the works in question, though this activity actually intensified only after I joined the firm. The company had a legal department consisting of two (later three) copyright specialists, in addition to a prominent law firm that represented SESAC in lawsuits and other important negotiations. My first step was to learn all I could about what constituted public domain and what were the limits of copyright protection — the reason for a performance-rights society's existence.

All three broadcast networks were licensed by SESAC on a "blanket" basis, meaning that they paid a yearly fee to us in exchange for the use of the entire SESAC catalogue. Individual stations had an option of choosing a blanket license or a "per piece" license, which meant payment whenever a SESAC copyright was used. Naturally, the former option was simpler and more desirable. However, except for the southern states where religious and gospel music (SESAC's strengths) were regularly broadcast, individual stations had to be convinced that any such licensing was necessary. Very often, such stations had to be monitored — a costly affair often involving heavy expenses and litigations. While these problems were only indirectly my concern, I soon learned that there was a collective sense of insecurity on the front-office level, at times resulting in widespread distrust and even paranoia.

My individual activities, however, proved very educational, and I made the most of them. SESAC was also the creator of a series of "transcription discs," produced by our staff on behalf of our affiliated publishers, and sold to radio stations. Robert Stone was in charge of these recordings but, as he was already approaching 70 and eager to retire, he gradually turned over that responsibility to me. Here, after having sold records for many years, I learned the mechanics of record production. I picked a substantial quantity of suitable SESAC music, engaged the respective arranger-conductor, and, on consultation, we narrowed our choices down to the number of selections used (usually 12) for a recording session at one of the established Manhattan studios. Stone (later I, myself, and my associates) then supervised the sessions, listened to alternate playbacks and processed the material onto LPs under SESAC's own specially designed label. That was the most varied and enjoyable part of my business life. Since SESAC was extremely anxious to maintain good contact with the CBS network, we frequently engaged CBS contract artists: Elliot Lawrence for pop music arrangements and Alfredo Antonini to conduct a series of light classical works (rarely exceeding four minutes in length) strictly for radio use. These "transcription discs" were not allowed to be sold in stores. As a matter of fact, the very concept of "transcription discs" became *passé* as LPs were gaining enormous prominence and accessibility, rendering that phase of the industry nonexistent by the time I left SESAC.

Maestro Antonini, who in those bygone days of radio, had a miniature CBS Symphony at his disposal, did several sessions with me, leading an orchestra consisting of the likes of Julius Baker, flute, Robert Bloom, oboe, Tony Miranda, French horn, Jimmy Abate, clarinet, and about a dozen concertmaster-caliber violinists, Harold Coletta, viola, and Harvey Shapiro, Lucien Schmitt, and George Ricci, cellists. On one occasion, in doing Provost's *Intermezzo* (the source of much SESAC income from the Ingrid Bergman film), the young Aaron Rosand played the featured violin solo. Aaron, a longtime friend, was then just starting on his wonderful solo career. He was still a young man, but who wasn't in 1956? Richard Hayman, who was just beginning to work for the Boston Pops in those days, did some of Antonini's classy arrangements. Hayman mastered several instruments, but none with more virtuosity than the harmonica, for which he was to create several pop hits. Nowadays he is a successful conductor all over the country.

Antonini and I became quite close. One day he called me on the phone, advising me that he was preparing Richard Tucker's next Columbia recording, devoted to Italian songs. I immediately suggested *Rondine al nido*, a wonderful song by De Crescenzo, published by Cerruti, a SESAC affiliate. Alfredo knew the song and wanted to come in and pick up a copy of the sheet music. When he did, he brought Richard Tucker with him. They informed me that their program was virtually chosen, except that Mr. Tucker also wanted to include the folk song *Tiritomba* that the ill-fated tenor Joseph Schmidt had made famous. Not having the music on hand, I suggested my visitors to contact the Ricordi publishing firm. The quick-thinking tenor asked me for their number and immediately called Franco Colombo, president of Ricordi, on my desk phone, receiving prompt assistance.

I was invited to the recording session at the Columbia studios, which happened to be an old church in downtown New York. I stayed long enough to hear Richard Tucker's beautiful treatment of *Rondine al nido*, which, along with *Tiritomba*, may be found in some collector's possession on the long deleted Columbia ML 5258. During one of the breaks, Tucker, who didn't speak conversational Italian but had a marvelous feel for the enunciation, asked Antonini's approval of the way he was handling a word containing a double consonant. Antonini's reply registered on my own mind forever: "Please remember, Richard, whenever you see two consonants in a word like "attenzione" or "fanciulla," imagine that there are *three* of them ("atttenzione") and enunciate accordingly. Terrific advice! During the musical takes, Richard's wife Sara was sitting with me in the hall. I was to become close to the entire family during my later, radio years.

I have fond memories of my principal production associate, Jack Francis, who eventually left SESAC to become a field representative for NARAS, and of Richard Flusser, the venturesome director of *After Dinner Opera* after his SESAC years. Among other gifted "youngsters" who went on to greener pastures were Leonard Marcus, eventually the editor of the magazine *High Fidelity*, and Robert Israel, a successful producer of TV jingles and interludes. John Koshel, one of SESAC's house attorneys, remained my close friend and occasional legal aid for many years after leaving the firm and establishing his own. George Calfo, whose promotional talents were wasted at SESAC, went on to a substantial career with a major insurance firm. I stayed on because SESAC paid me reasonably well, treated me with respect, and I used every opportunity to learn and expand. Some time around 1957, Robert Stone, my boss and mentor, did retire and I became director of program services, also inheriting Robert's place on SESAC's all-important "allocation committee," which determined the revenues allocated to each affiliate based on their quarterly activities. This went with highly increased prestige in the office as well as an enormous amount of extra work. Mrs. Heinecke, who presided, preferred to have these allocation meetings take place after business hours, and apparently enjoyed keeping those of us who were family men away from home. Before the meetings, we did go out for a delicious meal, however. In such matters, SESAC was always generous.

Bud Prager, whose title was "assistant to the president," was that indeed, but he was also Mr. Heinecke's son-in-law, the husband of Alice, the Heineckes' only child, who was born in 1930 and, as she was fond to say, "as old as SESAC." Bud and I took to each other early on. A fan of country music, he was anxious to expand the company into that area. We both felt that SESAC could ease into that lucrative field by way of our strong gospel music catalogue. Bud made the necessary Nashville connections — with initially reluctant approval from the "front office," which meant his mother-in-law — and he and I organized a gospel-country session with Faron Young and the Anita Kerr Singers sometime in late 1956. Nashville was Seventh Heaven for Bud and a big eye-opener for me. Faron Young was a happy-go-lucky young man, already a Nashville favorite. Anita Kerr was an all-around musician-singer and arranger. With the expert assistance of Owen Bradley, pianist and owner of the once legendary, if a bit primitive, studio set in a Quonset hut, our recording turned out very successfully, and we returned home in triumph. I was given a very generous bonus at the end of the year, and Nashville became a yearly stop for us thereafter. Anita Kerr turned into a crucial associate, and in future years, we went on to record the Jordanaires, Chet Atkins, Floyd Cramer, Boots Randolph, and Webb Pierce, among country artists. I attended the Grand Ole Opry in the Ryman

Auditorium and remained in awe of the innate musicality of country musicians who could, once agreed on the starting chord, deliver a flawless four-part vocal or instrumental arrangement without the benefit of written music. ("That score only confuses me," one of them once said.) It recalled my childhood memories with the gypsies.

As I am recalling my childhood, it is essential to remember that soon after I joined SESAC, a great historical moment changed my life in an exciting and dramatic way. It was the Hungarian Revolution, which began with sporadic protests on October 23, 1956, escalated into armed nationwide resistance to local communist authority, and soon forced the temporary withdrawal of Russian troops. Eventually, the turncoat minister János Kádár helped Moscow to defeat the heroic resistance. But a brief period of widespread rebellious blockades and passive resistance to the communist government created a loose situation internally, to put it mildly. The Austrian border was opened and within a few days in early November, nearly 100,000 refugees escaped to Austria on taxis, buses, horses, wagons, or on foot. Among them was my only sister, Évi. Her marriage over — easy access to divorce being one of the very few advantages of the prevailing system — she realized that her future was with her only brother. With an impulsive and daring decision, she contacted all her friends one evening and offered them all her belongings — furniture, carpets, tablecloths, lamps, kitchenware — for sale. What she couldn't sell, she gave away. The following morning, with the money she realized she rented a car that safely transported her to the open Austrian border. Once safely across, she telephoned us — it was a Sunday — and my joy in hearing her voice, safely out of danger, was boundless.

Hungary was the center of worldwide attention in those days, with all Western Europe united in helping the plight of the refugees. I wasted no time to act. First, I called my old army buddy, Joe Kestler, whose parents had resettled in Vienna, welcomed Évi and gave her immediate and comfortable shelter. Then I got in touch with the American Rescue Committee, which immediately responded to my (and many other people's) appeal. (I have been making regular contributions to the ARC ever since.) Jerzy Starczewski, a dear friend and representative of the Polish Publishers Association, a SESAC affiliate, also set some action in motion through his diplomatic connections. With American immigration regulations temporarily suspended during those unbelievably charitable days, Évi, a single person with no family ties, was spirited onto an airplane and arrived safely at Camp Kilmer, N.J., within a matter of days. As my presence was needed that day at SESAC, Hedy quickly drove to Kilmer, braving a snowstorm, and brought her to our place in Hollis. She stayed with us for a month or so, but wanted her independence and found employment as a housekeeper with a family fur-

With sister Évi, together at last (around 1962).

ther out in Long Island. Her English, tentative at first, improved at an accelerated pace, and within a year she began working as a bookkeeper with a manufacturing firm in Manhattan, living in her own little rented apartment. Needless to say, Hedy and I did our very best to help her, and so did members of Hedy's family. Nancy, age 9 then, was delighted to meet her only aunt and they spent a lot of time watching television together. As for Évi and myself, in endless reminiscences, we began bridging a gap that world politics had forced on two loving siblings, reunited in peace for the first time in 17 years.

Life is a game where the cards are sometimes dealt with brutal suddenness. On the morning of October 21, 1957, cousin George Turi, an expert horseman who had served in the Hungarian cavalry in his young years, went out on his weekly Long Island trot. His normally docile horse suddenly dashed into a frantic and uncontrollable frenzy, and threw its hapless rider. George broke his neck and never regained consciousness. His brother Charlie and I rushed to the hospital and stayed with George until near midnight, when the doctors told us to go home because we, or they, could no longer help him. I suppose the plug that was keeping him temporarily alive was pulled soon thereafter, because Charlie received word in the wee hours that his brother was gone. George was 44 years old, a survivor of the Normandy landing, a man of many talents. We loved each other like brothers, and his image with that mischievous Sinatra-like smile remains forever engraved in my memory.

Our home life, all these excitements aside, was reasonably placid. My father-in-law was restored to fairly good health and spent a happy season as violinist with the Orlando Philharmonic while continuing with freelance artistic work. I was even able, occasionally, to squeeze an engagement for him as a violinist-member of one of our SESAC orchestras. Hedy and I discovered a wonderful lakeside vacation lodge in the Adirondacks, perfect for growing children and swimming aficionados like myself. Hedy and Nancy would spend three weeks there, two of which I shared with them. But in 1959, we decided to spend four weeks in Europe with our daughter, visiting France, Italy, Germany, and Switzerland. With my sister safely in America, I saw no reason to visit Hungary under the communist system.

The well-planned journey was unforgettable for all of us. Those were the days of the strong dollar: we luxuriated in hotels that were to exceed our means in the years thereafter. Paris (Hotel Napoleón on Avenue Friedland) was wonderful in peacetime, and the special attractions (Versailles, the Tuileries and, especially, the Louvre) made a fabulous impression on 11-year-old Nancy. Though never a Francophile, I enjoyed it all immensely, but I drank Italy in with even more enthusiasm. In Rome (Hotel Eden), we finally met Dr. Ruffo Titta, son of the great baritone, and his lovely English-born wife Gabriella. They entertained us in their elegant home and drove us around the celebrated sights in and around Rome. Ruffo pointed out the palatial building where he had spent his childhood with his parents — it is now the Embassy of Bulgaria — and took us to an old palazzo where Titta Ruffo, as an apprentice ironworker in the 1890s, had once heavily labored on the ornate grills. We visited the Vatican, paid homage to the various sites associated with Puccini's *Tosca*, and visited the Terme di Caracalla and the Colosseum. Before our departure to Europe, I had suggested to Irving Kolodin that I would try to get an interview with Tito Schipa, the great tenor. To my delight, on checking into our Rome hotel, the first telephone call that reached me was from Schipa. In excellent English, he invited me to visit him at his condo on Via Cassia No. 19. Leaving Hedy and Nancy to explore the sights of the Via Veneto, I took a taxi through the winding streets along the Tiber — Rome was then preparing for the 1960 Olympics — and reached my destination, where my beaming host, then 72 years old, greeted me like an old friend. We settled down with a glass of vermouth and played some recordings (Schipa's own). I listened avidly to his comments and reminiscences, and learned that he would like to visit the States and do some teaching here. (I gained the impression, later confirmed, that he was not doing well financially.) Having divorced his second wife, Schipa was then living with his son Titino, then 13, and a housekeeper. Titino, who was wildly circling around with his bike to his father's increasing annoyance, eventually grew up to become a pop singer and, as Tito Schipa Jr., published a candid and quite wonderful biography of his father many years later. On my return home, I wrote to John Brownlee, then president of the Manhattan School of Music, who remembered Schipa lovingly, but couldn't offer any definite invitation for him at the school. Schipa did visit the United States in 1965, but died suddenly in New York before I could make contact with him.

We took the train from Rome to Florence and settled in the Hotel Lucchesi with a splendid view of the Arno River. As Rinuccio says in Puccini's *Gianni Schicchi*, the city opened up to us like "un albero fiorito," and we left no stone unvisited, ate at the best restaurants, and browsed through as much of the Uffizi Gallery as our stamina permitted. In all these ventures Nancy, whose artistic talent was a maternal inheritance, proved to be an endlessly stimulated and mature companion, way beyond her years. Following the time-honored "American tourist" pattern, our next stop was Venice. When we checked in at the Hotel Londra, I found the room not really up to my recently acquired finicky expectations. As I reached for a telephone, wishing to ask for another room, Hedy opened the window on the Grand Canal with the majestic view of San Giorgio exactly opposite us. The telephone fell out of my hand — that is not a view a sensible person would want to exchange for anything!

After three wonderful days in Venice, including a restful afternoon at the Lido, we took the very brief airline flight to Vienna, Hedy's birthplace and a unique city previously known to me either from my carelessly (was I really *ever* careless?) youthful period or in the city's war-torn and divided state. We took Nancy to the house where Hedy had grown up; I had revisited the Hotel Regina of my wartime memory, we explored the museums and Schönbrunn and ate sumptuously wherever we found the opportunity (quite often). We stayed at the Hotel Sacher (where else?) and, according to the playbill I safely treasured, we took Nancy to the Staatsoper on June 22, 1959. Herbert von Karajan conducted *Aida* with the mouth-watering cast of Renata Tebaldi (Aida), Giulietta Simionato (Amneris), Eugenio Fernandi (Radames), Tito Gobbi (Amonasro), Gottlob Frick (Ramphis). Opposite the Sacher, at the equally luxurious Hotel Kranz-Ambassador, I was delighted to discover the "Lehár Stube," an ornate room full of Lehár memorabilia. Also there, a newly acclaimed young American soprano named Leontyne Price, a Karajan protégée, was holding a press conference (two years before her Met debut).

Leaving Vienna by train, we spent a day in picturesque Innsbruck, a city so closely surrounded by tall mountains as to leave visitors oscillating between wonderment and claustrophobia. A rented auto then took us to Munich by way of Garmisch-Partenkirchen, the Alpine resort that had been the home of both Adolf Hitler and Richard Strauss. We didn't stop for sight-seeing anywhere. Actually, the war was still too keen in my memory, and we could have bypassed Germany entirely. But Hedy had spent several cherished childhood years in Munich, where her father had a little orchestra at a summer resort, and she wanted to visit the sweet Frau Penzkofer, her former private teacher, now elderly and virtually blind, with whom she had been corresponding since the end of the war. I, on the other hand, looked up my childhood friend George Hivessy. George and his wife Margaret escaped Hungary in 1956, as my sister did, but Munich was only as far as he wanted to go. His father, who had helped me obtain my passport back in 1939, had refused to swear loyalty to Szálasi and was placed under house arrest but somehow managed to find his way out of Hungary along with other former officials of Admiral Horthy's regime. Father and son were briefly united in Munich, but the old man died a few years later. George found an entry-level job with the giant Siemens organization, where, in succeeding years — after completing various advanced courses — he became a department head. We corresponded frequently thereafter and met in Germany once again some years later. My friend George eventually obtained German citizenship, but he never felt at home there. He retired from Siemens 25 years later, after Germany became unified. In due course Hungary, too, was freed of the Russian influence, but, unfortunately, by then George lost his wife, became ill himself, and decided to return home after a long self-exile. He died shortly after our last and rather sad reunion in Budapest in 1999.

In 1959 much of Munich was still in ruins, but not the fabulous Hotel Vier Jahreszeiten (ah, that strong dollar!) where we stayed and entertained the Hivessys, who rightfully regarded us as "you rich Americans." On the evening of June 27, while Hedy and her old teacher went to see a classic play, I took Nancy to *La Bohème* at the Bavarian State Opera (not yet in its official location). The performance, "auf deutsch," was on a high level, with the young Hermann Prey as "Marcel" in the company of good German artists of not quite international fame. Our wonderful month-long vacation ended in Switzerland (another important locale from Hedy's childhood), where we visited with Elisabeth Dürst, Hedy's former colleague at Prentice Hall. I loved the sights (Zurich, Lucerne, and environs), which we were to revisit frequently in later years. I remember celebrating the Fourth of July at the Hotel Weggis overlooking Lake Lucerne before embarking on our return home, full of wonderful memories. While at Weggis, feasting on the sight of the lake and the mountains, I finished my Schipa article, which saw publication ("Summer Day with Schipa") in the November 1959 edition of the Metropolitan Opera program.

Life seemed too prosaic after that luxurious month in Europe, but SESAC quickly returned me to normalcy — which meant overwork in my case. Sitting at my desk several months before our European trip, I had received a phone call from David Hall, then editor of the fairly new *HiFi Stereo Review*, inviting me to join their staff as contributing editor specializing in opera and vocal music. I jumped at the occasion, because the job represented a fairly decent additional income, even if it did mean long evenings of listening and many weekends of writing. As always, Hedy was supportive, but Nancy wasn't entirely convinced why it was necessary for her daddy to spend so many hours listening to so much music. (We had bought an upright piano and started her on lessons but, much to our disappointment, she never quite warmed to it. She was, however, drawing and painting relentlessly and very imaginatively.) My association with what was to become *Stereo Review* was a very satisfying one and, under the editorship of such appreciative colleagues as David Hall, William Anderson, William Livingstone, and James Goodfriend, lasted more than two decades. Irving Kolodin was displeased by my new connection, grumbling that "when you write for me you cannot be published all over the place." He would have had a point, but my freelance commitment to *Saturday Review* was of an occasional nature as opposed to the semi-permanence of my new connection. (Permanence in this line of work is a highly elusive concept.) After a few weeks of silence, Irving started sending me material as though nothing had happened.

My first article for *Stereo Review* was an interview with the brilliant Hungarian pianist György Cziffra, following his American debut. He had left Hungary in 1956, like so many others, and settled in Paris where he eventually became a French citizen and a very much appreciated artist. After our very pleasant conversation, he sat at the upright and played one of the Liszt Hungarian Rhapsodies for me. I found his *legato* unbelievably smooth and his liquid passagework almost violinistic. It came as no surprise when I found out years later that Cziffra was of Gypsy origin. In the United States, he was typecast as a Liszt specialist and, feeling under-appreciated, he hardly ever returned. My second article was devoted to Maria Callas, to be followed by an offer from the magazine's then publisher Ziff-Davis to write a biography of the soprano, whose activities in those days were displayed on the front pages of the international press far surpassing her considerable presence in the musical pages. Intimidated at first by the project, I nonetheless undertook it and began researching part of the material while in Rome and Florence. My *Callas, Portrait of a Prima Donna,* published in 1960, is still in print, in a soft cover edition, more than forty years later. The final chapters were written while my father-in-law, Charles Dicker, lay dying from a heart ailment. My book bears a dedication to his memory and "to a life devoted to kindliness, geniality, and music, which he personified." He was only 69 and, had he been able to benefit from the remarkable cardiac innovations that saved so many others (including myself), in later years, he would have lived another decade.

At SESAC, my activities seemed limitless. When I briefly visited Purdue University to record their famous band for our transcription library, Maxine Lefever, the assistant band director, who became a longtime friend to Hedy and myself, complained to me about the relative insecurity of her employment. I explained to her my personal theory of "working hard and making yourself as irreplaceable as possible. Therein lies your job security." Maxine questioned the ethics involved. I never did, nor did I ever regret living by that method — though two open-heart surgeries were the price I had to pay for practicing it.

The promotion of concert music in the SESAC repertoire was my responsibility. William L. Dawson, a noted composer and choral director in Tuskegee, Alabama, owned a valuable choral catalogue. He was also the composer of the *Negro Folk Symphony*, a three-movement work utilizing original and spiritual-derived themes in a very accessible neo–Dvořák style. Stokowski and the Philadelphians gave the symphony's world premiere in 1934. In the early 1960s, I approached the old maestro, then around 80 and conducting the American Symphony Orchestra, and he showed renewed interest in the project. If the financing could be arranged, Stokowski said, he would record it at the union wages (plus royalties, if any) "for the orchestra's sake." The financing was arranged by SESAC, and the recording was organized by American Decca, produced by my friend Israel Horowitz, Decca's A&R director. Stokowski briefly blew his top when a careless photographer flashed an intrusive photo during the rehearsals, but after that episode, he was relaxed and jovial. The LP remained in the active catalogue for many years.

Miklós Rózsa and Eugene Zádor, distinguished Hungarian-born composers, had major works in the SESAC-affiliated Eulenburg catalogue. Rózsa's *Theme, Variations, and Finale* (1933) was a work the composer himself had recorded in Germany at his own expense. Rózsa (1907–1995) was a three time Oscar winner, and his film scores made him a wealthy man, but he justly felt that his "serious" activities were never properly recognized, and a recording of this particular and quite outstanding work meant a lot

Leopold Stokowski (left) and William A. Dawson (center), recording the *Negro Folk Symphony* while I look on, ca. 1966.

to him. Is Horowitz and Decca again came to the rescue; they made a direct deal with Rózsa for the masters without any financial participation from SESAC but, of course, I got my share of kudos from the front office for having served as a conduit. Eugene Zádor (1894–1977) was a less celebrated but far more diversified (in the "classical" field) composer, and he too made a fortune in Hollywood as an orchestrator and teacher. (Lionel Barrymore was one of his students and, as he once told me, his investment advisor very much to Zádor's benefit.) I didn't succeed in getting his *Divertimento for Strings (1955)* recorded, but attended a performance with the Philadelphia Orchestra under Eugene Ormandy (Zádor's friend from youth). Briefly visiting Ormandy in the Green Room, Hedy and I had an opportunity to observe that he handled the adoring and effusive Philadelphia matrons with the same elegance and virtuosic skill he demonstrated on the podium.

Both Rózsa and Zádor became friends of mine but, unfortunately the two had become estranged over the years. Once, when some years later Hedy and I spent some time in the Los Angeles area and I offered to bring them together, Zádor eagerly welcomed my efforts, but Rózsa wanted no part of it. They died unreconciled for ancient causes never made known to me. In the 1970s, when Rózsa learned that I had visited Hungary, he said that he "would also return when the Emperor Franz Joseph [d. 1916] would return to the Hungarian throne." But he did go back briefly a few years later for what I believe was the 50th anniversary of his graduation from the Franz Liszt Academy. For Eugene Zádor I became the librettist of two of his late operas, *The Magic Chair* (Baton Rouge, La., 1966) and *The Scarlet Mill* (Brooklyn College, 1968). I am proud of both of these librettos, achieved as a challenge to myself, but had neither the will nor the time to "promote" them after Eugene's death. And I am equally proud to have been a friend to these two exceptionally talented men.

Radio Station WQXR in New York was very important to SESAC and enjoyed a blanket license as well as a complimentary service of the relevant section of our transcription library. I visited the station on a regular basis and became very good friends with program director Walter Neiman, music director Martin Bookspan, and senior writer Bob Sherman, all of them already established personalities on New York's musical scene. My writing career, of course, continued unabated, with reams of reviews for *Stereo Review* and several articles for *Saturday Review,* among which I fondly recall a report on my meeting with the silver-maned great tenor Giovanni Martinelli, still vigorous and volatile at age 75, whom I had visited in his New York apartment at the Hotel Buckingham across the street from Carnegie Hall. The veteran tenor sent me a cordial letter of appreciation, though expressed the wish that more of our conversation could have been retained. (Space requirements made this impossible — a condition all magazine writers must live by.) The sixth program of *The Vocal Scene* on February 7, 1969, five days after his death, called "A Memorial to Giovanni Martinelli," was dedicated to his memory.

At SESAC, the company engaged an interesting associate named "Red" Clyde, so named for his unusual pigmentation caused, as he explained to me, by some cardiac malformation. (I hope he is still with us, because his explanation sounded scary.) Clyde had good connections in the jazz field, and through him we engaged Duke Ellington to be the featured artist at SESAC's hospitality suite at the National Association of Broadcasters (NAB) convention in 1962. The Duke, with his courtly manners and elegant speech,

With Duke Ellington in Chicago, 1962.

was naturally a huge hit. He headed only an octet due to space limitations (the group included Johnny Hodges and other legendary associates), but we made arrangements to record the full Ellington Orchestra in New York soon thereafter. Red Clyde and I shared the producing chores starting at midnight (the band's preferred hour) at the Capitol studios on 46th Street, enthusiastically witnessed by the musicians' wives and girlfriends. SESAC then started a brief trend of recording big bands (Count Basie, Woody Herman, Warren Covington, and Les Elgart.) Business must have been good and Jack Francis and I enjoyed the experience thoroughly. Eventually, SESAC must have turned out too "square" an outfit for Red Clyde's liking, because he left us for places unknown but doubtlessly more swinging.

The remarkable Sy Oliver, formerly associated with the Jimmy Lunceford and Tommy Dorsey bands, was engaged through my and Jack Francis's efforts, and I will never forget our collaboration. Oliver, too, engaged a big 16-piece band, but his arrangements were so precise and transparent, his ear for balance so perfect that, after a brief run through, we ended up with single takes on all our selections. Sy sent the musicians home ahead of schedule and joined us in the control room to hear the playbacks. I couldn't help complimenting him thereafter in this fashion: "Sy, they'll love this in the office." His reply: "George, I don't give a ... if your office will love it. *I* love it!" I tried always to follow Sy Oliver's philosophy in setting higher standards for myself than those that were expected of me by principals, employers, and so on.

No show business personality was larger in those days than Jackie Gleason who, in addition to his enormous TV successes, had started a series of recordings featuring the Jackie Gleason Orchestra. Mrs. Heinecke decided that SESAC should somehow sign Gleason up "to do something for us." Realizing the absurdity of the situation, Jack Francis and I nevertheless made an appointment with The Great One's manager at the Park Central Hotel. He received us in this manner: "We are not interested in money. What can you guys offer us?" Baffled though we were, the manager (Durgom was his name) made a lot of sense. Gleason was then on top of the world, and we really had nothing to offer him. As we were ready to depart, Durgom casually added that we should contact Bobby Hackett, the trumpet soloist whose lush sound was largely responsible for the successes of the Gleason Orchestra. Wasting no time, we signed up Hackett with a small combo to support his voluptuous trumpet sound. Bobby was a delightful guy who once told me that, getting a finicky and rather unfavorable review of one of his jazz engagements, he responded by sending the critic a get well card. After continued successes in the field, Bobby Hackett died prematurely in 1976.

In December 1961, my sister Évi married Tibor Waldman, a well-established textile importer 20 years her senior. Tibor had been a longtime confirmed bachelor, but Évi made a nice home for the two of them at 35 Park Avenue, a walking distance from Tibor's office at the Empire State Building. Évi could have been useful at his office, but her husband preferred to have her serving good meals in their elegant home. They had a good marriage for 25 years, ending with my sister's untimely death. Tibor was active in Israel-oriented philanthropy, and our social lives rarely intersected, though we did have several mutual friends. Nothing, however, interfered with our brother-sister relationship, which remained forever intimate and frictionless. In 1962, Hedy and I celebrated our 20th wedding anniversary by taking 14-year-old Nancy on a western trip (Denver, Colorado Springs, San Francisco, Los Angeles). At the famous Biltmore Hotel at Colorado Springs, I discovered a wonderful portrait of Feodor Chaliapin, painted by his son Boris. Hedy and Nancy braved the heights of neighboring Pike's Peak, while my less adventurous self preferred the hotel's magnificent swimming pool. The San Francisco area helped Hedy and me revive memories of our Army days; we even visited the house where we briefly lived at 111 Monte Diablo Avenue in San Mateo. In the Los Angeles area, we visited several old friends, including the Rózsas and the Zádors, enjoying every moment with them, though our preference for Northern California, which was to play an important role in our later life, remained unshaken.

What was not unshaken, however, was the marriage of Alice Heinecke and Bud Prager back at SESAC. They broke up, with results that caused wide reverberations throughout the organization. The former "assistant to the president" became a nonperson virtually overnight, and the subsequent collective insecurity and persistent search for suspected enemies permeated the entire office. Being a close associate of Bud Prager, I began noticing that I was being left out of top-level planning and discussions, even though I remained a member of the coveted "allocation committee." I was 44 years old in 1964 and, my good salary notwithstanding, I began to be concerned with the fact that SESAC had no retirement benefit policies for its employees. While I was considering my options, one of our arrangers, Earl Sheldon, who had also been steadily working with Muzak, the large background music network, asked me if I would consider making a change. Muzak is a good solid outfit, as Sheldon explained to me and, since their music director had no recording experience, the expanding company was looking for a permanent recording director to replace the free lance person they were then employing. Sheldon thought that I would be perfect for the job, and put me in contact with John C. Andrus, Muzak's executive VP. We had a brief meeting and, fortified by Sheldon's enthusiastic recommendation, I was offered a job at a salary considerably lower than what I was then earning at SESAC. I was not surprised by Andrus's offer, particularly since the job of the recording director, as outlined to me, was nowhere near the complexity I was facing at SESAC on a daily basis. I told Andrus that I would give his offer serious thought.

Hedy and I discussed the matter and decided that money was less important than mental peace — an element that was sorely missing from my business life of late. I called Andrus and agreed that I would join Muzak, Inc., in two weeks. Then I turned in a two page letter of resignation at SESAC, outlining my reasons for leaving: primarily a sense of distrust on the part of top management. My statements found total noncomprehension at the front office, followed by an instant offer of financial betterment. When they realized that I was leaving for a position of *lower* remuneration, they were likely to have considered the state of my sanity. But I was leaving nonetheless, and leaving on the best of terms. SESAC gave me a very nice farewell luncheon, full of speeches of warm and cordial feelings all around. I recall my nine years there as an important cornerstone, a steady expansion into all phases of musical activities: publishing, recording, music rights, administration, legal matters. I had made important contacts throughout the industry, worked with fascinating musicians ranging over the entire field, respected them and earned their respect. Many of my former colleagues continued to remain my friends. Mr. and Mrs. Heinecke eventually passed on and, after some years, Alice sold SESAC to new owners. The company's headquarters are in Nashville now and, from what I hear, they are stronger and more meaningful than ever in the vastly changed arena of today's business of music.

The change in my "business life" affected my writing and reviewing activities not at all. Writing, in the years that followed, included those two opera librettos in collaboration with Eugene Zádor. I continued on my endless road of self-improvement, still living a life that combined my livelihood with music, my only hobby. Not a bad mix, and an even more perfect synthesis was yet to come within a few years.

19. Music in the Background

When I joined Muzak as recording director in 1964, the company was one of the divisions of the Wrather Corporation, established by Jack Wrather, a Texas oilman with vast holdings in the broadcast and entertainment fields. Muzak, the best-known dispenser of background music, was very successfully operating a network of domestic and international franchisers. The source of those harmless and innocuous sounds, somewhat contemptuously regarded as "elevator music," was Muzak's headquarters at 229 Park Avenue South. Audio and reproduction techniques have changed so much since 1964 that I shall waste no time in describing them, especially since I suspect that the entire "background music" industry, if it still exists, has since been altered to fit 21st-century tastes and techniques.

In any case, in 1964 I joined a prosperous firm headed by Charles Cowley, an urbane and elegant man in his sixties. John R. Andrus, the executive vice president who hired me, soon took me aside to tell me that, in addition to my obvious duties as recording director, I would have the responsibility of cleaning up an "administrative mess" of several years standing. I was introduced to the marketing and sales staff and, of course, to Donald O'Neill, Muzak's longtime music director, and the various programmers who would be working under me.

O'Neill was a sweet and soft-spoken man of deep frustrations, and a severe alcoholic. He was a systems man with an excellent grasp of the department's basic organization, largely established by himself, and improved over the years. He had a good knowledge of popular music, but no experience in studio work whatever, nor any willingness to learn its mechanics, relying on a freelance consultant to produce the recording sessions. The "administrative mess" Andrus had alluded to resulted from years of accumulated indebtedness to a large number of publishers of copyrighted music the company had used without paying for the required mechanical royalties. Donald simply ignored invoices, statements and other reminders, causing several publishers to refuse servicing Muzak — a financially solid and responsible organization. Given Donald's long association with the company, Andrus decided to remove him from dealing with that area, hoping that I would clean up the arrears. Having learned all about mechanical royalties at SESAC, where such delays would never have been tolerated, I assured Andrus that the matter would be taken care of. (It took two years to complete the project, but Muzak's relationship with its publisher creditors never suffered, once I got into the picture.)

Although Donald O'Neill was well liked, he was treated somewhat offhandedly by the Muzak hierarchy — a very decent bunch obviously aware of Donald's alcoholism and the psychological damage it caused, above all to his own career. He attended all my evening recording sessions, events usually preceded by a good dinner at a nearby midtown restaurant where I would have my usual solitary cocktail while watching in silent disbelief as Donald consumed three martinis, crowned by three bottles of beer with his dinner.

The sessions, however, were a lot of fun. I inherited several staff arrangers (like Earl Sheldon, who had brought me to Muzak), and brought in several previous SESAC friends like Richard Maltby, Elliot Lawrence, Frank Hunter, and the brilliant pianist-composer Dick Hyman (later to create the scores for all the Woody Allen movies). Neither they nor any of their predecessors ever considered creating "elevator music." We recorded the best arrangements of pop and country standards under optimum audio conditions. Once the masters were finished, they were turned over to the production department where all the highs and lows were equalized, neutralized, and otherwise emasculated to conform to Muzak-mandated sonic limitations. The company's stated purpose was to create light background music for stores and industries, not to "make workers dance in the aisles" but provide subliminal entertainment at a low audio level. In short, "elevator music." This, naturally, went with a great deal of aesthetic frustration on my part, but I took delight in the quality of the recordings inherent in the original masters, and the music-making itself was, of course, invariably rewarding. After the sessions, the programmers and I set up the necessary card files (organized by Donald O'Neill many years previously), assembling 15-minute units of great internal variety in matters of mood and tempo. What, of course, delighted me was that I was no longer limited to the SESAC repertoire, but had access to the music of all publishers, which meant the music of Gershwin, Cole Porter, Kern, Rodgers, Ellington, Mancini, the whole world of Broadway, light standards, current hits and even suitable material from the Beatles catalogue.

In the late summer of 1965, I combined a venturesome Muzak project with a personal adventure of my own. A live-wire Dutch jazz accordionist and arranger named Mat Mathews, with active international contacts, opened my eyes to the considerable sums the company could save by producing two sessions in Europe, paying all recording costs (arrangements and copying included) on location, using European artists. I projected the estimates, obtained the approval of John Andrus (who by now watched all my activities with an appreciative eye) and proceeded to set up two recording sessions, one in Amsterdam (with Mathews as arranger and local guide) and one in Stuttgart, Germany, utilizing the recording facilities of Muzak's German franchiser. Far from making it an entirely selfless business-oriented enterprise, the project involved two weeks in Holland and Germany, followed by a European vacation for myself and family. That, by the way, turned out to be the only four-week "vacation" in my entire life — the two weeks spent in works preparatory to the sessions, and the music-making itself, never seemed anything like work to me.

That auspicious trip also meant my first visit to Hungary after a 19-year absence. The wounds festered through all those years, making me unforgiving for my great personal losses. The country may have been driven into the Nazi orbit in my youth for geopolitical reasons, but a large segment of Hungary's populace at the time welcomed the Hitler philosophy. When, after the war, the Stalinist era happened, Hungary was again victimized by geopolitics. Though the excuses were obvious, I was still not in a forgiving mood. The rescue of my sister in 1956 went a long way toward easing my bitterness. I still had surviving members of my family there, several old friends, and bittersweet memories. Budapest was still dear to me and I wanted Nancy to learn more about my childhood and become an active element in a family continuity. Moreover, Hedy and I definitely wanted to include Vienna in our trip — it was her birthplace, after all, and a city I had learned to love without the bitterness that always intruded whenever thoughts of my birthplace had crossed my mind.

In Budapest, we were reunited with members of the family on both sides. Hedy's cousin Marianne (Marcsi) had married a childhood friend of mine, a Ph.D. in pharmacology, who was eventually to attain a high governmental position in his field. They had two daughters roughly Nancy's age, and the kids got along famously, managing the language barrier with the fun-filled skill of teenagers. I spent time with the remaining members of the Jellinek brood. My cousin Imre, a physician, seemed to be reconciled with the position the communist regime had imposed on his activities, though I never really believed him. My younger cousin Bandi, who was then managing a small industrial plant, had two small children to whom Hedy and I were known only from faded photographs. Imre's mother, my old aunt Melanie, was mentally alert and far more practical in all matters than her doctor son Imre. It was always a warm experience to meet my childhood friend George Besnyö (Braun), a friendship that began in 1925 and still exists nearly eighty years later. Relatives, being what they are, all wanted to monopolize their long-distant American visitors. It was impossible to satisfy all invitations during the limited time, so we took them out for dinner at the garden restaurant of the old and once romantic Hotel Gellért. As our party of about 20 listened to gypsy music, I enjoyed watching Nancy and her young cousins happily giggling, while thinking just how far I had come from regarding Hungary's atmosphere as anything like "home" to me. Nostalgia was not a sentiment people affected by the war's losses could honestly experience. My childhood belonged to a faraway past; the life I lived then seems to have happened to another person.

And yet, that 1965 European journey was a complete success in every way. It produced colorful additions to the Muzak library and, on the family level, we were able to include London, Amsterdam, The Hague, Munich, and Stuttgart, along with Budapest and Vienna, in that comprehensive adventure. Nancy, naturally, enjoyed it all, with a copiously kept journal detailing exciting new discoveries. On our return home, we picked up our established routine — Muzak for me, Prentice-Hall for Hedy, the last years of high school for Nancy.

My writing contributions kept pace, keeping my nights and some weekends busy with listening and writing. I had a regular column in the Met programs edited by Irving Kolodin, called "The Met on Microgroove," which listed the operas in the theater's current repertoire, along with the appropriate complete recordings in *my* order of preference. *Stereo Review* continued to keep me busy as a reviewer of opera and vocal music.

Even before our European trip, I had submitted an article idea to Irving Kolodin that, unlike most of my other submissions, never saw publication. Its subject was the late and great basso Boris Christoff. In those days, he was widely celebrated in Europe, and a great favorite with the Chicago opera audience. His absence from the Met had long interested me, as I suspected some background intrigues. In the early 1960s, Christoff gave a great concert at Carnegie Hall, which I attended, and my friends at Angel Records made arrangements for me to call on the artist at his suite at the Hotel St. Regis. A remote man with a King Philip–like austere demeanor, he grew friendlier and more communicative as our conversation progressed.

It seems that Rudolf Bing had approached Christoff in Italy in the mid

With Sir Rudolf Bing (left) and Robert Merrill (center) at WQXR, 1977 (photograph Olga Boenzi).

1950s and invited him to sing Boris Godunov in the Met's then English-language production, which the singer declined because he didn't think that the opera should be presented that way. In 1958, Bing approached him again, this time with *Don Carlo* in mind, which would have interested Christoff but, instead, Bing offered him the role of Mephisto in a new and rather controversial production of Gounod's *Faust*. Christoff intensely disliked that production (so did New York's critical fraternity) and declined again, causing Bing to remark that "true to your reputation, Mr. Christoff, you are a difficult man." According to my notes taken at the time, Christoff mused toward the end of our discussion, "I don't think Mr. Bing really wants me at the Met. Why is he suggesting roles he knows I would decline ... I guess he just doesn't like me."

I called Bing the following morning. He had no love for the press, but appreciated publicity of any kind, and listened to the essence of my Christoff interview with curious interest. "Mr. Christoff is wrong. I did want him at the Met and offered him two great parts, but he declined both. We cannot alter our productions for the sake of one singer even if he is of Mr. Christoff's eminence. As to my disliking him, it is nonsense. I am interested in artistic qualities and stay clear of emotional involvements. The Metropolitan has survived before without certain individuals, and we shall do our best to survive hereafter."

Those who ever dealt with Sir Rudolf Bing will recall these words as characteristic Bing-speak: cool, resolute, and unemotional. In my insistent optimism to do right, in my would-be article I put forward the following suggestion:

> Why not let Mephisto be done by other members of the Met [which at that time counted four star-caliber artists on its roster: Cesare Siepi, Jerome Hines, Giorgio Tozzi, and George London, not to mention Nicola Rossi-Lemeni, who had actually participated in that controversial production in 1953]. Do invite Christoff to do his Boris in Russian though the rest of the cast may adhere to the English text. Traditions will not be shattered since both Chaliapin and Pinza had appeared in "bilingual" *Godunov* productions that are gratefully remembered in Met history. Perhaps Christoff is a difficult man, but a theater able to accommodate Callas, Tebaldi, De Los Angeles, and Milanov in the same season, need not fear a basso.

Though it would have made an interesting article, it never saw the light of day. Kolodin didn't want to cause trouble for and with Bing. Manager and basso, both very stubborn men, remained estranged, and Boris Christoff never sang at the Met. Nicolai Ghiaurov, a fellow Bulgarian artist of almost equally formidable stage presence, made his debut there in 1965 as Mephisto and went on to great successes. The Met survived, as Bing suggested, but Boris Christoff would have added many stellar moments to its history.

My Muzak activities settled into routine and seemed secondary in importance compared to my writing commitments and family matters. We enrolled Nancy at the Art Students League, where she showed extraordinary promise. It was also the time to look at colleges for her. For reasons of her own, she was not interested in Radcliffe, Smith, and Wellesley (much to Hedy's and my disappointment because we loved those campuses). Encouraged by her principal, a Pembroke graduate, she applied there for early admission, but was not accepted — a decision Nancy did not take kindly. On the other hand, she was accepted at Clark University at Worcester, Mass. It was obviously a "second choice" for Nancy, but Hedy and I welcomed the fact that this only child of ours would remain within a reasonable distance from home. She concluded her senior year as a class valedictorian (her mother's daughter!) and delivered her graduation speech with a grace and panache that made me burst with pride. Pride, however, had played no part in an episode that had occurred a few months earlier, in a wintry morning, when I left our house by way of three icy steps leading to our walkway. "Careful, it's slippery!" were the last words I uttered before slipping on the ice and, in the fall, broke my left wrist. The surgery was only partly successful — the X-ray revealed that the tiny bones involved were beyond repair. I never regained full flexibility in the wrist, immediately ending my all-too-modest career as a violinist. I was also told that my left hand lost 30 percent of its strength, which meant that my left jab would have been indistinguishable from a caress — but then I never was a trained pugilist.

Some time in 1966 I received a call from Robert Sherman, my friend at WQXR, informing me that Martin Bookspan, the station's program director and another old friend, was leaving the station for a position at ASCAP. Bob Sherman was going to succeed him and, since there was no one on the station's staff qualified to be their music director, would I be interested? "I certainly would," was my reply, but it depended on the finances. Bob was going to discuss the matter with Walter Neiman, WQXR's general manager, and promised to call me shortly. He did, but the station's offer simply was well below my Muzak salary, a major obstacle for us, as Nancy was about to enter college. We ended our conversation to our mutual disappointment.

In the fall of 1964, Hedy and I attended our one and only Met opening night ever. I had never been attracted to such circus-like events, and even in later years, when I earned the privileges of the "working press," I stayed away from openings in the firm belief that all new productions would improve once past the opening-night jitters. We broke procedure due to the presence of our close friend Sándor Kónya, who shared that gala evening with Joan Sutherland and Robert Merrill in Donizetti's *Lucia di Lammermoor.*

I had been following the career of Sándor Kónya ever since his 1958 Bayreuth debut, and when I learned about his arrival to New York three years later, I immediately arranged an interview through his press representative. We met in the East Side apartment the Kónyas shared with friends. Although nothing publishable came from that meeting, it led to a lifelong friendship. Our common Hungarian roots cemented our relationship, and Sándor, a passionate cook, insisted on my staying for dinner. In fact, he called Hedy at our home in Hollis, explaining the situation, charmed her out of her wits, and I stayed for a delightful evening.

Sándor had left Hungary during the tumultuous postwar years to pursue his vocal studies in Germany. Married to a smart and strong-minded German woman, Anneliese, he obtained German citizenship after his professional debut in 1951. He also studied in Italy and modeled his career on the Italian style of singing. After early successes as a member of the Berlin Städtische Oper, he was invited to audition for Wieland Wagner who, in 1958, was determined to find a truly lyric tenor for his new Bayreuth production of *Lohengrin*. Unfamiliar with the Wagner opera which was to make him world famous, Sándor chose "Vesti la giubba" to audition for Wagner's grandson, but he was engaged anyway.

Sándor Kónya spent 14 seasons with the Metropolitan Opera, and we saw him in virtually every one of his 21 roles. Because he was a peerless Lohengrin and Stolzing, the American press labeled him a "Wagnerian tenor" and tended to belittle his excellence in such Italian operas as *Turandot, La Bohème, La fanciulla del West, Tosca,* and *Lucia di Lammermoor*. Bing, who appreciated Kónya's artistry, also cast him in the Met's revivals of Flotow's *Martha* and Weber's *Der Freischütz*, operas that did poorly at the box office through no fault of the artists involved. Sándor's first dozen years were certainly crowned with success in New York, San Francisco, Italy (*Lohengrin,* of course, in Italian), but he continued to spend most of his time in Germany. The Kónyas took an apartment on West 72nd Street, in the same building where Zinka Milanov then resided, and we shared many lively parties with them. Nonetheless, they did not really take root in their American surroundings. We kept in touch by phone while the Kónyas were in Europe, and shared their triumphs and frustrations. Sándor was a well-built, athletic man and, perhaps because he was so proud of his physical strength, he paid insufficient attention to a strange form of hepatitis that hastened the end of his career. When he finally retired in the early 1970s, he became a successful vocal teacher in Stuttgart. He and Anneliese brought property in Ibiza, Spain, where Hedy and I visited them in September 1993 to celebrate Sándor's 70th birthday. He looked well, and entertained a large party of friends and admirers from all over Europe. Anneliese, on the other hand, already showed signs of the illness that was to claim her a few years later. When we last saw Sándor, it was at a luncheon given by the Metropolitan Opera Guild during the Verdi year of 2001. He was a shadow of his former vigorous self, and a year later he followed his devoted Anneliese, dying quietly — a native Hungarian, a German citizen, ending his days in Spain, and by then virtually forgotten in the United States.

At the end of the 1965–66 season, the Metropolitan Opera departed from its venerable but rather decrepit initial home at 39th and Broadway. The occasion inspired me to write an extended tribute in rhyme, intended for publication in the Met program booklet, still under Irving Kolodin's editorship. Irving not only loved it, he even contributed two lines of his own — I no longer remember which ones. Everything, however, had to be approved

Sándor and Anneliese Kónya at Ibiza, 1993.

by the theater's management and, after hearing complaints that this or that artist's name was either left out or not properly treated, Irving lost his patience, and the piece called "Farewell and Hail" found a welcome outlet in the October 1966 issue of *Stereo Review*. Kolodin rewarded me by getting me a special pass for the unforgettable April 16 closing gala, in which 57 soloists and 11 conductors paid their final tribute to the house in the presence, on stage, of such immortals as Lotte Lehmann, Elisabeth Rethberg, Marian Anderson, Alexander Kipnis, Risë Stevens, Richard Crooks, Giovanni Martinelli, and other still living legends. Although my ticket specified merely "standing room," I was privileged to stand in the aisle up front, with a commanding view of both the orchestra and the stage. Met stars Leontyne Price, Birgit Nilsson, Zinka Milanov, Richard Tucker, Dorothy Kirsten, Robert Merrill, and their colleagues, took one star turn after another, and I recall an unusually torrid Gioconda-Laura duet from the Ponchielli opera with Régine Crespin and Biserka Cvejič as the venomous rivals. On a less distinguished level was the *Aida* Triumphal Scene where tenor Kurt Baum (only occasionally active by then and apparently a stranger to the new production) was handed Radames's lance and, for a moment, was visibly unsure what to do with the thing, while relative newcomer Zubin Mehta wielded his baton with acrobatic vehemence. A faded star of the past, soprano

Queena Mario, dazzled by the thunderous applause and the limelight absent from her life for at least a quarter of century, stayed beyond her accorded welcome, and had to be gently guided off the stage by a respectful usher. The long evening began with the Grand March from *Tannhäuser*, led by the distinguished-looking but ever unpredictable Leopold Stokowski, who used the occasion to raise his voice on behalf of "saving this beautiful house"—by then a hollow effort for a useless cause.

Apart from these festive events, in the normally unexciting confines of Muzak, important things were happening. Charles Cowley, the company's longtime president, announced his retirement. At the farewell party he introduced his successor, a gentleman named Muscio who, soon enough, made his presence felt. Unlike Cowley, Muscio wanted to take an active interest in the creative end of programming, offering one unnecessary suggestion after another to Donald O'Neill and me. Muscio's previous position was executive vice president of the Fedders Corporation, a leading producer of air conditioners. His observations suggested an attitude which regarded musical sounds and cool air pouring into the atmosphere as interchangeable phenomena.

Nonetheless, these unwelcome intrusions persisted and upset me no end, while the invariably placid Donald O'Neill accepted them with weary resignation. Hedy, at home, called me a "tyrannical employee," and not without reason. Things came to a breaking point when Donal Henahan, then chief music critic of *The New York Times*, asked me to lunch one day to discuss the background music industry in general, preparatory to a major article he was preparing on the subject. I explained to Henahan Muzak's program policies, the various orchestras we employed, and the types of music we considered suitable to our purposes. The article, which appeared in the November 28, 1967, edition of the *Times*, was fair and factual, in no way hostile to Muzak, though colored by the general condescension classical musicians shared toward the entire background industry. Henahan, naturally, quoted me by name quite profusely, identifying me as Muzak's recording director, which I was.

Muscio was quite indignant and let me know in no uncertain terms that no one but he was authorized to act as Muzak's "spokesman to the media," disregarding the fact that Henahan's lunch invitation had been extended to *me* as the writer's longtime professional colleague. After a lengthy and upsetting discussion, I went home and told Hedy that I was on a collision course with the company's president, which meant that it was time to call Bob Sherman again to see if the WQXR position was still open. As always, Hedy encouraged me to heed my instincts and not to allow salary to be the object. Bob told me that, no, they hadn't found a music director yet and that I would do *both of us* a favor by accepting the position. As I recall, I told Bob that "if WQXR would make an upward adjustment while I would lower mine, we would be in business." A few days later, I joined him in WQXR's conference room, along with Walter Neiman and Bob Krieger, the station's sales manager and vice president. We came to terms very shortly, shook hands, and Walter asked me when I would join the company. I suggested the normal two week's notice, but Walter asked me to make it four weeks. "There will be some personnel changes, like early retirements, in the staff," he said, "unrelated to your arrival, and I don't want you to come in the middle of such things." I agreed with pleasure, not yet knowing that Walter Neiman's thoughtful gesture was typical of many more like it, in the years ahead.

The following day, I went straight to Muscio's office to announce my resignation, stating with a straight face that, being aware that I would leave the organization without a recording director, I was willing to stay for four instead of the customary two weeks. Muscio thought that mine was a very gentlemanly offer, we shook hands and parted on the friendliest of terms, both being glad to be rid of each other. O'Neill and the programming staff understood the situation perfectly. So did John Andrus, who said goodbye to me with the apologetic remark, "Too bad it had to happen." Bill Werner, the marketing director, playfully inquired: "Does this mean that we are going to lose Nancy, as well?" (I had gotten a temporary summer job for Nancy in the sales department, and she charmed them all.)

Nancy did leave for Clark University in the fall, and it brought a huge change in our lives. A few days before driving away, she told me the following: "I am not worried about Mom because she will know how to adjust, but I am worried about *you*. You should have had another child." She was right about the first part — it took me years to adjust. But never for a moment did I regret having an only child.

My lame duck month at Muzak went by in a somewhat intensified fashion because I had squeezed in another recording session to make the transition easier for Donald O'Neill. They did not engage another recording director while I was still there, and I lost touch with the organization thereafter. Some time in the interim, demo material came to me from one of the major publishers, heralding the forthcoming opening of a musical that would "take the city by storm." I went over the material and decided that there was nothing in it to warrant my attention. The rock musical *Hair* opened soon thereafter. There was nothing in it to make me alter my initial impression, but — even without envisioning the future with its subsequent infusions of heavy metal, acid rock, rap music, and hip hop — the time had obviously come for me to leave the pop scene behind.

20. Early Radio Days

Once, many years ago when I was still in my teens, my father wanted to know if I had any plans for a future career, should work in a restaurant no longer satisfy me. When I expressed the desire to become a journalist, my father quickly dismissed the idea because, based on his limited experience gathered in associating with the theatrical crowd, he regarded journalists as a flighty and irresponsible breed. As I first entered the venerable premises of *The New York Times* building on West 43rd Street on the morning of April 15, 1968, and many mornings thereafter, my thoughts were racing back to that faraway time more than 30 years ago. All right, I was in radio, but this was perhaps the most important newspaper in the world, and I was going to be rubbing elbows with the likes of James Reston, Clifton Daniel, Russell Baker, and their journalistic peers!

My reception couldn't be friendlier insofar as Walter Neiman and Bob Sherman were concerned, and I quickly made friends with WQXR's legendary cadre of announcers: the ever-genial George Edwards, the urbane and multi-talented (actor-portraitist-versifier) Lloyd Moss, the rich-toned Peter Allen, and the unique, unpredictable, and frequently indescribable Duncan Pirnie. The attitude of the music staff was coolly businesslike. There were at least three junior colleagues who had wanted my job, and Walter immediately warned me that I might anticipate some hostility, but that I could count on his solid support. I spent my first few weeks watching and learning about the daily routine and my responsibilities as music director. Nothing that I observed seemed to present a real challenge; I quickly learned the duties of each individual and found that, collectively, the station was slightly overstaffed and that, with some redistribution of forces and a more concentrated effort from certain individuals, matters could be tightened and made more efficient.

I had a lot to learn about what was really meant by a "commercial" radio station, and how important it was to generate the kind of income that would guarantee fiscal sanity so we could properly fulfill our aesthetic mission to broadcast great music to our listeners. With my long experience in the musical field, I have never lost sight of the fact that in our society music is unavoidably linked to the marketplace and depends upon it for its survival. Our source of income at WQXR depended on the generosity and interest of our sponsors and on the expertise and business contacts of the station's sales staff. To my surprise, very few of these sales representatives were knowledgeable about music. Larry Krents, a delightful guy and an ace salesman, told me himself how little he knew, and I was wondering how he could effectively *sell* a product (music) without knowing what he was selling. When I consulted Walter Neiman and, being an "eager beaver" by nature, offered to accompany Larry on one of his sales pitches just in case some musical expertise might be needed, Walter demurred. "George, you have a lot to learn about commercial radio," he said. "I pay both of your salaries and, believe me, Larry makes a lot more money than you do. Let him go after the clients. If he feels he needs you, he will be happy to call on you." Yes, in that area, I had a lot to learn.

Otherwise, my first months went with interesting challenges. In addition to our carrying the Met "live" on Saturday afternoons, and the Chicago Opera by delayed broadcast for several Saturdays following the Met season, we programmed recorded operas every Sunday night, sponsored by Delta Airlines. It seemed natural that I should write detailed scripts for those recorded operas, to be read by the respective staff announcers. I also took over the programming of George Edwards's morning program, into which I inserted a half-hour mini-feature on some topicality (summer music, storm music, the pizzicato in music, marches, etc.) that George and I enjoyed probably as much as our audience did.

But the silent hostility toward me within the staff continued, and I decided to take action. Setting aside a lunch hour for myself and my three principal antagonists, I had lunch brought into my office and, in a closed-door session, began to talk to them in the following manner: "Listen, I am no fool and I know that you resent my being on this job. You are probably familiar with my résumé and know that I am qualified to be here. What you probably don't know is that I was an infantry officer in the war, and there is *nothing* you guys can do here to scare me away. I want this job and I will stay here. On the other hand, if any of you are unhappy, you are free to leave. I've been here several months now and I know what all of you are doing. I am ready to step into anyone's shoes at any time. No one here is indispensable. Any questions?"

There weren't many. I cannot say that I won an instant popularity contest, but eventually they all became reconciled to my presence and, after the departure of one gifted but continuously under-achieving programmer-writer, we developed into a tighter and more focused ensemble. While still in 1968, a curious intersection of music and the world of big business brought about an interesting challenge for WQXR and myself. A major oil producer, Texas Gulf Sulphur Company, was charged by the Securities and Exchange Commission with insider trading violations. Under heavy adverse publicity in the press, Texas Gulf needed a prestige radio program to create a favorable culture-oriented image. WQXR's head of sales, Robert Krieger, an affable man with considerable diplomatic skills, made the right contacts and sold Texas Gulf on an idea of a panel of nationally known critics moderated by a popular WQXR personality (Lloyd Moss), reviewing brand new recordings. Such a panel had long been a favorite idea of Walter Neiman and Robert Sherman, but its budget needed a major sponsor and now, thanks to corporate malfeasance and Bob Krieger's quick action, we had one.

Walter, Bob Sherman, and I quickly agreed on the panel of our critics: (1) Edward Downes, popular moderator of the beloved Texaco Opera Quiz, (2) Martin Bookspan, a longtime WQXR personality, also active on PBS television projects at that time, and (3) Irving Kolodin, the nationally known author and critic. Not coincidentally, as Irving had been my long-time mentor, it was now "payback time" for me. Though our choices were unanimous, it must be said that with Walter Neiman the "one man one vote" principle rarely applied. The program *First Hearing* went on the air shortly thereafter, initially produced by Bob Sherman, who soon thereafter handed the producing reins to me. It was hugely successful at the outset, constantly gaining acceptance, and generating strong and controversial responses ranging from "What a helpful and constructive way to learn about music!" to "How can you feature critics who don't know the first thing about music?"

The original panel stayed intact for the four years the program remained under its Texas Gulf sponsorship. And they were quite an impressive three-some. Edward Downes was a quietly authoritative presence who wore his far-ranging scholarship with an unaffected, easy grace. Kolodin was a writer, not a facile speaker. He delivered essays in well thought-out paragraphs, interrupted by weighty pauses that necessitated some editorial tightening for the benefit of our listeners. His outward appearance may have been austere, but Lloyd Moss occasionally engaged him in easy, irreverent, and mollifying banter. Martin Bookspan was Kolodin's opposite: a natural and experienced broadcaster, a constant fount of historic and phonographic data, which he supplied with firm authority in carefully structured phrases.

Early on, convinced of the program's favorable audience reaction, I suggested to Bob Krieger to invite some of the Texas Gulf bigwigs to sit in on one of our sessions. This prompted the following reply: "George, these guys don't care a hoot about music. They want the cultural image and they are satisfied in getting it from us. There are no complaints, and the bills are being paid. Let's leave them alone." *First Hearing* with Lloyd Moss as host and myself as producer stayed on for 25 years. (Texas Gulf Sulphur eventually merged with another organization, and the name disappeared from the Wall Street radar.) In time, Kolodin found our schedule difficult to accommodate with his commitments at the Juilliard School, and Bookspan's busy activities resulted in reduced *First Hearing* sessions. Ed Downes stayed with us to the end, but it became desirable, for variety's sake, to present a different critical threesome for every session. I continued choosing the music and the panelists, and Lloyd Moss invariably hosted the program in his customary witty and imperturbably sophisticated manner. Our alternating panelists came from the top echelon of New York musical life: conductors Antonio de Almeida, Erich Leinsdorf, Jorge Mester, David Randolph, Julius Rudel; violinists Aaron Rosand, Erick Friedman, and Gabriel Banat, clarinetist Gervase de Peyer, cellists Michael Rudiakov and Lynn Harrell, flutists Eleanor Lawrence and Carol Wincenc, pianists Ruth Laredo, André Watts, Barbara Nissman, Susan Kagan, and practicing music critics from magazines and newspapers all over the country. They usually enjoyed the music and said so when they didn't, often calling for adverse reaction when our audiences disagreed with their judgments. I found that many active musicians enjoyed stepping into the roles of critics on occasion. But there were exceptions: Pinchas Zukerman declined my invitation because he "didn't want to sit in judgment on his colleagues."

On one memorable occasion, André Watts took severe objections to the recording of a fellow pianist. Realizing that he might have gone too far in his criticism, I noted an expression of despair on his face as he looked at me, sitting behind the glass window that separated the studio from my control room. When Lloyd Moss finally identified the distinguished performer (obviously not one of André's favorites), André's face eased into a benign smile. (It was one of the cardinal rules that critical views, once expressed, would stay on the tape, not subject to corrections or editing of any kind, except for some tightening of "pregnant" pauses.) In a different instance, flutist Eleanor Lawrence delivered a somewhat too severe criticism of the playing of clarinetist Gervase de Peyer, a close friend of hers and a tennis partner of Eleanor's stockbroker husband (incidentally, a distant relative of mine). Eleanor was upset, but took my advice in persuading her husband to invite Gervase to play tennis with him during the time period when *First Hearing* went on the air.

I invited the late Alexander Schneider one morning to join the panel. We opened with a chamber work by Ernst von Dohnányi (we usually did not identify composers of unfamiliar works to leave the panelist free of prejudices, a restriction that did not apply to well-known pieces generally familiar to most listeners). When Lloyd made the identification, Schneider delivered a stinging opinion of the work — the kind of rapid-fire indictment I usually cautioned panelists to avoid because I knew how most listeners disliked that kind of personalized and self-important attitude. He then expressed doubt in the wisdom of putting that particular selection on the air — which, of course, had been my decision and responsibility. Alexander Schneider was never re-invited. But *First Hearing* continued to be a provocative and unique audience favorite. Unfortunately, it never gained the understanding and appreciation of Walter Neiman's successors and, lacking insufficient management motivation to gain sponsor support, the program went off the air after some 25 years of audience-pleasing activity.

Two exceptional broadcast experiences stand out as I recall my earliest radio days. We honored Leopold Stokowski, then 86, on the 60th anniversary of his first American engagement as conductor of the Cincinnati Symphony Orchestra. The all–Stokowski hour contained a brief interview I recorded at the Maestro's apartment at 1067 Fifth Avenue, with the very talented Ray Neuman as my engineering assistant. Stokowski received us in his private study, a large but sparsely decorated room full of scores, manuscripts, a working table, some books, and memorabilia. The old man was mentally alert, somewhat measured in his speech and reactions, but very friendly, treating me to some unusual recollections of 1908 Cincinnati, a city culturally dominated by its German-oriented population and reluctant to accept any kind of "different" music. Stokowski warned me on several occasions that he had difficulty remembering names and, indeed, in trying to recall the great 20th century works that he premiered during his legendary Philadelphia tenure, he couldn't remember the name of Manuel de Falla. None of these hesitant instances became evident in our radio broadcast, thanks to the magic of tape editing. WQXR carried the broadcast on its long-established *Symphony Hall* hour on the evening of November 2, 1968. I maintained frequent contact with the Maestro after that event, and received several complimentary notes from him about the station and my activities. Four years later, he sent me an invitation to attend his last concert with the American Symphony Orchestra at New York's Town Hall. I was saddened by the scanty attendance despite the unusual program (including Britten's *Serenade for Tenor, Horn, and Strings*). In the same year (1972) I attended Stokowski's 90th birthday tribute — along with some 400 other invited guests. Then this one-time perennial presence in the American headlines (and not only musical ones) quietly returned to his native England and signed a recording contract that would have carried him into his centennial. But he died in his 96th year on September 13, 1977, in a quiet English village.

During that same initial period, WQXR was contacted by an organization dedicated to saving the city of Venice from the elements. Douglas Fairbanks, Jr., the celebrity spokesman for the group, volunteered to give a brief talk for the occasion, and I wrote a special radio script combining history, poetry, and Venice-related instrumental and vocal music. The whole project was very dear to me and, it turned out to be "a superb program, in every way a credit to the station, of which you can be justifiably proud," according to Walter Neiman's characteristically thoughtful memorandum that I have treasured among other mementos of this great friend. Because of the poetic content, the entire program was eloquently delivered by Peter Allen (soon to leave WQXR to become the broadcast host of the Metropolitan Opera), but it certainly inspired the thought that, eventually, I should also establish my own vocal presence to lend another dimension to my activity as the station's music director.

With Nancy in college, Hedy was editor at the National Bureau of Economic Research, working on books and periodicals by internationally noted scholars — a position she cherished. But in the same year when I joined WQXR, her office was moved to Harvard University and, while she was invited to go with the staff, she declined and soon accepted a similar and quite interesting job with the federal government in statistical projects under the U.S. Labor Department. With our only child in college, we soon became familiar with the "empty nest" syndrome. Our modest house in Hollis, N.Y., became suddenly too large for us, the domestic chores ever less attractive and, sadly facing the possibility that Nancy would eventually not be coming back to us, we sold the house where she spent her childhood, and moved to a comfortable apartment on Hillside Avenue, Jamaica, a walking distance from the subway terminal. Naturally, a room was left open for Nancy's occasional visits, and we were fortunate enough to find a small apartment for Hedy's mother in the same building.

After completing her sophomore year at Clark University, Nancy transferred to Barnard College and briefly returned to live with us. Majoring in English, she graduated *magna cum laude* and in August 1969 married a Rutgers University graduate majoring in political science. A handsome young man in perfect physical shape, he was, of course, ready for military duty. The Vietnam War was on and Mark followed my advice, joined the ROTC program, and soon went to Vietnam as an Army lieutenant. Nancy began working for a New York publishing firm, the first step on the path that was to lead her to a satisfying career as an editor in the medical publishing field. Fortunately, Mark returned safely a year later from hazardous overseas service, and the two of them settled down in Mark's native Massachusetts. We kept in close contact, but it took me years to accept the fact that my "little girl" no longer needed my care and protection.

Before the end of 1968, I decided to correct what I regarded as a serious imbalance in WQXR's programming: the inadequate representation of vocal music. We carried several occasional programs contributed by some excellent specialists, Robert Lawrence and Boris Goldovsky among them. They wrote very fine scripts with appropriate musical examples, but left the choice of those illustrations to the station's music staff. This resulted in programs well written but lacking personal involvement. The quality of the singing and the element of excitement were somehow left unexplored. Since I was sure that this failing could be remedied, I approached Walter Neiman with the idea of a one-hour program, as yet unnamed, to be written and presented by me and devoted to the art of the greatest singers of past and present, offering a wide spectrum of the vocal art — opera, Lieder (long neglected on radio), operetta, and other areas of interest to the vocal aficionado. Walter asked me to submit an outline in the form of an audition tape to allow him to judge how I would sound on the air. He took that tape home with him on a Friday afternoon and surprised me the following Monday morning by asking me to prepare the first program of what was to become *The Vocal Scene* for the first Thursday of 1969. "Let's run it for 13 weeks," Walter said, "and see what happens." I am pleased to say that it has run uninterruptedly for 36 years and has turned out to be the "magnum opus" of my professional life.

When I expressed my concern about how listeners would react to my subdued but still noticeable Hungarian accent, Walter brushed it aside, remarking that the station's most popular on-the-air personality had been the late Jacques Fray, who had once attracted a huge audience by sounding like Charles Boyer. And so, the first of nearly 2000 consecutive weekly broadcasts of *The Vocal Scene* was aired on January 2, 1969. It was called "To Love — with Opera." And thus, a self-confident musical administrator, but still a novice and far from fearless broadcaster entered tiptoeing into untested waters.

21. Beginnings of
The Vocal Scene

Since my first broadcasts confirmed my suspicion that I was a novice at this game, I turned to my old SESAC colleague Jack Francis, who had done some radio work, for an objective appraisal of my efforts on the air. His reaction was to the point: "George, I know that you are writing your own scripts, but they don't sound right. You are *reading*, not talking." Jack was absolutely right — I needed coaching, and quickly. WQXR's chief announcer, Albert Grobe, took me under his wing and gave me essential pointers about the value of short sentences. Writing for publication is one thing, he stressed, writing for broadcast is quite another. I learned to insert brief breathing pauses, as singers do, to avoid running out of breath in mid sentence. My coach also persuaded me to slow my natural speech "for greater intelligibility." This proved not to be good advice, because some weeks later Duncan Pirnie took me aside and asked, "George, are you trying to sound like Al Grobe with an accent?" That incident taught me that my coaching days were over and I had to be my own person, for better or worse.

It took me two years and about a hundred broadcasts to acquire complete confidence in my work. I may have been too self critical, because already in the second year I heard favorable comments about the program, which was conceived from the outset as a series of spoken essays, each devoted to a specific subject. As a matter of fact, for the first two months or so, every program was introduced as an "essay in sound." But Walter Neiman didn't like the idea: "George, that 'essay in sound' business sounds pretentious and not like you. It is unnecessary." So I dropped it from the script, but the format remained an essay in spirit yet quite spontaneous in sound, as I was receiving increasing signs of appreciation from my listeners.

I did five interviews in *The Vocal Scene*'s first year: My guests were Sándor Kónya and Irving Kolodin, by then old friends of mine, and Julius Rudel, who was to become one as the years progressed. A more formal conversation occurred when Leontyne Price came to visit me at the station. That was my first encounter with the great soprano. While she was extremely gracious, it was too early in the game for me to create a true rapport between us. Surprisingly, an aura of true joviality permeated my first and only encounter with Lauritz Melchior, the great Dane, who exuded informality and good spirit. The program was intended to honor the tenor's 79th birthday on March 20. Beniamino Gigli (d. 1957) was born on the same day in 1890, a remarkable coincidence I did not neglect to celebrate in *The Vocal Scene*'s later years.

Melchior had come to Manhattan to greet the winners of the Lauritz Melchior Foundation, a generous award he had established to foster the careers of young heldentenors-to-be. (William Cochran and John Russell were the co-winners in 1969). In our conversation, Melchior asserted that "true heldentenors are made, not born. They should develop in their late twenties and early thirties, the age when young artists are preoccupied with family and financial responsibilities. That is where my foundation comes in." It is a well-known fact that Melchior had begun his career as a baritone. When I asked him how eight years of constant singing in the lower range affected his tenorial career, he gave me a memorable reply:

"A skyscraper cannot be built on sand. A strong foundation in a low range is essential to a heldentenor. Without it, he cannot develop his high notes." He was distressed by the fact that such great Wagnerians as Birgit Nilsson lacked tenor partners of her worth. "Imagine, today's Isoldes and Brünnhildes must live without their heroic boyfriends!" Melchior made no secret of his disapproval of the Bing administration. His Met contract had ended abruptly during the first Bing season and, at the closing gala concert in the old house, when such past Wagnerian luminaries as Lehmann, Rethberg, and Kipnis were honored on stage with torrents of affection from their fans, Lauritz Melchior was conspicuous by his absence.

In my studio, Melchior's giant figure was unbent, but he moved about with some difficulty and complained about his impaired hearing. He was on his way to Copenhagen to help celebrate his older sister's birthday and was planning to undertake his third African safari with some California friends. After our microphones were silenced, he turned to me and asked, "Mr. Jellinek, are you a drinking man?" "A moderate one," I replied. "Why?" "The next time I pass through New York, I'll take you to my favorite Scandinavian restaurant, and we'll have some aquavit, with a beer chaser." To my great regret, it was not to happen. The old Viking died on March 18, 1973, two days short of his 83rd birthday.

In late 1969, quite apart from my radio activity, *Stereo Review* sent me

for a weekend to Cleveland where the great Russian violinist David Oistrakh and cellist Mstislav Rostropovich were appearing with the Cleveland
Orchestra. Both artists had contractual arrangements with Angel Records
then, and I was engaged to cover the recording sessions, interview Oistrakh
for the magazine, and contribute some additional Angel publicity material.
Together with Angel Records executive George Sponhaltz, we set up shop
at a motel near Severance Hall and presented ourselves at the first session
of the Brahms Violin Concerto. The recordings were closed to the public,
so George Sponhaltz and I were ushered into the august presence of music
director George Szell for his imperial approval to our being there. The maestro glacially proclaimed that "we are here to make music. Interviews are
unimportant." His discouraging attitude notwithstanding, we were allowed
to stay. Our immersion in some wonderful music making was tempered by
maestro Szell's disapproving glances during the orchestral breaks, culminating in his telling me just before the lunch break: "Since I have to discuss
things with Mr. Oistrakh at the end of the day, I don't see how he will find
the time to talk with you." At that moment, I couldn't help wondering
whether the maestro's attitude would have been different if my assignment
had been a "Szell interview" instead of an Oistrakh one. In the meantime,
George Sponhaltz was determined to make sure that our Cleveland journey
at Angel's considerable expense would produce the desired results. He talked
to the Cleveland press relations people and they assured us that "some time"
will be set aside to meet Mr. Oistrakh at the end of the day. So, after a pleasant lunch in an Italian restaurant, during which the name of George Szell
provided peppery seasoning to our veal scaloppini, the two frustrated
Georges returned to Severance Hall for more exquisite Brahms.

Finally, in late afternoon, a weary David Oistrakh sank into an arm-
chair. "It has been a long day," he began in German, the only language in
which we could communicate, "I am not a young man any more." He had
flown straight from Moscow to Cleveland, and was scheduled to return to
Prague after the concerts to resume his European tour. But he did not regard
recording a familiar work several times a tiresome experience. "This will be
my fourth recording of the Brahms Double Concerto, but each attempt
brings a new approach, a new kind of rapport with a fellow artist, all different individuals. And the same goes for the Violin Concerto which I had
already recorded with Klemperer, and now I am doing it with Szell, both
great conductors." He showered praises on Szell and the Cleveland Orchestra, but was quick to express his enthusiasm for the Boston and Philadelphia ensembles as well. It was the year when Oistrakh was expanding his
activities as a conductor, and shared with me his recent enjoyment in conducting Shostakovich's Tenth Symphony in Russia.

At age 60, Oistrakh found the life of a touring virtuoso exhausting. "My wife and I spend our summers in Estonia, about six weeks every year. It is very restful after being always on the go. But don't think that my life is generally more relaxed in Russia. With my 40 students at the conservatory, I can be as tired in Moscow as I am now." On the current scarcity of young American string players, Oistrakh remarked that Soviet Russia did not experience a similar shortage. "The explanation lies in the governmental structure. The state has succeeded in making the life of a concert violinist or an orchestral musician more appealing to a young person. Apparently in America, fewer youngsters are drawn to a life that requires so many sacrifices. Their priorities and ambitions are different."

As the fading late-afternoon sunlight filtered into the dressing room in Severance Hall, Oistrakh looked his 60 years, his face like that of a benign professor radiating a sad wisdom. But the following day, recording the Brahms Double Concerto with the exuberant Rostropovich providing an amusing contrast in personalities, Oistrakh gave no evidence of aging. He was playing Brahms, music full of mellow and autumnal feelings, and the violinist seemed like the embodiment of ripe and ageless musicality. After those wonderful recording sessions, we had to return to New York without attending the concerts. Both Brahms works, incidentally, earned Grammy nominations as "best recordings of the year."

In 1970, Hedy and I went to Europe — without Nancy, this time — primarily to attend a family wedding in Budapest. But first we stopped in London for a few days and visited the Pordes family, Hedy's childhood friends. I also met Martin Cooper, music critic of the London *Daily Telegraph,* and, after conveying Irving Kolodin's greetings, asked him to contribute an article for the forthcoming Beethoven bicentennial issue of *Saturday Review.* Budapest was the next stop on our rather over-crowded schedule. We visited cousins and their families on both sides, leaving both factions disappointed because we could not spend enough time with them all. Under the communist system, our relatives lived under extremely modest circumstances, and they had every reason to expect more companionship from their distant and presumably well-to-do American cousins. Whatever time we did spend together, however, was extremely pleasant and full of bittersweet old memories. We visited the recently established Bartók Archives in the historic Buda side of the city, where I called on Bence Szabolcsi, Hungary's most eminent musicologist, to extend, in Kolodin's name, an invitation to contribute to *Saturday Review*'s Beethoven issue. Dr. Szabolcsi, a man of advanced age, kindly showed us around the archives, but for the article he suggested Dr. György Kroó, a younger colleague at the Franz Liszt Academy. That led to a new and valuable friendship. György Kroó and I shared not only our first name (along with tens of thousands of Hungarians), but we were both broadcasters. He gave us an interesting article on Beethoven's significant relationship with Hungarian culture which, in my translation, appeared, along with Martin Cooper's contribution, in *Saturday Review's* November 28, 1970, issue.

Vienna was our next stop, and we spent a memorable day at the Grinzing home of Robert Stolz and his dynamic wife Einzi. We played quite a bit of Viennese operetta music on WQXR in those days, and Einzi and I had already been corresponding regularly. Robert was already 80 years old

Robert Stolz plays for us in Grinzing, Austria, 1970.

(Einzi some 20 years younger) and, to quote the much-married Robert, "my fifth marriage was the best, like Beethoven's Fifth." He was a lively, ever-optimistic man, reminisced quite a bit about his fabulous career, and played some of his immortal Viennese songs for us on his old piano. The Stolz home, on Grinzing's Himmelstrasse (Heavenly Street), treated us to a commanding view of Vienna below, causing Robert to remark, "If the call comes from above, I don't have far to go." But in 1970 he was very much alive, touring, conducting, and recording his own works and those of his great contemporaries and onetime friends: Lehár, Kálmán, Fall, Benatzky. He survived them all. I was to devote several programs to Stolz's music, and the tireless Einzi kept me constantly posted on what she, with her business acumen, eventually built into a veritable Stolz industry. Before leaving, I did a quick recorded interview with the Stolzes for *The Vocal Scene*, and took abundant photographs in their home, which we were fortunate enough to visit again three years later. Robert passed away in 1975 while visiting Berlin on a conducting tour. Einzi, with whom we regularly corresponded for years thereafter, and visited several times in Vienna and New York, died in 2004.

From Vienna, we flew to Milan for a very brief but significant stay. Through previous arrangement with my friend Roberto Talignani at the Italian Government Tourist Office in New York we had reserved two tickets for La Scala. The opera was *Don Carlo*— my all-time favorite. Flaviano Labò, a very short tenor with a brazen voice, sang the title role; the towering Martti Talvela, whom I had previously admired at the Met as the Grand Inquisitor, portrayed King Philip, and Shirley Verrett brought the house down as the exciting Eboli. That was our first visit to Italy's most venerable lyric theater, and what a glorious windup it turned out to be for a fast-paced but unforgettable European journey!

Looking back on the 1970 schedule of my *Vocal Scene*, it brought my first interviews with Bidú Sayão and Robert Merrill, both to become dear friends in the years ahead. I also offered an 80th birthday tribute to Beniamino Gigli— with a guest appearance of my longtime friend, the Hungarian-born Metropolitan Opera tenor Gábor Carelli. Gábor had been Gigli's protégé in his youth and a lifelong devoted friend later on. Jan Peerce also came to *The Vocal Scene* under unusual circumstances. Our sales department was approached by a commercial sponsor who wished to engage Peerce to be the host of a special program. Knowing that Peerce and I knew each other, I was asked to approach the popular tenor with the idea. I no longer recall the details of that moribund plan but, when I outlined them to Jan on the phone, he cut me short:

"George, for a commercial project like this, WQXR could not afford my fee. If it were a benefit, you could have me for nothing."

"I fully understand, Jan. By the way, I am planning a tribute to the memory of your late colleague, Leonard Warren. Would you be my guest?"

"Any time, George."

And he came in (for nothing) to lend his loving and amusing asides to my reminiscences of Leonard Warren, whom I never had the pleasure of meeting personally.

My friendship with Jan Peerce had begun in 1953, and had come through an unlikely mutual friend, the Rev. Juniper B. Carol. Father Carol, a Franciscan monk, was a theologian who had spent several years at the Vatican and spoke fluent Italian. He was also a great opera lover, and later taught opera classes at Siena College near Albany. We became good friends and he visited us in our Hollis home on the occasion of my sister's arrival in 1956. As a theologian, Father Carol had serious reservations about the Mass in the vernacular and, though I never ventured to discuss the particulars with him, I had the distinct feeling that his principles made him unpopular within the hierarchy. ("Obedience is the toughest among the priestly obligations"—that much he was willing to admit.) He joined Hedy and me at the Met a few times, and once, after a performance of *Don Giovanni,* he took us to Jan Peerce's dressing room for our first meeting with the tenor and his wife Alice. Jan made no secret of his poor eyesight: he was guided by his instincts on stage, and became aware of Father Carol and the two of us only when Alice quickly put on his very strong glasses.

It was also in 1970 when *The Vocal Scene*'s growing popularity attracted Neil Currie, head of Parkway Productions, a national syndicator located in Washington, D.C. Neil took the program on and when his company was reborn as Radio Features Corporation, introduced it to virtually all classical radio stations in the country. His wisdom and personal devotion has been essential for the show's nationwide success through the ups and downs of classical radio in the 35 years that followed.

When I honored the late Alexander Kipnis on his 80th birthday in 1971, he regaled my listeners and me with the following bit of autobiographical reminiscence: "In my childhood in Ukraine, Jewish parents of musically gifted children had several options. If they were wealthy, they bought a piano for their kid; if they were middle class people, they bought a violin. My parents were poor, so I became a singer." When I asked for his thoughts on why there have been so many distinguished bassos among Russian singers, he quite seriously attributed that fortuitous phenomenon to the cultivation of vodka.

It was my friend, the late John Coveney of Angel Records, who suggested that I call on Victoria de Los Angeles at the Regency Hotel on Park Avenue for an interview. I had long admired her recordings, loved her Metropolitan Opera Marguerite, Micaëla, and Manon, and looked forward to meeting her with a thoroughly non-objective anticipation. When I entered her suite and greeted her in my still respectable Spanish, I felt that we got off very promisingly. Since I had a portable recording machine with me, our dialogue did not register with the proper studio clarity and resonance, but the musical selections (Manon, Violetta, Spanish songs incomparably sung, especially her fabulous "De España vengo"), all later added at WQXR's studios, assured me of a thoroughly charming hour. The show went on and Victoria and I remained friends for several years thereafter. She later revisited me at the station for an afternoon chat after her memorable joint recital with pianist Alicia de la Rocha. On one of my *Vocal Scene* programs, I openly named her "my favorite soprano," which may not be the proper thing to say for a critic, but it was the truth. Her voice was not large but always full and pure in her golden years, and the winning smile that was her trademark was unmistakably present in the richness of her tones. Hedy and I were once invited to a special luncheon given by Spain's Consul General in Victoria's honor — the other distinguished guests were the sister of King Juan Carlos and her husband, the Duke of Badajoz. I have forgotten the names of the other invited guests at that rather intimate luncheon, but Regina Resnik was also there among us commoners. I last met Victoria at her 1991 concert at the Manhattan School, continued celebrating her art on *The Vocal Scene*, honored her 80th birthday in 2003 but, as those things usually happen, our communications eventually ended. Hedy and I visited Barcelona twice, but intruding on her privacy was not in my nature.

With *The Vocal Scene* buzzing nationwide on all cylinders, drawing enthusiastic response everywhere, it occurred to me that I should contact what was then the *Texaco Opera Quiz* to see if I could become at least an occasional panelist. Walter Neiman, who was the station's only direct link with the Texaco crowd, advised me against taking the initiative. "Geraldine Souvaine [producer of all the intermission features] is a very difficult woman," Walter said. "She hates advice of any kind, and, should you call her, she would immediately think of you as a pushy person. By now, she knows who you are and what your program has done for opera. She will contact you whenever she finds it convenient." And she did, very shortly thereafter. Souvaine was indeed a difficult woman, full of bitterness and venom, but I started my association with the Saturday afternoon intermission features in 1972, a link that continued, with a brief interruption due to Ms. Souvaine's temporary displeasure, for more than 30 years. When Richard Mohr became the program producer, the *Quiz*— with the wonderful Edward Downes as moderator — enriched me and my fellow panelists with many tension-free and unforgettable memories.

22. The Workaholic Years

I first met André Kostelanetz in 1972 as he visited WQXR as a guest on Bob Sherman's long-running morning program, *The Listening Room*. When he complimented me on my work on *The Vocal Scene*, I lost no time in inviting him for a future program called — the idea was born in that instant — "Singers I Have Worked With." It happened soon thereafter, and Lily Pons, Lawrence Tibbett, and Rosa Ponselle, among others, were fondly remembered. André even supplied private and then unavailable recordings of Ponselle, whose powerful voice, as he recalled, presented occasional problems for the audio engineers in search of the proper orchestral balance. We became very good friends thereafter, had dinners together, and visited each other's homes. André was living in a penthouse condominium at 10 Gracie Square. In the old days, Lily Pons was a joint owner; after their divorce, André bought out her share — after long and costly negotiations. They remained friends, though André assured me, "Lily was a tough business-woman."

The place was tasteful and elegant, with Renoir and Miró originals decorating the walls. André was not only a gracious host but also an altogether wonderful human being. An avid world traveler, he reminisced about the war years when he and Lily were concertizing for the troops, particularly in the Far East, a corner of the globe that had a special fascination for André. It so happens that we were born on the same day 18 years apart, and we would congratulate each other annually when he was in the States. He would also send me cable salutations from wherever his adventurous life would find him on that day.

Lily Pons, who had come out of retirement for a special concert with the New York Philharmonic, carefully planned and conducted by André in 1972, died on February 13, 1976. We duly honored her memory on WQXR and, about a year later, I wanted to remember her on *The Vocal Scene*, and

André joined me for an evening of music and tender recollections of their many years together. Naturally, I promised to provide a copy of the program for André's own library. But he was a very busy traveler, and the evening of that particular program found him in Los Angeles, preparing for a concert at the Hollywood Bowl. Shortly before my program went on at 10

P.M. New York time, as Hedy and I were preparing to retire, the phone rang. It was André: "George, my friend, I am calling you from Los Angeles. I know that you'll be reserving a duplicate of our program for me, but I am anxious to hear it right now. Let us listen to it together." And so we did. With the phone

Top: Bob Sherman (right) and I honor Arthur Rubinstein (left) on the occasion of his 90th birthday in 1977 (RCA Victor). *Bottom:* The 12th anniversary of *First Hearing,* 1980, with Martin Bookspan, Larry Krents, Irving Kolodin, Walter Neiman, myself and Lloyd Moss (photograph WQXR).

receiver placed close to my radio, we heard the entire one-hour program, commenting on it during the commercial break and at the end of the hour. It was a unique experience for both of us.

True to form, André Kostelanetz passed away in Port-au-Prince, Haiti, on January 13, 1980. His will contained the following proviso: "If there is contemplated a gathering of family, friends and associates in New York City or elsewhere, I direct that such a gathering shall be a cheerful get-together." Within a few weeks after his passing, such a gathering took place in the giant foyer of Avery Fisher Hall, with the participation of hundreds of André's friends and associates. André's brother, attorney Boris Kostelanetz, spoke briefly and affectionately, as did Carlos Mosley of the New York Philharmonic, paying homage to André's long association with the orchestra, a connection cherished by both parties. With all the members of the Philharmonic present, Hedy and I were among the invited guests at the party where good spirits and warm memories ruled, just as that remarkable man would have wished.

Shortly thereafter, Walter Neiman approached me with a thought: "George, you are an experienced broadcaster by now, and *The Vocal Scene* is going great. But that is a taped show, and there is nothing like live radio. How would you like to have another program, between 2 to 3 P.M. every weekday? After a brief trepidation, I said yes, perhaps prompted by that wonderful Verdian phrase from *Falstaff*, "Dalle due alle tre." My colleague and longtime friend Karl Haas was to precede me on tape between 1 and 2 P.M., and Walter regarded the new change important enough to persuade *The New York Times* to carry a full-page ad devoted to several WQXR personalities, including Karl and myself in rather silly poses. In any case, this was the prelude to an 8-year tenure of *Music in Review*, a one-hour program offering interviews with musical personalities, commenting on musical events, and topical subjects in my kind of sometimes-surprising juxtapositions. I avoided giving special stress to vocal music, to safeguard the integrity of my other program. *Music in Review* was a source of unending pleasure for me; an hour of totally "ad lib" talk was an invaluable lesson in timing and discipline. Menacingly looming before me every day was the clock to remind me not to miss ending the show at 2:58 to make room for the news and the preceding commercial.

Through the kind assistance of Dr. Peter Marboe, then cultural attaché of the Austrian government in New York, Hedy and I received an invitation to attend the famous ball of the Vienna Philharmonic, one of the primary festive events of the Carnival season. I never was a "party animal," but that formal affair in Vienna's Konzertverein, the locale of the annual New Year's celebration televised all over the world, was a temptation impossible to resist. We flew to Budapest first, greeted our relatives in our customary loving but hurried fashion, and finally paid our respects to my old opera idol, the baritone Imre Palló, whom I lovingly treated in my earlier chapter devoted to youthful memories of the Royal Hungarian Opera House. We had been regularly corresponding in the intervening years with "Uncle Imre" and his wife Dussy, but it was a special thrill for me not only to visit with the Pallós but also to take them to dinner on top of the Hotel Intercontinental, gazing at the fabulous Danubian view of the illuminated city with its bridges and ancient sites radiant in their almost pre-war splendor.

Prior to our dinner, the old baritone regaled me with stories of the bitter wartime years. After the war, the Opera House (no longer "Royal") reopened among the ruins with surprising alacrity, to serve an audience in a needy state but starving for the consoling power of music. Palló was still singing some of his old roles, but eventually accepted the theater's directorship on an interim basis. Our conversation eventually turned to politics, and I expressed my pleasant surprise on finding relatively open political discussions among the people, and the virtually invisible Russian presence. *Imre bácsi* (Uncle Imre), as he was affectionately addressed by his juniors in the traditional Hungarian manner, explained with a wink in his eye: "My dear George, in this entire country of ours there is only one communist. Our problem is that we don't know who he is."

A couple of years later, the Pallós came to New York to visit their conductor son and their new grandchild. With pre-arrangement with Imre, Jr., I played some Hungarian music on my afternoon program, including some of his father's singing, and I addressed Imre, Sr., with a few words in Hungarian. That was the last time that I met this lovable link to my youth. He was ill in the hospital the next time I visited Hungary, and died in 1978, at age 86.

In Vienna, our road led to Grinzing, with a lively visit to the Stolz villa, where we found Einzi Stolz as animated as ever, and Robert still vigorous and involved in planning new activities. And then came the Vienna Philharmonic Ball, a celebrated annual event since 1924. The hall of the Musikverein was turned into a giant flower garden. The concert hall served as a dance floor, surrounded by ornate boxes occupied by Vienna's elite: government officials, diplomats, and various celebrities. "White tie and decorations" were the approved attire, but dinner jackets were tolerated to accommodate at least one ill-prepared American. The ceremonies opened with a brass fanfare Richard Strauss had composed especially for the Vienna Philharmonic in 1924. The procession of dignitaries included honored members of Vienna's operatic aristocracy, among them Hilde Gueden, Jarmila Novotná, Irmgard Seefried, and Paul Schöffler. The Vienna Philharmonic opened with the *Donna Diana* overture by Reznicek, conducted by young Riccardo Muti, then a new local idol. After that, however, the members of the Philharmoniker became participants rather than entertainers, making the way for a large dance band. Young debutantes and their squires soon filled the hall; Johann Strauss waltzes and polkas sparkled and, as I was to write in an article describing the event in *Saturday Review*, "champagne and wine flowed generously, and somewhere the unrelated Strausses, Johann and Richard, must have smiled. The world at large may go to the dogs and, who knows, maybe Vienna goes with it, but wherever it goes it sure is in no hurry to get there; music is still king in this outpost of a bygone era." (The gloomy undertone in my writing was influenced by the Vietnam War, still beclouding our thoughts.)

From Vienna we flew to Zurich, a city Hedy remembered from her childhood, but it was the first time for me, and that model of Swiss orderliness nestled in idyllic surroundings has remained one of my favorite European spots ever since. My colleague Bob Sherman once referred to me as a "world traveler," but I was really nothing like that. When I traveled, and I did quite a lot in the following years, it was always in the USA or Europe. As for the Far East, *Madama Butterfly, Turandot,* and Lehár's *The Land of Smiles* satisfied my adventurous needs.

Back home, I settled into my rather busy routine, enriched by several important changes. I began teaching an evening seminar on opera history at New York University in 1975 — an association that lasted for more than 15 years and, in 1982, earned me an "Award for Teaching Excellence." I was pleased, of course, but surprised, too, because I never thought that, temperamentally, I had the makings of a good teacher. Nevertheless, some years later, one of my faithful radio listeners, a retired professor, wrote to me, "Mr. Jellinek, after listening to you for years, I think I know what makes you tick: you are a teacher masquerading as an entertainer." That description has stayed with me, because it may not be far off the mark.

In that same eventful year of 1975, our only grandchild, Amy, was born. Nancy and her husband, Mark, moved to Chappaqua in Westchester County and, to be near them, Hedy and I left Long Island after many years, and found an apartment in Hastings-on-Hudson. While it eventually proved not ample enough to accommodate my books and records, it offered us a magnificent view of the river, and with Danubian echoes persistent in my mind, all shortcomings became irrelevant. Walter and Muriel Neiman were our first visitors, and they found us surrounded by 25 huge boxes, still unopened. The Neimans came unannounced from neighboring Ardsley, but brought an apple pie and all the utensils, and we had a delightful time with them on our terrace in messy but convivial surroundings.

With Joan Sutherland, 1976 (Olga Boenzi, WQXR).

I owe my first meeting with Beverly Sills to my NYU classes. Bob Sherman also taught there, offering a series of seminars with prominent musical personalities, and he found himself in a schedule conflict on the evening when Beverly Sills was booked. I happily welcomed the opportunity to substitute for Bob, with the understanding that Hedy and I would pick up Ms. Sills at her apartment on Central Park West, drive her to the university, and deliver her back home after the class. We pulled up our car at the appointed place, and I was ready to tell the doorman to ring her, when out came the diva herself, already waiting for us. First name terms followed immediately and, when I told her that inquisitive students have a way of asking indiscreet questions, in which case I would interpose myself and fend them off, Beverly reassured me "to let them ask what they want; I'll take care of it." That was the time when she was already thinking about retiring from the stage, so anticipating that it might come up in class, I brought up that subject for my own curiosity. "I am booked years in advance, and I intend to honor all my commitments," she replied. "I am no longer looking for new bookings, but if offers should come in for a few more years, I will consider them one by one." Needless to say, she had the class in the palm of her hand. Ready wit, prompt and frank answers always with a friendly smile — these were the qualities that made me invite her not to *The Vocal Scene* (that

With Beverly Sills, ca. 1980 (Olga Boenzi, WQXR).

would come later, and more than once) but — for novelty's sake — to be a guest panelist on *First Hearing*. With Irving Kolodin and Edward Downes as her distinguished fellow panelists, she participated in an all-vocal program and, to no one's surprise, gave a stellar account of herself, engaging the urbane Lloyd Moss in some light banter. I might add that she came to the station early enough in the morning to join me for a cup of coffee at *The New York Times* cafeteria. The Star soprano, opera director, eventually chairman of the Met board of directors remained a good friend through the years, and the last time I interviewed her for *The Vocal Scene*, we met in the boardroom of the Metropolitan Opera as she was reminiscing about her "Tudor Queens" in Donizetti's *Anna Bolena, Maria Stuarda, and Roberto Devereux.*

Among my guests on *The Vocal Scene* in that period was the delightful Marilyn Horne, on the occasion of the Met's revival of Meyerbeer's *Le Prophète* in 1977. We discussed the opera itself, her role, Fidès, and its historical interpreters, the special vocal challenges and, in general, the art of embellishments, and who but Marilyn Horne could treat that subject with her kind of authority? Two years later, in the Met's new (and still current) production of *Don Carlo*, Marilyn ("Jackie" to me and her other friends) sang the role of Eboli for the first time. She used a few transpositions to highlight the best register of her voice, which caused some adverse critical reactions. They prompted me to send her the following card:

> What's the right tonality?
> From arguments the heads are ringin'...
> But as for me, the proper key
> Is the one HORNE elects to sing in!

It brought in one of the many charming and appreciative comments she has sent me through the years.

Somewhat earlier, I had the unforgettable experience of spending an hour with Tito Gobbi at his rented apartment near Lincoln Center. He had come to sing Iago at the Met's new Zeffirelli production of Verdi's *Otello*, but Gobbi found the director's ideas of Iago's character and relationship to Otello totally uncongenial to his own concept, and canceled his performances. I had already admired Gobbi's interpretations of Scarpia and Falstaff, both richly documented in recordings, and envied the audiences in Chicago, where Gobbi was welcomed on an annual basis for years. The Chicagoans were privileged to enjoy his absorbing portrayals in a large variety of roles — Rossini's Figaro, Verdi's Rodrigo, Giordano's Gérard, Puccini's Jack Rance — all vividly and eloquently commented on in our conversation. Even sitting across the table, Tito Gobbi appeared to me larger than life. I recall his observation that he had given up some roles associated with his younger years. "I no longer do Figaro. I can still sing the role, but I can no longer *dance*

Marilyn Horne, ca. 1975.

it," meaning that Figaro was meant to be sung by a younger artist, fast and mercurial in his movements. He was kind enough to remember our interview in his autobiography (*My Life*, Doubleday, 1980), recalling that he was "in a loquacious mood" on that occasion. It was true, but nothing he said was without interest, and I was left with enough material to create not one but two programs devoted to Gobbi's art and colorful personality.

Baritone George Cehanovsky (1892–1986), who had sung more than 1700 performances at the Met during his long career, and worked at that time as the theater's Russian diction coach, spent an entertaining hour with me. We had met a while earlier as fellow members of a panel of judges, and became quite friendly — a friendship further cemented by a vodka-enhanced luncheon after the interview. George did some Silvios and Schaunards in his younger years, but later he was used by the Met in important character parts (the smuggler Dancaire in *Carmen* 172 times), and that suited him fine. "I shared the stage with the greatest singers of my time, the most imposing of them all in terms of stage presence was Chaliapin. He was also full of mischief. When I did Tchelkalov to his magnetic Boris Godounov, he suggested that I should do my lines in Russian and he would inform the conductor about the plan. Chaliapin did no such thing, and the conductor Vincenzo Bellezza was caught by surprise." (The language of the Mussorgsky opera was Italian in those days.) Titta Ruffo was also recalled as great theatrical personality, and a vocal phenomenon. There was a time when Giuseppe de Luca was already aging and frequently ailing, and Cehanovsky was discreetly covering the older baritone's roles. On the air, we remembered all those artists with a special homage to the great soprano Elisabeth Rethberg (Mrs. Cehanovsky at the time) and her friend and occasional rival Rosa Ponselle. But we also left room for one of George's own private recordings, Mercutio's "Queen Mab Ballade" from Gounod's *Roméo et Juliette,* which he delivered beautifully. With a little backstage gossip my guest recalled from his 40-year career, time passed very fast.

Through the assistance of my longtime friend Oscar Evans who, as a super at the Met for some 25 years and a devoted friend of Carlo Bergonzi, documenting in scrupulous detail all of Carlo's appearances everywhere, Hedy and I became acquainted with Carlo and Adele Bergonzi. Naturally, an invitation soon followed. Carlo was reluctant to be heard on the air because his English was a bit deficient and, as he explained, he didn't want the listeners to think that he had no vocabulary to speak of. When I encouraged him to lapse into Italian at any time, relying on my instant translation, he acquiesced, and our conversation progressed smoothly, enhanced by his uniquely appealing singing. Carlo told me about his beginnings as a baritone and how, realizing that his early teachers had misidentified his voice, he turned himself "from a third rate baritone into a good tenor" on his own. My subsequent Bergonzi programs on *The Vocal Scene* became great audience favorites.

Those were memorable years for tenors. Richard Tucker came to our studios on several occasions for brief promotional visits, and stayed for an intimate and heartfelt conversation with me in 1974, prior to going to Europe on a brief concert tour. He talked most enthusiastically about his favorite role (Des Grieux in Puccini's *Manon Lescaut),* about his recent visit with he widow of Beniamino Gigli, and about his almost obsessive interest in Halévy's *La Juive.* He had already performed the heartrending role of

With Carlo Bergonzi (right) and mutual friend Oscar Evans (center) 1979.

Eléazar in various venues, but felt confident that the Met would get around to scheduling the opera that had crowned Caruso's career in 1920. It was not to be — Richard Tucker died suddenly on January 8, 1975; I was in the crowd of thousands attending the funeral of the only singer ever held on the Met stage. Immediately thereafter, I made several textual changes in my original Tucker script, and rebroadcast its essence within a few weeks as a "memorial tribute." It is hard to describe the eerie effect of hearing Richard's familiar voice in conversation so soon after his untimely passing. Here are a few lines from the "Afterword" I wrote to his biography by James L. Drake (E. P. Dutton, Inc., 1983): "There is an element of self-confidence that radiates from Tucker's singing.... This kind of self-confidence was part of the man's makeup. Richard Tucker knew his worth: there was no false modesty about him. He not only knew he was good, he simply did not know anyone who was better."

The groundwork of the Richard Tucker Music Foundation was laid soon thereafter, with Richard's widow Sara and son Barry in the apartment of Karen Kriendler Nelson, a longtime friend of the Tucker family, who became the foundation's executive director. I have been a fairly active member of the advisory board ever since, and a judge at the annual auditions for more than 20 years. Some of the prestigious Tucker Award winners are now the current stars at the Met (Renée Fleming, Deborah Voigt, Dolora Zajick, and Richard Leech, among others). The foundation's annual gala — always broadcast on WQXR, frequently with my commentary — is by now one of the festive events of New York's concert season.

Jan Peerce was Tucker's brother-in-law, but the two tenors had strained relations ever since their early years and, unfortunately for those who admired and befriended both artists, they never reconciled. Jan's very entertaining memoirs, co-authored by Alan Levy, were published in 1976. Hedy and I attended the book party, and we found the 72-year-old singer in an exuberant mood. Thanks to a delicate operation by an outstanding eye surgeon (an honored guest at the party), Jan had regained the unimpaired vision of his youth. He subsequently visited me on my live afternoon program *Music in Review*, and the rich material in his book, *The Bluebird of Happiness*, gave us a great deal to talk about. I paid tribute to Peerce's art on *The Vocal Scene* as well, aired on June 2, 1983, and what happened before the airing was uncanny. Jan suffered a series of strokes and eventually lapsed into a coma. By the time my program went on the air, he was unconscious. His devoted wife Alice put the radio on at 10 P.M., but afterwards she told me that while Jan was listening to it with a peaceful smile, no one could be sure whether he realized what was going on. As I had been informed of his comatose condition beforehand, I rewrote the last paragraph of my original script, turning the program into a kind of memorial tribute, just as I had for his brother-in-law and longtime rival Richard Tucker several years earlier. Jan continued in this vegetative state until his death on December 15, 1984. His sister Sara, Richard's wife and equally estranged from Jan, was mortally ill at the time, but their son Barry Tucker told me that he had paid his respects to his uncle in his final hours.

In those "workaholic years," with the NYU classes continuing, with appearances on the Met Saturday afternoon broadcasts, frequent lectures in New York and elsewhere, several European travels and, of course, *The Vocal Scene* enjoying nationwide recognition, my daily *Music in Review* continued growing in local popularity. A youthful and somewhat reticent young Hungarian exile named András Schiff had contacted me, and was treated to his first American interview. Now he is one of the world's most celebrated pianists, but — countless concerts and award-winning recordings later — he chose to establish his home in Austria, with frequent visits to his eventually liberated homeland. On another memorable afternoon, Victoria de Los

The first radio interview of the very young András Schiff, ca. 1974.

Angeles visited me, and I tried my best to behave like a dispassionate critic and not, to quote the operatic Duke of Mantua, "schiavo de' vezzi suoi" (a slave of her charms), but I am not sure that I succeeded. Christa Ludwig (whom I had previously interviewed on behalf of the Metropolitan Opera) spent a very lively hour with me. When I complimented her on the still fairly recent recording of Bellini's *Norma* (where she sang Adalgisa opposite Callas and Corelli), she surprised me by admitting that she was still not fully at home in Italian roles. Later I learned that she had been coached in 1968 by Zinka Milanov in preparation for her first Lady Macbeth in Vienna. During our brief conversation before going on the air, I asked her to name her three favorite conductors, so that our on-air conversation would be built around her choices. She unhesitatingly named Karl Böhm, Herbert von Karajan, and Leonard Bernstein. When I asked Christa about Otto Klemperer, with whom she had done some immortal work on records, she explained (not on the microphone) that one day when she was recording with Klemperer, the word came of Bruno Walter's death. Klemperer's reaction to the news was so disrespectful and personally venomous that Christa lost all her "respect for that conductor." When Leonard Bernstein died some years later, Christa and some members of the Vienna Philharmonic honored the New York Philharmonic's special tribute to their Lenny with one of Mahler's appropriately mournful songs at Avery Fisher Hall. According to Christa, Bernstein had been a major influence in her understanding and interpretation of Mahler. Before her departure, I presented Christa with the music of the Verdi song, *Perduta ho la pace*, which is based on the Italian translation of the Goethe lyric best known to us from the Schubert song "Gretchen am Spinnrade." The last thing Christa Ludwig needs (considering her enormous song repertoire) is a suggestion of this kind, but the Verdi song was unfamiliar to her. Besides, I am an inveterate program builder, and imagined that the Schubert-Verdi sequence could give her a most unusual double encore. Although I doubt that she ever followed up on my recommendation, I still think it was a good idea.

Victoria de los Angeles. Photograph taken around 1970.

Radio Station WQXR is a highly prestigious bulwark in New York's world of classical music and, usually, the artists I contacted either directly or through their press agents gladly came to use my programs as a nationwide publicity tool. In rare instances, certain artists felt that such a visit to the station was inconvenient or, perhaps, below their dignity. Some of my planned interviews did not materialize for one or the other reason, but I did want to commemorate Zinka Milanov on *The Vocal Scene*, so, properly accompanied by one of the station's engineers to create the necessary audio ambience, I presented myself one afternoon at Madame Milanov's West 72nd Street apartment. She treated us in a courtly, diva-like manner, answered my questions in a no-nonsense fashion, without evasions of any kind, always with a cool self-assurance. When I praised her classic *Aida* recording of 1955 (with Björling, Barbieri, and Warren; Perlea conducting), her brief summation was: "Yes, but Björling had a smallish sound; Del Monaco and I would have blended better." When discussing singers of the younger generation, she reacted rather pensively in this manner: "What they generally lack is ... modesty. There has to be modesty in our art." How true, but how surprising it is to hear that wisdom expressed by an artist whose regular habit had been to make a grand entrance at a rival soprano's performance, majestically gliding down the center aisle, acknowledging the applause of fans just as the lights were about to dim! Looking back on the days when Callas and Tebaldi were still frequent presences at the Met, I asked Madame Milanov about her own relationship with the controversial Sir Rudolf Bing. Another pensive reply: "It was pretty good because ... Mr. Bing, you know ... needed me." Going back to the studio and, in my usual fashion, completing our brief interview with musical excerpts dating from Milanov's best years, I found that, except for the "modesty" reference, all of her sometimes startling statements were somehow validated by her singing.

One day I received the call from the noted Italo-American artist and opera enthusiast Luigi Lucioni. He said: "Mr. Jellinek, how come you have never featured Franco Corelli on any of your programs?" I assured Mr. Lucioni that I was a great admirer of Corelli, but he was generally known for a certain unpredictability, and I didn't think he would be interested. Lucioni persisted and offered to deliver Franco Corelli "in person." We set the date for my live afternoon program — which was listed in *The New York Times* with the name of my guest identified, thus guaranteeing a considerable amount of attention. The two gentlemen arrived on time, as promised — Lucioni rather prideful of his achievement, Corelli friendly but somewhat diffident, and I, rather relieved. Corelli turned out to be a charming and utterly sympathetic guest. Since his stage fright was proverbially known, I asked him — off mike — whether he would mind discussing the subject on "live" radio. "Not at all," he said. "Ask anything you like."

With Franco Corelli, ca. 1990 (Richard Tucker Foundation).

Corelli did not describe that phenomenon as "stage fright," but attributed it to an enormous amount of accumulated tension that could be released only by virtually throwing himself onto the stage. (According to some reports, sometimes his wife Loretta did the actual "throwing.") I asked him about the press reports relating to an angry confrontation with basso Boris Christoff. Corelli identified the incident as a tense dispute arising from his alleged upstaging the basso during a *rehearsal* prior to a 1958 performance of Verdi's *Don Carlo* in Rome. Christoff rather forcefully objected to Corelli's stage behavior, Corelli stood his ground, and, equally unbending, Christoff withdrew from the cast. "We all have our egos," Corelli admitted. "These things happen between singers." There was no anger in his voice, nor was there any sign of regret. As my guests departed, seeming very pleased with the radio visit, I asked Mr. Lucioni if he would be good enough to "deliver" Mr. Corelli once again for a *Vocal Scene* interview where we could discuss some technical matters, in particular his marvelous *morendo* effect on diminishing high notes. "Give me your card, and I'll contact you," Corelli said resolutely. We were to meet on different occasions in the following years, and I left a few more cards with him, but I had to be satisfied with honoring his art later on with a special tribute without that forever handsome but forever withdrawn and unpredictable tenor's participation.

The tempestuous career of Maria Callas ended in troubled solitude on September 16, 1977. On December 4, hosted by Robert Jacobson, then editor of *Opera News,* a group of musical people — all personally or professionally associated with Callas — paid tribute to her before a capacity audience in the auditorium of New York's 92nd Street YM-YWHA. John Coveney of Angel Records, Dario Soria, the earliest champion of Maria's recordings, Francis Robinson of the Metropolitan Opera, and authors Irving Kolodin, Andrew Porter, Gerald Fitzgerald, and myself comprised the panel, all contributing our individual memories. Seven years later, I wrote an epilogue to the newly published soft-cover edition of my 1960 Callas biography. Here are the concluding lines: "History will deemphasize the image of the tempestuous diva. As the most influential and significant operatic personality of her age, she will continue to inspire singers, to stimulate controversies, to excite and to mystify. That is what legends are meant to do."

What I earlier referred to as my "workaholic years" were hardly different from earlier decades. I am a "type A person," unfamiliar with the art of carefree relaxation, for whom the borderline separating work in my chosen field and having fun is thin to the point of invisibility. Music is my only hobby, and vocal music and recordings have been my lifelong passion. Honoring my 10th year on *The Vocal Scene* in 1979, Thomas P. Lanier wrote a very complimentary article on me for *Opera News* with the title "I Love My

Maria Callas in 1966 (Angel Records).

Work," and that just about sums it up. At one point, the article quotes me: "This [the radio station] is a restless place.... I am responsible for a lot more than my own programs. I have to deal with internal matters as well as sponsors, artists, record companies, and constant administrative work to make the station more efficient and interesting."

Yes, I worked hard, but my efforts did not go unrewarded. In addition to a huge amount of mail from appreciative listeners nationwide, and total support from station management, I received two national awards, both in 1978. The first was the Ohio State Award, presented to me in Washington, D.C., for "Napoleon, a Musical Saga," (Program No. 415 in a total of nearly 1900). The second was the 14th Annual Armstrong Award, named after Edward Howard Armstrong, the inventor of FM broadcasting. That came in recognition of my broadcast tribute to Maria Callas (No. 457). When my late friend and colleague Robert Jacobson congratulated me on that occasion, he suggested that I should do an annual program highlighting various aspects of Callas's art around her birthday (December 3), an advice I faithfully followed on *The Vocal Scene* ever since.

23. Matters of the Heart

During those "workaholic years," Hedy and I traveled to various parts of Europe almost annually — I as a musical guide for opera and concert tours, initially under the auspices of New York University and later with various travel organizations. Hedy's trip was included in my honorarium — never extravagant but always worthwhile considering the mind-expanding circumstances. Needless to say, sea travel was still not on my agenda as I held fast to my 1946 pledge of oceanic abstinence. We met many congenial music lovers in these journeys, and kept a friendly relationship with some of them afterwards. But every once in a while we treated ourselves to trips *en deux*. Outstanding in my memory was a 7-day package tour by Italian Airlines to Naples, Pompeii, Amalfi, and Salerno, and a visit to the French Riviera centered on Monte Carlo, with brief sojourns to Nice, Cannes, and San Remo. The latter trip brought only one disappointment. Having read much about the Monte Carlo Opera's golden years with all those legendary singers around the turn of the century, I wanted to tour the insides of that theater. Well, the building, constructed by the famous Charles Garnier, the architect of the Paris Opera, turned out to be an elegant wing of the casino itself, not an independent edifice. We admired the whole thing from the outside, invested $20 to satisfy our gambling instincts, quickly lost it, and moved on.

After a memorable trip to the Canadian Rockies, with a brief interlude in Seattle, Hedy's mother died of a stroke in late 1979 at age 82. She had carried the heavy burdens of widowhood remarkably well, and enjoyed the joys of being a great-grandmother for nearly five years. She lived in our apartment complex, well cared for, but retained her independence and enjoyed being the matriarch of the extended Turi family. Her initial doubts of my being worthy of that family had vanished long ago, and eventually she had even displayed signs of being proud of her son-in-law.

In the spring of 1980, Hedy and I both felt that another non-professional vacation would serve us well, and we chose Bermuda. That was our second visit to that wonderful island, which attracted us with its relatively short distance from home, its breezily moderate climate, inviting sea beach, and its aura of total relaxation. One of the persistent dilemmas was choosing between the beach and a pool where they were serving cocktails to customers standing half-submerged in the water. A combination of the two usually solved the problem. We did visit Hamilton and other attractive sights once or twice, but our hotel offered excellent accommodations, and we (at least I) rarely wished for the enticements of nightlife. The friendly locals and the perfectly well-behaved schoolchildren in their neat uniforms delighted us and, visiting a land with a 25 miles per hour speed limit and the delicate humming of tropical birds replacing the variegated noises of the big city seemed to be this New Yorker's temporary paradise.

I swam a lot in Bermuda, but otherwise exercised not at all. One day, walking from our cabin toward the dining room for an afternoon tea, British style, I suddenly felt a shortness of breath that forced me to pause at a nearby bench until my breathing returned to normal. It was but a passing moment but, having experienced a similar episode a few weeks earlier, walking in Manhattan with Walter Neiman toward the funeral services of our mutual friend Dario Soria (victim of a sudden heart attack at his desk), I felt that a medical consultation was necessary. My cardiologist, Dr. Daniel Macken, whom I called immediately on returning home, gave me a thorough examination that called for an angiogram, with a bypass operation to follow. At New York's Columbia Presbyterian Hospital, the angiogram graphically showed me more than I cared to learn. What turned out to be a quadruple bypass followed almost immediately thereafter. I was in my 60th year; several of my acquaintances, including my close friend George Calfo, had luckily survived a similar experience. Nonetheless, while I did my best to show an optimistic attitude, inwardly I felt that my chances were 50-50 at best.

Hedy, Nancy, and my sister Éva rushed to my bedside; my five-year-old granddaughter Amy was present and highly indignant when she was not allowed to pass beyond the reception room. I had fairly extensive and quite emotional individual moments with Hedy, Nancy (who had recently divorced her husband Mark but still lived in Westchester County), and my sister. Then I was wheeled into surgery, given anesthesia, and the rest turned into a blur with faint memories of intense pain relieved by occasional morphine shots. In short, I luckily survived and was eventually returned to my room, where I rather groggily kissed my anxious wife, and moments later turned on the radio to listen to WQXR.

Dr. Macken saw me on a daily basis during my brief post-op hospital stay. When I asked him about returning to work, he said that I needed at least two weeks of convalescence and suggested that Hedy and I should go "somewhere in Europe." The doctor used good psychology by reminding me that I should no longer regard myself as a heart patient but one who had had a brief "cardiac episode." A European trip was, of course, out of the question. Hedy and I spent a two-week vacation alternating between our two favorite places in Connecticut: the shoreline by Old Saybrook and Essex and Litchfield County, near Lake Waramaug.

Prior to my hospitalization I had received an assignment from the San Francisco Opera for an article relating to their revival of Verdi's *Simon Boccanegra*. In a letter, I explained the condition that made it impossible to complete the article on deadline. For reasons no longer remembered, that letter was returned to me several days later, unseen and unopened, just before we departed for Connecticut. Consulting the calendar, I decided that, weakened though I was, I could finish the assignment *near* deadline. Most of the writing was done at the Essex Public Library under Hedy's disbelieving but always attentive care, and the article, eventually titled, "The Real Boccanegra and the Political Verdi," appeared in the *San Francisco Opera Magazine* in the fall of 1980.

During my hospitalization and convalescence, my colleagues at WQXR continued airing earlier programs of *The Vocal Scene*, but my "live" afternoon series of *Music in Review* had to be suspended. When I returned to the air, my first program was devoted to "The Heart," featuring some appropriate Schubert songs, Lehár's "Dein ist mein ganzes Herz," Dalila's "Mon coeur s'ouvre a ta voix," and other cardiac-related music. Although my commentary was lighthearted, it was not unmindful of my own "episode," and duly credited Dr. Macken and my outstanding surgeon Dr. Frederick Bowman for making it possible for me to resume the work I love.

On March 17, 1981, my afternoon program celebrated the 40th anniversary of my arrival in the United States. It featured popular and classical recordings released in 1941, all previously assembled, without discussing it with anyone at the station. My commentary, however, was ad lib, as I tried to recreate the atmosphere of pre–Pearl Harbor New York in music — Gertrude Lawrence in Kurt Weill's *Lady in the Dark,* Horowitz and Toscanini in the Tchaikovsky piano concerto, and Freddy Martin's pop arrangement of the concerto's opening theme — among others. Neither Duncan Pirnie, the mid-day announcer, nor Walter Neiman had been aware of the very special nature of my program, but Walter quickly organized a champagne party to celebrate the occasion, as I came off the air at 3 P.M.

The centenary of the birth of Béla Bartók was in 1981, and the American Hungarian Foundation celebrated the occasion with a black tie banquet at the Waldorf Astoria on March 26. I was invited to act as master of ceremonies and to deliver a short talk honoring the memory of that great composer and humanist. Yehudi Menuhin, Bartók's lifelong friend and devoted interpreter, received the foundation's annual "George Washington Award." Seated at the same table, I enjoyed brief conversations with the great violinist and future Knight of the British Empire, a very shy and withdrawn man, but his wife Diana provided all the talk needed, and then some.

Another delightful event had been in the making ever since late 1979, when Dr. Peter Marboe, cultural delegate of the Austrian government, informed me that my name had been submitted for a decoration honoring my longtime services on behalf of Austrian music. While inwardly I felt that honoring Mozart, Schubert, the waltzing Strausses, Richard Tauber, Christa Ludwig, Leonie Rysanek, and other Austrians of their caliber should call for no special recognition, I was in no mood to dispute the honor. I was awarded the "Cross of Honor for the Arts and Sciences, First Class" by Consul General Thomas Nowotny. Family and a few close friends attended the intimate ceremony at the Austrian Consulate, and I also had the foresight to invite Sidney Gruson, then executive vice president of *The New York Times*, and an appreciative listener of *The Vocal Scene*. Had it not been for Sidney's presence, *The Times* would have passed the event unnoticed in the manner it had usually managed to overlook WQXR's other contributions to the city's cultural image.

In late spring 1981, Hedy and I took a nostalgic European vacation, which started in Zurich and the lake region of Switzerland, in the company of Hedy's former colleague and our longtime friend Elisabeth Duerst. We visited Hedy's only surviving cousin Sylvia, then a resident in the Italian region of Switzerland. Then, using Elisabeth's car, we drove into Italy with the following itinerary: Bergamo (visiting the birthplace and final resting place of Donizetti and his teacher Giovanni Simone Mayr), the Lake Garda shores, Verona, Mantua, Busseto, with its tiny but dignified Teatro Verdi (also Verdi's humble birthplace at Le Roncole, and the Villa Sant' Agata), Cremona, a violinist's Mecca, with a visit to a noted violin maker of Hungarian extraction, and the museum where Paganini's four violins were on display. Then on to Parma, Pavia, Lake Como (where I telephoned Titta Ruffo's elderly daughter at her brother's request). The whole trip was an Italophile's dream, but it came to end in Zurich, where my childhood friend Miklós Róna, by then a Swiss citizen, and his wife drove us through fabulous Alpine resorts like Flims and Bad Ragaz and to the Zurich airport, where our unforgettable journey finally ended.

The year 1981 was rich in other memorable events for me. All my radio

Consul General Thomas Nowotny awarding me a decoration from the Austrian government, 1980.

programs were running full steam. I entertained Nicolai Gedda on *The Vocal Scene* and tried to learn the unlearnable from him: how to obtain those incredible "voix mixte" sounds that are best illustrated in his recording of "Magische Töne" from Goldmark's *The Queen of Sheba*. The ambiguous term "falsetto" hardly applies here, because Gedda's tone is firmly supported by a delicate but still noticeable chest resonance. What Paganini had allegedly said about his peerless violin technique — "We all have our secrets" — may go for Nicolai Gedda, as well. When I complimented him on his exemplary vocal charm in the classic Viennese operettas, Gedda surprised me by calling them "merely recording roles." He never performed them on stage because he could identify neither with operetta plots nor with their tenor principals.

I continued deriving much enjoyment from the unpredictability of my live afternoon programs. Eleanor Steber came in one day, well past her prime years, and rather heavy in appearance. I had always admired her in several roles, particularly in Mozart operas. When our conversation turned to Italian opera and the recently re-issued 1949 recording of *Madama Butterfly*, Miss Steber delivered the following question/statement, as the fine singer she was, all in one unbroken *legato* arch: "Have you heard my *Butterfly?* It's definitive!" It was one of those occasions when the interviewer's lot is to bite his tongue and withhold comment. I never failed to remember André Kostelanetz's birthday on December 22, a birthday he shared with Puccini, so these annual programs of mine were dual celebrations. Actually, triple ones. Peppered with my seemingly insignificant allusions to the nice warm feeling connected with such a pleasant time of the year, I modestly concealed the fact that André and I (and Puccini) shared the same birthday.

Nonetheless, 1981 was the year when my afternoon program ceased operations. WQXR's sales department, the very people who seven years earlier enthusiastically embraced the consecutive mid-day presences (1–3 P.M.) of Karl Haas and myself, now declared to management that those two hours should be devoted to more generic ("no personality") broadcasts. Such things often happen in the revenue-oriented business of commercial radio. Then and now, the sales staff of WQXR consists of able and industrious colleagues who totally lack any appreciation of classical music.

I accepted management's decision stoically, especially considering Walter Neiman's personal assurance that another hour would be found for me on the station's schedule. It happened soon enough, and it was called *Music Magazine*, an hour-long monthly musical essay relating to contemporary events. In October 1982, it brought me the important "Gabriel Award" by UNDA-USA "for outstanding achievement in radio." The piece so honored was "Poland's Search for Freedom," a vital subject in those days of the

Cold War. I received the award personally from Archbishop (later Cardinal) Joseph Bernardin of Chicago at the grand ballroom of the Palmer House Hotel. A few months later, before *Music Magazine* ran its brief but rather successful course, I was given another national award by the San Francisco State University Broadcast Conference for "FDR Remembered," an essay honoring (in words and music) President Roosevelt's centenary. As I remember, Robert Conrad, general manager of WCLV Cleveland, accepted the award for me.

More lastingly, I began a very unusual series called *Italy in Music*. Its genesis had been WQXR's carrying the Italian Radio's (RAI) live transmission of Bellini's *Norma* (with Montserrat Caballé and Tatiana Troyanos), from La Scala, Milan, via satellite on January 18, 1977 — the first such opera broadcast ever. With Duncan Pirnie breaking in with news and weather reports at appropriate moments, my live commentary filled the lengthy intermission time with stories on Bellini, the opera itself, and famous interpreters. The broadcast, a stimulating experience, was brought off without any technical glitches, and it cemented a lasting friendship with Renato Pachetti, RAI's top New York executive. Eventually, RAI decided to sponsor *Italy in Music* with the understanding that, while I would be free to write the program and make the musical choices, RAI would also provide me with suitable material from their own archives. I was cautioned not to lay stress on opera, but should rather concentrate on Italian chamber and orchestral music, which suited WQXR and me just fine.

The sponsorship eventually passed to other organizations, thanks to our Italian-born new sales manager, Simona McCray, who regarded *Italy in Music* as a special personal project. It developed a highly responsive afternoon audience and, for me, a creative challenge to seek out rarely heard nuggets of Italian culture. Here was my chance to feature the music of Tartini, Boccherini, Salieri, Cherubini, Clementi, Respighi, Pizzetti, Casella, even Puccini's forebears, all musicians in Lucca. I offered Italian music presented by violinist Salvatore Accardo, pianist Arturo Benedetti Michelangeli, and assorted lutenists, guitarists, and gambists. Nor did I neglect the Italian connections of Berlioz, Liszt, and Tchaikovsky. Always devoted to thematic programs, I was delighted to create special essays like "Ancient Rome in Music," "Commedia dell'arte," and other fascinating topics. With several interruptions when sponsorships were lacking, *Italy in Music* continued to be heard for several years.

In 1981, *The Vocal Scene* had lost a starry listener, the great soprano Rosa Ponselle, one of the legendary Normas I had been happy to praise during the satellite transmission from Milan, to say nothing of the several programs I had devoted to her. I never met the great Rosa, but she heard *The*

Vocal Scene on my syndicated program from Baltimore and sent me several appreciative notes, even an autographed portrait inscribed as follows: "To George, for all he has done for the Old Druid, affectionately, Rosa, 1977." Individual sponsorships of *The Vocal Scene* were always welcome, but no longer essential to assure the program's survival, thanks to its impressive nationwide audience, which, in its peak years, represented 75 affiliated radio stations.

A fondly remembered sponsor was the late Robert B. Rivel, former president of the Union Dime Savings Bank. As a devoted operagoer and constant listener, Bob disregarded the negative advice of his own public relations management in choosing *The Vocal Scene* as a source of concentrated publicity for his bank. Some years later, when Union Dime was merged into another organization, Bob Rivel floated away on the proverbial "golden parachute," but not away from my life. One day he took me to lunch at the New York University Club and introduced me to his friend Bill Sullivan, an aspiring singer in his youth, but by then a prosperous broker of industrial insurance. Bill was also the vice president of the Bagby Foundation, a charitable organization devoted to assisting singers and musicians fallen into financial hardship in their declining years. At Bill's recommendation, I was invited to become one of the Bagby trustees, and it was my honor to serve in that capacity for 20 years, until my own retirement in 2003. Among my distinguished fellow trustees over the years: Licia Albanese, Rose Bampton, Schuyler G. Chapin, Alfred Hubay, Anna Moffo, Jarmila Packard, Paul Plishka, John Steinway — all lively and cherished companions. F. Malcolm Graff and Blanche Lark Christensen served as presidents and Winthrop Rutherfurd, Jr. was our general counsel — all philanthropists active in the world of opera. Bagby serves a good cause with no fanfare, but the recipients of the foundation's generous but discreet grants have included many illustrious names of the past.

In 1982, Hedy and I celebrated our 40th wedding anniversary by revisiting our military years in Sacramento and Reno. While Reno had grown a lot, most of the growth affected the casino environs. Going from a remembered landmark downtown, and following my instincts, I had no difficulty in finding our romantic old abode at 440 Hill Street, remarkably well preserved. We briefly stayed at the Hyatt Lake Tahoe, a spectacular lakeside resort, before driving by rented car to Sacramento, a city of sweet wartime memories. Now it has grown to three times its original size, but locating our old apartment on K Street posed no difficulties. The imposing Capitol building and its surrounding park were richly renovated during Governor Ronald Reagan's long tenure, and a friendly passer-by took a picture of the two of us sitting at what seemed like the same bench and in a pose we remembered from 1942. We revisited the Sacramento Auditorium where we had seen *Carmen* with Petina, Jobin, and Pinza in that year. In one of the countless photo albums documenting our memories, we long treasured a picture of Hedy sitting on a stone rim astride the auditorium steps, at age 20, showing a lot of shapely leg. Forty years later, duplicating the same posture, I was happy to find her in a new photo still quite sexy for a woman pushing 60! Our California stay ended with meeting old friends in the Los Angeles area.

Earlier, we had spent a few days in Aspen, Colorado, visiting our friend, conductor Jorge Mester, and attending one of his orchestral concerts. We stopped for a brief visit at radio station KVOD in Denver, a longtime *Vocal Scene* affiliate, where I was able to greet my listeners on the air. There we stayed with the Goroves, devoted radio listeners of mine, overnight.

There was an international conference on Béla Bartók at Indiana University in 1982, organized by its Music School, which, at that time, was heavily tilted toward Hungarian dignitaries. Pianists György Sebök and Bálint Vázsonyi, cellist János Starker were among the members of the faculty, and scholars from England, France, Hungary, and the United States were invited to present papers on various aspects of Bartók's art and personality. My contribution, "Bartók the Humanist" was eventually published in a volume edited by György Ránki, along with other entries written by Robert Layton, György Kroó (my old Hungarian friend and broadcaster colleague), Tibor Tallián, Bálint Vázsonyi, and others. Attending the seminars but not otherwise participating was the great violinist-teacher Joseph Gingold, with whom I quickly struck up a nice friendship, and who was singing the praises of his star pupil, young Joshua Bell. Befitting the occasion, Mr. Bell performed Bartók's Violin Concerto No. 2 to the enthusiastic acclaim of all attending. Mr. Gingold and I pursued a friendly correspondence until his death a few years later. I remember sending him a tape copy of my parallel tribute to Kreisler and Heifetz, and receiving a highly valued compliment from him.

Less than two weeks after that joyful event, on the morning of Tuesday, March 20, 1983, I was in the middle of my *First Hearing* taping when Louise McKellip, Walter Neiman's executive assistant, stormed into my control room, sobbing uncontrollably. "Walter has died in the hospital!" Separated by a soundproof glass enclosure, Lloyd Moss and the *First Hearing* panel continued doing their job, but Lloyd immediately noticed something strange in my behavior, and rushed to the corridor to join Louise and me. The entire office was thunderstruck. Many of us knew that Walter was briefly hospitalized for what we had assumed was a cardiac examination. He had been experiencing inner ear problems which I understood to have been somewhat similar to heart symptoms, and his physician thought Walter should have an angiogram "just to be safe." That same night he called me at home, pretending to be jovial and saying: "Imagine, I am at the Columbia-Presbyterian, 'your old hangout' and scheduled for an angiogram in the morning. What will it be like?" I reassured him that, based on my earlier bypass experience, he did not need to worry. We both carried on in our usual lighthearted fashion, but I sensed a fearful presentiment on Walter's part, a feeling I inwardly shared. He died during that procedure.

Our entire station was totally unprepared for the sudden loss of a very popular and respected leader in his 57th year. Walter and I frequently rode home together on Metro North, and at one time, we were contemplating our eventual retirements. "You and I should leave together, George. We'd have a helluva retirement party." I replied that he was six years my junior, and I wasn't going to wait that long. Hedy and I immediately rushed to visit Muriel and Walter's two sons, and they asked me to deliver the eulogy at the funeral service.

There, among my many words delivered audibly and visibly shaken, I recalled that "Walter liked to call himself a problem solver, and business life has a way of making sure that he never lacked problems to solve. He was proud of us — his associates — and gave us considerable leeway. He believed in delegating responsibility, but on occasion he was quick to remind us who was 'the boss,' just in case.... We frequently second-guessed him — second-guessing is easier than decision-making — and we recognized that it was *his* responsibility to make those decisions.... He had an even temper which I, for one, sincerely envied, and a stubborn streak which I may not have always appreciated but, being a man similarly inclined, clearly understood. I certainly owe him a deep gratitude for furthering my career...."

As I recall lighter moments of our times together, there was a "management meeting" (a weekly ritual attended by the station's department heads) where Walter announced a decision that didn't sit well with Bob Sherman and myself. As we voiced our objections virtually in unison, Walter gave us a characteristic Neimanesque reply: "You guys are talking logic again!" Another time, he virtually stormed into my office, protesting: "George, what is that God-awful music we are listening to, and it's been going on endlessly?" It was some Indian specialty played by the distinguished Ravi Shankar on the sitar. I tried to convince Walter of Mr. Shankar's eminence, but left him dissatisfied, especially because of the length of that particular selection. I had to take him to our old-fashioned card-file (a system later rendered obsolete by computerization, but not really improved) to prove that the "offensive" music was less than 4 minutes in length. Walter stormed out, shaking his head and, with silent apologies to Mr. Shankar, I removed the selection from the WQXR library. Walter loved music but was not musically trained. He listened to our programs with the ears of a sophisticated music lover, in other words those of a typical WQXR listener. It was not our mission to make such listeners unhappy, even for four minutes.

On April 25, 1984, Hedy and I attended a musical tribute in Walter's memory at Brown University, Walter's alma mater, in Providence, R.I. Marilyn Horne sang music by Rossini and Copland, accompanied by Martin Katz, and received an honorary doctorate. The university established "The Walter Neiman Archive of Sound," with an endowment supported by the Neiman family, *The New York Times* Foundation, the Concert Music Broadcaster's Association, and other friends of Walter. Moved by the occasion, I pledged to donate a large quantity of my record collection, which, as a result of further annual contributions, has amounted to more than 1000 LPs and CDs in the succeeding years, housed in a special wing in the Neiman Archives, bearing my name.

A logical choice, Warren G. Bodow, vice president and general sales manager, succeeded Walter at WQXR's helm. Warren and I had a very cordial relationship, but Walter's passing reinforced my decision to retire. We agreed that I would give up my position as music director, take my pension from *The New York Times*, and continue with WQXR as a consultant and, in Warren Bodow's eloquent phrase, an "emeritus presence." I would continue with *The Vocal Scene, First Hearing*, the Sunday evening *Delta Opera House*, and the still flourishing *Italy in Music*, and remain available to the station for special projects. I was 64 years old, it was time to slow down, and, besides, the station was entering a new era of computerization, a procedure that was to require a transitional phase of more than a year. I was the first to admit that a younger and more "with it" generation should inherit the joys of that lengthy transition.

On March 15, 1984, I was given a wonderful retirement party at a restaurant on Sixth Avenue, near the Times Building. Attended by the entire WQXR staff, including June LeBell, the station's first woman announcer, and Nimet Habachy, our new siren voice for the midnight hours. With family (Hedy, Nancy, Gil, and Amy), and many friends attending, it was a happy occasion. I greeted my old SESAC colleague Jim Myers, Is Horowitz of Decca Records, Tony Caronia of Angel/EMI, Richard Mohr of RCA, Bill Livingstone of *Stereo Review*, Peter Allen of the Metropolitan Opera, Martin Bookspan, David Hall, Karl Haas (*First Hearing* panelists) and Muriel Neiman. My sister Éva, who had been a cancer patient for several years, unfortunately could not attend.

It was a "This is Your Life" affair. Warren Bodow started off with a warm introductory speech, followed by Bob Sherman, Bob Bragalini, my longtime associate music director (who was to inherit my job), and rounding out the ceremony, Lloyd Moss reacted to my retirement with his characteristic verbal virtuosity. Here are Lloyd's closing lines:

> But then, forsooth, the happy truth at once allayed my fear,
> He'd not be far from QXR. Each week he'll still be here.
> No need, indeed, to panic, or be manic, or to grouse:
> He'll make, I mean, *The Vocal Scene,* and *Delta Opera House,*
> And *Italy in Music,* and that one *we* do; you know, [*First Hearing*]
> So we didn't have to worry, or to carry on quite so.
> It's surprising, realizing how much time he'll spend with us.
> Will somebody please tell me then: What the Hell's all this fuss?

I acknowledged the company's generous gift, briefly reminisced on what WQXR had meant to me for the past 16 years, and entered a new life as a retiree, a *former* employee of *The New York Times,* and a "freelance contractor."

24. A Pseudo-retirement

My new status as a retiree began auspiciously. On June 1, 1984, I received an honorary doctorate from Long Island University for "distinguished and multifaceted contributions to the world of music." Naturally, this did not happen overnight. Professor Elliot Seiden, who had been instrumental in my getting an Oral Communication Award from LIU in 1979, again acted as the benevolent spirit who had submitted my name to the board of trustees. My fellow honorees were Howard K. Smith, the noted author and news commentator, and the Rev. Gardner C. Taylor, a community leader and civil rights advocate. It was Mr. Smith who delivered the commencement address at LIU's Brooklyn Campus. The formal event, part of LIU's graduation exercises, was followed by a lively party attended by other celebrants, university dignitaries and, of course, my family and close friends. My sister, in and out of the hospital in those days, was there to share this new honor with me. Among the many congratulations I received was a warm letter from Arthur Ochs Sulzberger, publisher of *The New York Times*.

Relieved of the multiple administrative responsibilities of a music director, my daily presence at the station was no longer required. But WQXR listeners continued referring to me in my previous capacity. Radio listeners, by the way, are a wonderful but occasionally strange lot. Meeting many of them in person, I had become accustomed to hearing some unusual questions. Most frequent among them: "Mr. Jellinek, what do you do when you are not on the air?" Non-professionals really cannot imagine that, when they turn on their radio and hear instant response (be it music, news, weather forecast, or commercials), there are many people behind the scenes to make that instant response possible. Another unusual comment I recall hearing from a fellow Hastings resident: "Your programs are on tape, that must make it easier for you." Well, yes, if you discount many hours of research

Honorary doctorate at Long Island University, with George Calfo, Warren Bodow, and Karen Nelson, June 1, 1984.

and planning, about two hours of actual recording and editing, the rest — listening to the finished product while reclining comfortably at home — is easy indeed.

As previously agreed with management (I never had a written contract in all my years at WQXR), I continued programming and writing scripts for our Sunday night *Delta Opera House*, but eventually Delta Airlines withdrew its sponsorship. WQXR's management and sales department shared the view, gradually spreading among the nation's classical broadcasters, that vocal music was not very popular with the majority of listeners. Therefore, despite protestations by our own listenership, our full-length opera broadcasts on Sunday evening came to a halt. As an "emeritus presence" with an extremely limited influence in programming matters, I expressed my views and, getting nowhere with them, I resigned myself to the station's way of doing things.

Sideline activities I had plenty. With my regular appearances on the Metropolitan Opera's *Texaco Opera Quiz* and other Saturday afternoon intermission contributions, my voice continued to be heard nationwide. I lectured in many venues, including the New York City Opera, radio station WHYY in Philadelphia, on behalf of the Richard Tucker Music Foundation in Baltimore, and at the Art Song Festival at the University of Central Arkansas, where I honored the centenary of John McCormack. Syracuse University (Warren Bodow's alma mater) invited me for a pleasant session with its Opera Club, and John Ettelson of WQXR's Sales Department organized an informal round table at the Lotos Club in New York, where John introduced me as "the only man he knows who owns a Spanish-Hungarian dictionary." I began a longtime association with the New York Singing Teachers' Association, a very congenial and worthwhile group that was kind enough to honor me with an award on two occasions within a decade. I moderated a celebratory event honoring Arturo Toscanini at the Met, hosted a panel at the American Scandinavian Foundation in which mezzo-soprano Sylvia Lindenstrand and baritone Jorma Hynninen were the performing artists, and joined the newly formed scholarly magazine, *The Opera Quarterly* as contributing editor, a prestigious connection though devoid of remuneration. My longtime series with New York University, however, had to come to an end to allow me to pursue other "retirement" possibilities.

In the meantime, *The Vocal Scene* continued in its established pattern. I began sharing my enthusiasm for Spanish music and the zarzuela legacy with my audiences. With such artists as Victoria de Los Angeles, Teresa Berganza, Pilar Lorengar, Alfredo Kraus, and José Carreras assisting my cause, the response was quite enthusiastic, and certainly not limited to the sizable Hispanic listening audience. (Hedy was forever puzzled by this special fascination of mine. How could I, a confirmed non-dancer and luke-warm balletomane, respond to Iberian rhythms with such enthusiasm? Well, those two years in Cuba must have been partly responsible.)

Back in 1983, I had a lunch date with my friend Tony Caronia, head of Angel Records' New York office. The day before our date, Tony informed me that he had invited a friend to join us for lunch. The friend turned out to be Alfredo Kraus. We had a delightful time at an Italian restaurant opposite Carnegie Hall, and our entertaining conversation resulted in my inviting the courtly and cultivated tenor for a broadcast interview. With his fluent English, we covered many subjects. His self-confidence arose from his full knowledge of what he vocally could and could not do, and he credited his artistic longevity to that sound appraisal of his gifts. He surprised me by admitting that he was not a Mozart enthusiast because Mozart "didn't do much for the tenor voice." When I reminded him of his outstanding Ferrando in Angel's *Così fan tutte* recording, Kraus seemed unmoved, and I decided not to bring up "Il mio tesoro." A gentleman of the old-fashioned breed throughout, he left me smiling outwardly and inwardly as he departed. I remembered all those effortlessly produced high notes on stage, his graceful bearing and unvaried good taste and discipline. Kraus inspired my admiration to the end of his days, though at times I did feel that his singing lacked a certain amount of visceral excitement.

Several delightful divas of the past deserve to be recalled as lively guests and warm friends. I had been introduced to Bidú Sayão by Terry McEwen, longtime director of London Records and, later, general manager of the San Francisco Opera. We shared many Saturday afternoons as fellow panelists on the *Texaco Opera Quiz*. Terry worshipped Bidú; an idol of his early youth, and it was indeed easy to adore the lady with her chirpy voice and outspoken manner. She lived at the Hotel Ansonia and, later, at the Salisbury on 57th Street. Recalling memories of her early American years at the Met and San Francisco, she grew quite emotional remembering tenor partners like Björling and Schipa, and our listeners were treated to splendid souvenirs of those partnerships. When she learned that Hedy had singing aspirations in high school, she graciously twittered: "You shouldn't have given up singing. I, too, had a small voice, but it developed under my good teacher (Elena) Teodorini. You should have persisted." As she must have, because great ambition and tenacity lay beneath Bidú's gentle ways. Eventually, she settled permanently in her Maine home, which she and her late husband and coach, Giuseppe Danise, had purchased decades before. In 1992, I paid tribute to her on her 90th birthday. We exchanged holiday cards and phone messages until her voice was permanently stilled soon thereafter, but I don't think she ever admitted her true age.

Risë Stevens was eleven years younger than Bidú, and I had the pleasure of celebrating her 70th, 80th, and 90th birthdays on the air, not only on *The Vocal Scene* but also during the relevant Saturday afternoon broadcasts of the Metropolitan Opera, where she was long honored as a member of the board and active advisor for the Young Artists Development Program. At one of those events, before a live audience at the Kaplan Penthouse at Lincoln Center, she still exuded the glamorous aura that my generation associated with her Hollywood years in the 1940s, when she starred with such bygone luminaries as Nelson Eddy and Bing Crosby.

Jarmila Novotná shared so many important roles with Risë Stevens at the Met (Cherubino, Octavian, Orlovsky, Orfeo) that I never felt inquisitive or indiscreet enough to delve into their personal relationship, if any. The friendship I cultivated with these wise and elegant ladies was more important to me than searching for background gossip. In the post World War II years, Jarmila made Vienna her home with her husband, Baron George Daubek. When the Baron died, Jarmila settled in the United States, on the Upper East Side of Manhattan, to be near her daughter, Jarmila Packard, her son George, and her grandchildren. She became a U. S. citi-

With Licia Albanese and Jarmila Novotná at Bagby Christmas party, ca. 1990 (Bill Mark).

zen and I believe she at least partially forgave the Czech state for having confiscated much of the Daubek properties during the Communist regime — something her daughter could never do. One of Jarmila's many endearing traits was that she was singing *sotto voce* or humming all the time. She did so when I interviewed her on *The Vocal Scene*, and on an amusing photograph taken at one of the Bagby Foundation's Christmas parties. There I am sitting between the bemused Licia Albanese and the exuberant-looking Jarmila Novotná— caught singing, of course — while I seem to be having the time of my life.

❖ ❖ ❖

Ever since my early childhood, I have felt a great fondness for Finland. Finns and Hungarians share a common Asiatic origin, and many centuries ago probably spoke different dialects of the same language. The great migrations transformed both languages, but traces of their common origin still remain, and history has bound the two nations, separated by thousands of miles, into a strong cultural alliance. In the 1980s, a gentleman named Tatu Tuohikorpi, then Finland's cultural attaché in New York, informed me of his mission to promote the works of Finnish composers throughout the United States. As far as the American public was concerned, Finland meant

Sibelius, but as a result of Tatu Tuohikorpi's efforts, eagerly embraced by me, WQXR opened the way to the songs of Kilpinen, and orchestral works of Klami, Madetoja, Merikanto, and Kokkonen, not to say previously obscure and unrecorded works by Sibelius, who indeed had cast a giant shadow over the Finnish musical landscape during his long life (1865–1957).

It was through Tatu Tuohikorpi that I met Martti Talvela, the great Finnish basso, who had made his Met debut in 1968 as the Grand Inquisitor in *Don Carlo*. He was a giant of a man, six feet and seven inches tall, imposingly built and sporting an Old Testamental beard, the shape of which he would adjust to the requirements of his many substantial operatic roles. He needed minimal physical enhancement to become the giant Fasolt, the priestly Sarastro, the philosophical Prince Gremin, the scary Sparafucile, the wicked Osmin, the kindly Padre Guardiano and his more savage-looking but equally spiritual Russian counterpart, the martyred Dosifei. Equally appropriate was Martti's prophetic appearance in the role of Paavo Ruotsalainen, the 19th century country preacher in the Finnish opera *The Last Temptations*, written by Joonas Kokkonen especially for him in 1973. But his most talked-about portrayal in the 1980s was the title role of *Boris Godunov*, whose precipitous dying fall from the throne in the new Met production caused much comment at the time. On my 1984 broadcast I inquired about the physicality involved within the dramatic context, and Martti calmly explained that "only the first step had to be planned and calculated, the law of gravity would take care of the rest." (And suitable bodily stuffing, I suppose.)

Hedy and I became great friends of the Talvelas and the Tuohikorpis. Tatu and Nenne Tuohikorpi then resided in New Rochelle, and we saw them often. Both they and the Talvelas sang the praises of the annual music festival at Savonlinna in southern Finland, which under the artistic leadership of Martti (1973–1979) was brought to international prominence. Tatu arranged an official invitation for us to visit Savonlinna in the summer of 1985, an experience that turned my distant youthful Finnish fantasies into enchanting reality.

We fell in love with Helsinki at first sight — a modern and immaculate city, boasting of a daringly imaginative architecture by such masters as Saarinen and Aalto and their disciples. The Tuohikorpis introduced us to Finland's two most distinguished composers, Joonas Kokkonen and Aulis Sallinen. We called on Mr. Kokkonen at his home, a building designed by Alvar Aalto, for a mid-day cocktail, and enjoyed a delightful dinner with Mr. Sallinen at a scenic restaurant on a tiny island in Helsinki bay, carved out of an ancient building with characteristic Finnish ingenuity. We paid our respects to Ainola, Sibelius's onetime residence and now a museum about 25 miles from Helsinki.

Then we met Martti and Annukka Talvela at Savonlinna, a 45-minute plane ride from Helsinki. The town is surrounded by winding lakes dotted with countless little islands, a 17th century settlement, but now a modern-looking town of some 30,000 inhabitants. The Talvelas lived on a huge sheep farm in nearby Inkila, but they drove to Savonlinna to have lunch with us at a lakeside café. He told us that, while the Finnish government always regarded the patronage of arts a high priority, elevating the Savonlinna Festival to an international level required the kind of unprecedented largess that kept him, as the longtime artistic director, in constant financial battles with government bureaucrats. There were lighter moments, though. He recalled casting an opera requiring both American and Russian singers during the "Cold War" period. As the performance drew near, the Russian government decided not to allow its nationals to participate. Martti decided on a political move of an unconventional nature by inviting the Russian ambassador to his home for a dinner with the traditional toasts followed by the equally traditional Finnish sauna. As Martti further elaborated: "I cannot think of a more mollifying method than have two adversaries naked and slightly besotted, playfully smacking each other with the birch twig that goes with the tradition of the Finnish sauna." The party ended in a jolly spirit, the ambassador made the right political moves at the Kremlin, and the opera took place with the originally planned cast. Nonetheless, while remaining an honored Savonlinna participant — by now an artist in great international demand — Martti turned the administrative reins over to pianist and conductor Ralf Gothóni, another leading light of contemporary Finnish culture.

The operas at the festival are staged at the Olavinlinna Castle, an imposing 15th century structure preserved in excellent state. The 2,200-seat auditorium built within the castle walls is nearly always full because the entire six-week season is usually sold out far in advance. The castle is a short walk from the center of town; the audience enters through a narrow bridge — Olavinlinna stands on its own island — and makes its way over ancient cobblestones. Entering the castle is fun, but emerging from it after the performance near midnight into the long-lasting Scandinavian daylight is unforgettable. The stage is limited in depth but wide enough to accommodate scene changes remarkably well, and the openings in various shapes and sizes built into the ancient walls pose a real challenge for resourceful scenic designers and stage directors.

In our initial Savonlinna season — several visits were to follow in the years ahead — we attended an ingenious production of *Der fliegende Holländer,* a Finnish-language *Zauberflöte,* and Aulis Sallinen's brand new work, *The King Goes Forth to France,* a historical opera of sorts set to a bizarre

Hedy and I with Martti and Annukka Talvela in Savonlinna, 1985.

libretto by the modernist playwright Paavo Haavikko. Sallinen's music, however, supports the play's pessimistic and capricious moods with extraordinary skill. He knows how to write effectively for voices and create music that is varied, brilliantly scored, and never fails to hold one's attention. Sallinen was present, of course, and we were delighted to express our enthusiasm to him. In the title role, the baritone Jorma Hynninen, by then internationally famous, performed with athletic vigor and a magnetic stage presence. We became friendly later on, and I interviewed him both for *Opera News* and *The Vocal Scene* on my next Savonlinna visit a few years later. An inward person and a man of few words, Hynninen's transformation into a dynamic stage personality was astounding, as the Met audiences could also witness in such varied roles as Verdi's Posa, Mozart's Almaviva, and Wagner's Wolfram.

A young Russian baritone named Vladimir Chernov was Talvela's protégé at that time, and we attended his song recital at Savonlinna together with Martti and Annukka Talvela. That same evening we were all invited to the Talvelas for dinner, followed by what Martti called "a little *Hausmusik*." Chernov's accompanist was a member of the party, so Martti suggested that he and Chernov treat us all to the entire Filippo-Rodrigo duet from *Don Carlo*. They both sang magnificently, and hearing such an extended scene from my favorite opera really crowned my Savonlinna sojourn. A few years later, Vladimir Chernov would make his American debut with Eve Queler's Opera Orchestra of New York, and was to spend a few successful seasons at the Met in various roles, culminating (somewhat prematurely, I thought) in the title role of *Simone Boccanegra*.

Back in Helsinki, we had a choice of taking an overnight cruise to either Leningrad or Stockholm. Our relations with the Soviet regime were still strained in 1985, so we chose Stockholm and never regretted it. And so, this "old salt" broke the pledge he had held on for 39 years, and braved the waves to the extent of a surprisingly calm Baltic Sea voyage on the Silja Line. Small islands reassuringly calmed my nerves — the "shore" never seemed far away — and we were rewarded with a sunny autumn day in Stockholm, sightseeing and a night of ballet before returning to Helsinki a day later, and then flying home.

Personal matters overshadowed professional obligations in the immediate future. My presence at WQXR was no longer required on a daily basis and, while the casual observer may not have noticed any change from my "workaholic" pattern, I knew the difference. In 1985 Nancy, husband Gil, and 10-year-old Amy moved to Marin County, north of San Francisco, where Gil continued his successful practice and Nancy could maintain her editorial work via computer from home, with occasional trips to ghost-write articles for famous doctors and to report on medical conferences, including one in Florence and another in Yokohama. The San Francisco area held wonderful memories for Hedy and me from our army period, but giving up the family closeness represented a major change for us, as did the three-hour difference in telephone communication. We planned our life around at least bi-annual family visits, and also re-established contacts with old friends and colleagues Byron Belt and Joseph Valicenti. Byron, a music critic for the national Newhouse newspaper chain and frequent *First Hearing* panelist, had often singled out my broadcast work for eloquent praise. Similar much appreciated compliments were also rendered to me by music critics of Washington, D.C., Newark, Pittsburgh, and by other musical commentators, always excepting *The New York Times*. Being WQXR's corporate owner, *The Times* rigidly adhered to its policy of non-partisan neutrality, an attitude, not being a citizen of Utopia, rarely merited my approval.

At the station, I continued with *The Vocal Scene* and *First Hearing*, as well as with various other projects, but the venerable *Saturday Review* ceased circulation, and Irving Kolodin's editorship and my longtime contributions vanished as well. Irving joined the faculty of the Juilliard School but, already in failing health, he died in 1988 at age 80. He was honored at a well-attended memorial tribute at Riverside Church, with Harold C. Schonberg, chief music critic of *The New York Times*, delivering the eulogy. I would have been honored to remember him because, aside from his innate grouchiness, he had always been supportive of my career, but Harold was also his friend and he knew Irving even longer than I did.

On April 7, 1986, Hedy and I embarked on a 16-day musical tour centering on Vienna, Budapest, and Prague. Several personal friends joined the usual assemblage of music lovers, and we had a great time visiting Schönbrunn, the Staatsoper (*Der fliegende Holländer*), and a brief but always enjoyable encounter with the ever-active Einzi Stolz. A side trip by bus to Eisenstadt was also part of the trip; we paid a silent homage to Haydn's tomb, and were treated to a brief chamber concert at the Esterházy Castle. Our journey then continued to Budapest by way of the *other* Esterházy Castle at Fertöd, on the Hungarian side. We found it in a deplorably neglected state due to the unfortunate conditions then prevailing in the country. Aside from the customary cordial times with members on both sides of the family, and an evening at the Erkel Theater viewing an unspectacular *Carmen*, our visit in Budapest was relatively short. We regretfully bypassed an excursion to the still very rural city of Kecskemét (Kodály's birthplace) in order not to offend our disappointed cousins even deeper. I had spent two teenage summers with my unforgettable cousin Pali in Kecskemét in Hungary's Great Plains, the center of the country's apricot market, in the old days. Now my traveling companions were enchanted with the virtuosic horsemanship (Rodeo *all'ongarese*) the local cowboys displayed for their benefit.

There was some business to be done in Budapest before our departure. The Hungarian State Opera was closed for major renovations, but I did find the time to interview its general director, András Mihály, for a piece that was to appear soon thereafter in *Opera News*. Part of the opening paragraph of my article, called "Centennial in Budapest," went like this: "I have a tendency to judge a city by the prominence it accords its opera house. Vienna and Paris gained my early admiration for the dominant location of their lyric theaters, while disapproval is an understatement of my feelings when I first laid eyes on London's Covent Garden and New York's old Met. This admittedly lopsided view was conditioned by Budapest, the city of my birth, where the opera house occupies a full block on a beautiful tree-lined boulevard, in the very heart of the capital — where, in my judgment, an opera house rightfully belongs."

Professional duties done, my group and I took to our bus heading, optimistically, for Prague. Unexpectedly, we were detained at the border of what still was Czechoslovakia for an extremely long examination and interrogation obviously mandated by communist paranoia. Eventually the border guides, disappointed in not having found a single spy or double agent in our ranks, allowed us to continue. Bratislava, our first stop, was once an historical Hungarian city with a multilingual (Austrian/Hungarian/Slovak) culture. I would have welcomed a longer city tour there because what we were able to see disclosed little of real interest, except the discovery that Bratislava's opera house was a duplicate of the one in Zurich. Bratislava is an important Danubian port between Vienna and Budapest, but the river area seemed insignificant. Besides, due to the extraordinary length of time wasted on the Soviet-style welcome to tourists at the border, our tour organizers were compelled to move on to reach Prague before darkness.

The Prague of 1986 was far from the lively and cosmopolitan city it was to become a few years later. But, like all cities intersected by a river, in this case the Vltava (Moldau), which appropriately flowed by the bust of Smetana, Prague had a special beauty of its own. Because it was a complex of several ancient settlements, this first-time visitor had a difficult time determining which of the city's several centers was the real "downtown." We visited the historical Hradcny Castle, remembered in history for various defenestrations, and the art museum where female guards who looked like Russian discus throwers cast menacing glances at anyone daring to approach certain paintings from a closer than desirable distance. The famous churches of Prague were justly admired, as were the ancient synagogue and the adjacent much-photographed Jewish cemetery. One of the fine restaurants featured a gypsy band, but my attempts to address the excellent *primás* in Hungarian brought no success — Czech was the only language he knew. No one spoke English, or dared to. In our reasonably comfortable hotel, only Czech-language newspapers were allowed, even journals from neighboring (still communist-ruled) Hungary were taboo. Our rooms had television, but the language was always Czech and, while I love the sport, there was a limit to the number of ice hockey games I could tolerate.

Fortunately, we had a good-natured English-speaking tour guide named Miloš, a source of much planned and unplanned entertainment. During the Hungarian part of our journey, some of my fellow passengers had asked politically indelicate questions from our local tour guides so, before arriving to Prague, I seized the microphone and asked our friends to refrain from questions of a political nature to save our guides from embarrassment or worse. Imagine our surprise when the jovial Miloš greeted us in this manner. "My name is Miloš; I am a tennis pro and an experienced sportscaster. Unfortunately, the current government deprived me of my original profession, so here I am, but I do speak English, and am happy to welcome you to Prague."

Prague has two ornate opera houses, and we were treated to both of them. On our first evening, we went to see the opera *Karlštejn* by Vitežslav Novák at the National Theater (Narodny Divadlo). I had been familiar with certain orchestral and choral works by Novák (1870–1949), an eminent Dvořák pupil, but this opera *Karlštejn* unknown to me. During our brief bus ride to the theater, I asked Miloš to tell us briefly what *Karlštejn* was about. He correctly identified the venerated emperor Charles IV as an important character in the action, but the rest of his narrative was absolute balderdash, as we quickly found out on locating a multi-lingual synopsis inside the house. *Karlštejn*, based on an historical anecdote but done in a contemporary setting, turned out to be bright, charming, and sophisticated. We enjoyed Smetana's *The Bartered Bride* and Janáček's *Kat'a Kabanová* on successive evenings, and our diverting 16-day tour ended with a spirited farewell dinner with wine and cognac consumed in generous quantities, as several all-too-realistic photos taken by various fellow travelers eventually attested.

Back home, I quickly adjusted to my "emeritus presence" status as a rarely consulted "consultant." My colleagues — among whom I never found an antagonist in all my many years — continued to regard me with affection and perhaps with growing respect due to my advancing age. Two dear friends visited me on *The Vocal Scene*: tenor Robert White, always a jovial companion, a master punster, and a life of all parties, and baritone Robert Merrill, no longer active at the Met, but full of wonderful backstage stories and entertaining reminiscences of his youthful days with the NBC and, of course, of his significant Toscanini association. I met Bob Merrill and his lovely wife Marion many times in the years that followed; the warmth with which they both recalled their devoted friend Jussi Björling moved me deeply.

In 1961, the American Hungarian Foundation created the George Washington Award, inspired by a statue of Washington erected in the City Park of Budapest in 1906, a gift of Hungarian immigrants living in America. That award annually "honors persons whose eminent contributions are in the broad field of human knowledge, the arts, commerce, industry, and sciences." For the most part, Americans of Hungarian birth have been the recipients of the award, and scientists like Dr. John von Neumann and Dr. Edward Teller were among the first Washington laureates. In the field of music, Fritz Reiner, Antal Doráti, János Starker, Joseph Szigeti, Tibor Serly, and János Scholz had been so honored, and I was deeply touched when the foundation chose me for the award in 1986.

The event took place on December 4, 1986, at the Waldorf Astoria, the same place and in similar surroundings to the black-tie affair at which I had acted as master of ceremonies honoring Yehudi Menuhin six years earlier. My friend, the renowned restaurateur and author George Láng, was my fellow laureate. His longtime friend (and mine), János Starker, delivered the appropriate tribute, while Warren G. Bodow, president and general manager of WQXR, did the honors for me, with good humor, warmth, and eloquence.

Several dear friends shared that celebratory event with me, an occasion that inescapably resonated with a mixture of feelings within me. It brought back the bitterness surrounding the abrupt closure of my Hungarian past, mingling with a certain amount of pride in my own accomplishment in creating my new American identity. No one would have deserved to share that special event with me more than my adored sister Éva, who was on her death bed at the time, with only three more months to live.

She and her husband Tibor lived at 35 Park Avenue and, in more settled times, the two of us had lunch every week at a coffee shop on Madison Avenue, equidistant between her home and The New York Times Building on 43rd Street. During her hospitalization, Hedy and I visited Éva frequently but, as her condition steadily worsened, she wished to return to her apartment where she received all imaginable care. Éva knew that her days were numbered; her thoughts frequently turned toward her childhood and our lost parents, deriving a measure of consolation in that terminal period. Tibor, in his 80s and totally unprepared to lose a wife more than 20 years younger, provided all the love he could, but my sister had to ask *me* to make an arrangement to have her transferred to a hospice. Her oncologist had prepared me that in the final hours terminal patients are gradually distanced from their normal surroundings and frequently abstain from talking. And so it happened. On March 14, 1987, a day or so before the hospice people were scheduled to call, my sister quietly passed away in her 63rd year, taking with her all the personal links to my early life.

We spent more than 30 years together in mutual affection and spiritual closeness. At her funeral, broadcast professionalism was overcome by my emotions, and I could not complete these final lines of my eulogy: "Éva made it easy for me to be a good brother. It was my singular good fortune to be a recipient of an outpouring of a virtually uncritical sisterly devotion all my life."

Éva's loss sent me to my typewriter. Memories of my early life gushed forth into what had been intended as a family document for Nancy and Amy. But its dedicatees persuaded me to submit the resulting text, "The Gold Watch," to the editor of the *About Men* series in the Sunday edition of *The New York Times.* There it appeared on June 28, 1987, bringing me a substantial and heart-warming nationwide response.

25. Years of Travel

As our granddaughter Amy was approaching her 12th birthday, she asked us to take her to Europe and visit our childhood sites, just as we had done with her mother in 1959, when Nancy was also about to turn 12. Learning about one's roots was a frequent topic in schools in those days, and we were flattered that she chose us and not her parents to be her travel companions. It was a propitious time for us, too. Hedy had retired from her federal job as economist for the Bureau of Labor Statistics, and my broadcast and free-lance schedule was flexible enough to allow us to spend some extra time. Besides, after my sister's death, I was ready for such a vitalizing change in our lives. I had mixed feelings about Hedy's retirement. She had too much talent to leave unexplored and, by nature, she was too much involved in family matters (husband, daughter, granddaughter) to seek other side activities. But we all benefited from her devotion and at times exaggerated concerns, and accepted her decision. As I was already seriously planning to write another book, I knew that Hedy would be enormously helpful in that endeavor. So, off we went to revisit Switzerland (where Hedy's family had spent several summers in her childhood), Vienna, and Budapest in that order.

It was very interesting to observe the reactions of Nancy and Amy as they explored the identical sights at the same age many years apart. Amy was much more forward and uninhibited than Nancy had been at age 12. She was also more interested in people than visiting museums and enjoying nature for its own sake. Switzerland gave us a good example. Train rides in Switzerland, with their endless vistas of lakes, rivers, mountain peaks, and forests, now concealed now emerging from tunnels, revealing ever fresh and bucolic Alpine scenery — a joyful and nearly spiritual experience — left Amy surprisingly uninvolved. Hedy's childhood favorite place, the mountain resort of Weggis on Lake Lucerne, registered only a mild impression, but she immensely enjoyed the strutting giant peacocks, the prime attractions in the mini-zoo of the town of Zug, the area of the William Tell legend, where our old friend Elisabeth resided. Elisabeth was then president of a cheese factory, and she took us to a plant were the migrant Turkish workers labored on giant mounds of Ementhaler cheeses, all shaped like a bass drum. Amy enjoyed the whole setup as much as her mother once did; we, her grandparents, never ceased to find the experience instructive and amusing at the same time.

Hedy's only surviving cousin on her father's side, Sylvia, widowed and residing in Lugano at the time, rejoiced in meeting Amy, whom she had not seen since her babyhood, and so did my childhood friend Miklós Róna and his wife. They were childless and Miklós, 63 at the time but something of a child at heart, surrounded Amy with the same rapturous attention with which he had greeted Nancy back in Hungary in 1965. The Rónas took us on a beautiful trip to the Black Forest where the Danube, still a tiny rivulet, originates — a new experience for the three of us, but then Switzerland is full of such fascinating sites.

The historic Baroque architecture of Vienna didn't produce much excitement in Amy, but the Prater did, especially the Riesenrad, the gently revolving giant wheel, pausing periodically in its rotation to reveal unique overviews of the city. Nothing, however, excited her more than the ride on the city's famous "Fiakers" (horse-drawn stage coaches). We scheduled no musical entertainments for Amy — opera wasn't her thing. But she did visit the house and the surroundings where her "grandma" had spent her childhood.

We took the hydrofoil from Vienna to Budapest. It is the most enjoyable way to go (in a pleasant season) down the Danube, passing by Bratislava, Komárom (Franz Lehár's birthplace), the ancient castle of Visegrad, at which point the river bends south, past the commanding Basilica of Esztergom, offering the visitors a sight of uncommon beauty as Hungary's capital appears on the horizon. This was essentially a family visit, and we were joined there by Charlie Turi, his wife Ava, and their physician son George with his wife Susan. Charlie, who had played a very important part in my life in Cuba and the war years, had dropped out of my chronicle in the past several pages. We were pursuing different paths and, with our growing children occupying the center of our lives, we had been seeing each other less frequently than we did in our younger years. But the family link remained very strong. Charlie had become a very successful manufacturer of gold jewelry in the intervening years. Always devoted to family ties, he treated us all to a sumptuous dinner at Budapest's famous Hotel Gellért, with three generations of the Turi relations participating. Amy finally had two distant cousins, roughly her own age, to communicate and giggle with through the language barrier.

I had long hoped to show Amy the sights of my own childhood, my grandfather's house, our erstwhile family residence, quite shabby now, where I had spent my early years, and my gymnasium, whose sturdy brick walls had bravely survived the war and showed little decline in the postwar years. I attended the 50-year reunion of my class, with our old mathematics teacher still surviving. While I immediately recognized all my classmates, they all appeared older than myself or my friend Joe Marton, who had come from Silver Springs, Md., to attend the ceremonial dinner. Only 12 of us from our graduating class of 32 were present, with 4 expatriates in far-flung corners (the United States, Brazil, Israel, and Germany) greeting us from afar. There was a subdued roll call as we discussed the reasons why our number had decreased, and what we did know about the fate of the absentees. Some had fallen in the war, or become Holocaust victims, others — like Joe Marton and I — had chosen emigration. Illness had claimed quite a few. Twelve aging 68-year-olds sat around a big table, eating, drinking, and reminiscing. The event left me with sadness and bitter memories.

Even sadder was a visit to my family's erstwhile villa on Lake Balaton. With my cousin Imre and my sister dying a few days and a continent apart, I was now the sole owner of the property, but that knowledge filled me with nothing but painful memories. That was the last visit I paid to the site of my teen-age summers. Soon thereafter, I began the cumbersome process of selling it to a local resident.

In search of a more cheerful episode, we attended an open-air performance of Kálmán's *The Violet of Montmartre,* a rarely performed 1930 operetta, even in Hungary. Its central tune is the lush tango "Heut' Nacht hab ich von ihr geträumt." Recordings by Jussi Björling and Nicolai Gedda have long enchanted those in the know, but the practical Viennese made certain of the tune's immortality by inserting the tango into the Volksoper's current production of Kálmán's *Die Csárdásfürstin.* How it fits the story line is unclear in my mind, even though I saw that particular production at the Volksoper, but story lines in Viennese operettas are a secondary matter. In any case, on that memorable occasion, Amy found the Hungarian-language performance, with my *sotto voce* instant translation, entertaining.

Foreign languages no longer mattered to Amy as we flew to England for a brief visit with the Pordes family in Windsor. They embraced Amy just as they had done with Nancy several years before, toured Windsor Castle with us, and gave us a quick tour of London. Around Buckingham Palace, the automobile traffic, aggravated by countless tour buses, forced us to halt a few hundred yards from the palace gate. Our hosts stayed in the car while

Hedy, Amy, and I made our way through the throngs and ran into the loving embrace of Nimet Habachy, my WQXR colleague, a fellow accidental tourist. Our brief English visit was crowned by an excursion to Stratford-on-Avon, where we were all treated to an excellent performance of Shakespeare's *Twelfth Night*. Although Amy would become quite a traveler in her later years, I am sure that this well-planned and diversified European journey left many lasting imprints on her mind.

Returning to station WQXR, I found important and, in its wider ramifications, ominous changes. Classical radio stations throughout the nation were beginning to disappear. Nationally syndicated programs, like *First Hearing* and my *Vocal Scene*, were losing affiliated outlets, as long established classical stations changed their format to either country music or rock. Classical music had always attracted minority audiences in most markets, but in recent years, the classical vs. pop ratio had changed for the worse to a worrisome degree. We were obviously losing the young audiences, and station managers were desperately trying to regain them. Many classical stations fell in line with the false prophets within the industry who advocated compromising standards by reducing or eliminating vocal music, depriving symphonies of their slow movements, and other similarly misconceived changes. These "innovations" antagonized the faithful without making any impression on a generation that had grown up without any appreciation of music in their schools. This was a youth whose *parents* already preferred Elvis Presley and the Rolling Stones to either Schubert or Sinatra. The changes in taste reflected a gradually widening divide between generations.

WQXR, under the benevolent umbrella of *The New York Times*, did not fully buy into a full endorsement of the "dumbing down" phenomena, but did not remain unaffected by classical radio's new idealogues, either. General Manager Warren Bodow sought to surround himself with a younger group of top administrators. Bob Sherman, our longtime program director, became "executive producer" and lost his well-established and very important two-hour program, *The Listening Room*. Also dropped from the station's schedule was *Adventures in Good Music with Karl Haas*, another longtime feature and strong audience favorite. My successor, Robert Bragalini, was eased into early retirement, to be replaced as music director by Margaret Mercer, formerly with radio station WNCN, our foremost competitor. Bragalini had been my associate music director for more than a decade—an experienced and knowledgeable administrator devoted to his work. Unfortunately, he did not make himself very popular with the staff, and seemed unskilled in the ways of office politics. Even more important, two longtime announcers—George Edwards and Duncan Pirnie, virtual institutions at the station—were fired in a sudden and humiliating manner. Both eventually sued the station for age discrimination, a suit that was settled out of court but at a considerable cost to *The New York Times*.

Even in my privileged status as an "emeritus presence," these developments had me emotionally involved, casting a shadow on the station's thoughtful remembrance of *The Vocal Scene*'s 20th anniversary in 1988. Among other things, I had serious doubts about the future of *First Hearing*, due not only to the national upheaval affecting classical radio, but also to management's continued lack of appreciation. So I relinquished producing the show in favor of Bob Sherman, whose lightened schedule could easily reclaim *First Hearing*, a program he had initially launched in 1968.

But *The Vocal Scene* soldiered bravely into its third decade. With the charming and eternally youthful Marta Eggerth, we honored the legacy of her late husband, the tenor Jan Kiepura, as well as Marta's varied and brilliant *leggiero* artistry on rare recordings. Her remarkable voice and technique has remained nimble and accurate into her nineties. Samuel Ramey, whom I had already befriended in his New York City Opera days, after his spectacular Met debut and increasing international fame, recalled the past decade with the engaging openness and lack of artifice that continued to enrich his personality. I also welcomed Roberta Peters, who was delighted to be confronted with her first RCA Victor LP (*anno* 1957) for which I had written the annotations, and promptly obliged with an affectionate autograph. I also conducted an interview via telephone to Montreal with the great Mozartian tenor Léopold Simoneau. The musical illustrations were outstanding, but the audio sound of our conversation left much to be desired, prompting me to pay tribute to Simoneau's valued artistry with another program emanating from my comfortable and acoustically superior studio several years later.

In early 1988, a travel organization made me an offer I could not refuse, requiring my services as a guide on a "16-day tour of Italy for music lovers." Here is the itinerary: Rome-San Gimignano-Siena-Florence-Bologna-Venice-Verona-Cremona-Milan. The tour turned out to be full of scenic and musical delights, and temporarily drove all my anxieties about classical radio from my mind. In Rome, we had a wonderful get-together with Ruffo and Gabriela Titta and attended Rossini's *Mosé in Egitto* with Ruggero Raimondi in the title role and Rockwell Blake, by then something of a Rossini specialist, as Osiride. Rome's Teatro dell'Opera, an architecturally indifferent building, is situated on the Piazza Beniamino Gigli. In Florence, it was Puccini's *Trittico* with Diana Soviero as Suor Angelica and Elena Suliotis as the forbidding Princess. I had met Diana Soviero years earlier, and she was very happy to welcome us during the intermission in her dressing room. Suliotis, who had a meteor-like career as a soprano, was a dominating stage presence with mezzo tones like Gabriel's trumpet. I no longer remember the *Tabarro* cast, but Rolando Panerai was an outstanding Gianni Schicchi and Italo Tajo virtually stole the show as the conniving and doddering Simone. (An interesting sideline: Rockwell Blake and Diana Soviero had been Richard Tucker Award winners in 1978 and 1979 respectively, with me on the panel of judges on both occasions.)

Lucca had not been advertised in the tour's literature, but we enjoyed a brief tour of the city where Puccini and generations of his musical ancestors were born. We visited one of the Puccini residences and admired Lucca's famous towers, all related to various Renaissance events. I couldn't avoid photographing a street sign referring to the "Piazza dei Malcontenti," letting my imagination conjure up various 14th-century mischiefs. While our tour of Bologna was all too brief, Venice yielded its unforgettable landmarks and newly discovered (by us) buildings related to the 16th-century Ghetto. It all brought Ponchielli's *La gioconda* to my mind. As a matter of fact, a street sign honoring "S. Alvise" prompted me to send duplicate photographs to Paul Plishka and Samuel Ramey to remind them that the villain they have so convincingly portrayed in the opera had been named after a saint.

An opera entirely different from *La gioconda's* ominous atmosphere awaited us at Venice's celebrated Teatro La Fenice. It was Donizetti's delicious two-act farce *Le convenienze ed inconvenienze teatrali* ("Theatrical conventions and mishaps"), a hilarious romp involving backstage intrigues in a provincial opera company. While rehearsing a new opera, the temperamental prima donna behaves miserably not only with her colleagues, but also with the librettist and the composer. In bursts Mamm'Agata, a stage mother from hell who demands a more prominent role for her daughter, the seconda donna. Resisting the temptation to relate the rest of the opera, let me add that the Mamma is sung by a baritone, the hapless tenor driven mad by the intense jealousies around him is a German guest artist who speaks and sings with a German accent, and Donizetti's score is replete with musical parodies of other contemporary operas. Our baritone (Leo Nucci), in a dialogue with the Impresario (the Spanish bass-baritone Carlos Chausson) at one point lapsed into an ad-lib Spanish tirade no doubt unknown to Donizetti, but typical of the opera's relentlessly farcical spirit. Eventually, chaos prevails when several principals choose to abandon the venture, and the curtain falls almost by its own weight on a frantic finale that resolves nothing. Donizetti must have had a lot of fun concocting this crazy tale in 1827. After several 19th-century revisions, the opera was reshaped in 1963 and has received several modern stagings ever since. I don't know how much of its utter silliness impressed my fellow travelers, but I enjoyed the experience hugely.

Cremona followed, my second visit to the city of the great violin makers, and then Milan where the daily *Corriera della Sera* greeted us with the huge bold-face headline LUTTO NAZIONALE (National Mourning). Suspecting something really awful, we learned that Italy's soccer team had been defeated by Denmark. La Scala was still closed for the summer, so the rest of our operaphiles and I had to settle for the Kirov Ballet's visit with *Swan Lake* at the Teatro Lirico, which was not a mean alternative. We did visit the Scala Museum, in addition to other imposing monuments, including the peerless Galleria, the center of Milanese social life. Hedy and I paid our respects to the dignified marble gravesite of Titta Ruffo, the great baritone who had been the prime inspiration of my becoming a record collector in my teens (thus influencing the shaping of my path in life many years later). The Cimitero Monumentale is the final resting place of Toscanini and many of Italy's immortals and, as a matter of fact, on our way to the exit we passed by the gravesite of Arrigo Boito. Milan is a relatively modern city compared to Florence and Venice, and enjoys less respect with certain American tourists given to a kind of artistic snobbery. My plebeian taste found the city's ample boulevards and its mixture of stately antiquity and buzzing modernity endlessly stimulating.

As I resumed my reduced WQXR activities but continued writing and lecturing, I was contacted by Arthur Dembner, a New York publisher and regular *Vocal Scene* listener. He wanted to know if I might be interested in writing a book about my radio experiences — a kind of *Vocal Scene* in book form. I wasn't particularly attracted to the idea, but I did tell Mr. Dembner of my long-held desire to write a book no one had done before, a survey of operas inspired by history. Now it was Mr. Dembner's turn to be baffled, because he didn't find that elusive idea very commercial. We had a few more discussions on the subject, and somehow I managed to sell my plan on *History Through the Opera Glass* to him. We signed a contract but, as luck would have it, a few weeks later Mr. Dembner collapsed and died on his way to his daily health spa. Our contract became history, but I was fortunate enough to get Thomas P. Lewis, owner of Pro-Am Music Publishers, a small White Plains publisher, interested in the project. Tom had been familiar with my work, and he was adventurous enough to take me on. And so, for the next five years, *History Through the Opera Glass* became the center of my musical activity.

In the spring of 1989, another musical trip beckoned, this time a Scandinavian tour built around the Bergen Festival. Helsinki was our first stop, and this time we were given an excellently planned tour of the city, visiting various parks and historical sites, with lots of time for shopping, as well. It was too early for Savonlinna, but we did attend opera in Helsinki's nearly

100-year-old Opera House, to be mercifully replaced by a splendid modern building some years later. The performance that time was *Naamiohuvit*, better known to us as Verdi's *Un ballo in maschera*. Given the subject matter, a dark page from Swedish history culminating in the assassination of King Gustavus III, the work was given in Swedish, a language known to many Finns. But, as I was to reassure our tour participants, we were to get Finnish surtitles, which no doubt brought consolation to those in our group who were unfamiliar with the plot. To make the evening even more memorable, the tenor engaged to sing the part of the King came down with an attack of hoarseness during the second act, and he finished miming the part, with a semi-prepared substitute doing the singing from the orchestra pit. The following morning we departed for Stockholm via the delightful Silja Line, where the circumstances of that unusual *Ballo* were recalled with much amusement.

This old sailor thus returned to the sea for the second time since 1946, but, to mix a metaphor, the Baltic Sea was already familiar terrain for me, and Stockholm's little islands with their canals and bridges, to say nothing of the city's captivating architecture, delighted us all. A small boat took us to the Drottningholm Palace and Theater Museum, a Baroque structure still in use during the summer season, sustaining the memories of the ill-fated King Gustavus who, according to our tour guides, bankrupted the national treasury with his excessive generosity to music and the fine arts.

On a more modest but highly entertaining level, we were treated to an exceptionally spirited performance of Rossini's *The Barber of Seville*, done in Swedish not by the Royal Opera but by the "Folkoperan," an enterprising local ensemble. With minimalist but highly inventive stage settings and sporting a youthful cast — with only the Doctor Bartolo represented (appropriately) by a fiftyish artist — the opera's fleet action rolled on with irresistible charm. Adding castanets to Rossini's orchestration of the joyous final ensemble was a novel and delightful touch. After all, the Swedish language notwithstanding, we were witnessing a play about Spaniards!

There were no musical events for us in Copenhagen, but lots of time to enjoy that lovely city with its mixture of new and old, quaintly painted houses, picturesque canals, and the Tivoli Gardens, a giant amusement park where one of our fellow passengers, an elderly lady and avid photographer, took one shot too many and, detaching herself from the group, managed to get lost, driving our tour guide nearly insane. With the aid of the park guards, she was eventually located and able to rejoin us for a calm overnight cruise to Oslo. Our ship took off on a breezy, sunny afternoon, and I was amazed to witness how speedily the Scandinavian passengers on board undressed ready for sunbathing. For Northerners rarely treated to such luxuries, I suppose, a little sun goes a long way. That overnight cruise, by the way, represented the final sea voyage of my life. In that respect, and in a few others, I have never changed.

I found Oslo a pleasant but not too memorable city with a colorful seaport, ample parks and excellent museums — in and out of doors. The museum devoted to Norway's wartime German occupation was a particularly moving experience for us. A very fine performance of Wagner's *Der fliegende Holländer* awaited us at the local opera house, the foyer of which proudly displayed a bronze bust of Kirsten Flagstad. The true scenic charms of Norway, however, were to be found outside the capital, beginning with the Stalheim Hotel way up in the mountains. Getting there through a canyon by bus is nothing short of frightening, and I admit that frequently I chose to travel with my eyes closed instead of admiring the magnificent scenery. The descent was no less scary, and I was amazed that my camera remained steady enough to perpetuate that ride with a dozen beautiful photographs.

Sightseeing on a less adventurous level awaited us at the village of Flaam in the fjord country where we cruised on a small ferryboat, spellbound by the splendid landscape. From Flaam a scenic railway high on the mountains took us to the city of Bergen, whose seaport preserved the aura of the ancient shipping industry and the Spartan conditions in which those old mariners, like Wagner's Daland, earned their living. Walking leisurely through the city, Hedy had just remarked how physically different Norwegians looked compared to Swedes. As we often do discussing personal matters in foreign lands, we conversed in Hungarian. Sure enough, a beaming visitor soon accosted us in the same language, asking our help to recommend a good Hungarian restaurant. In Bergen, Norway, of all places!

We were then transferred to Grieg country with a visit to his villa at Troldhaugen, now a very attractive mini museum. There are several concert halls in the immediate area, all participating in the Bergen Festival. The informative program booklet on the festival listed a recital with Victoria de Los Angeles for May 25, with Elly Ameling for June 2, and with Isaac Stern for June 3. How much fun would it have been to greet at least one of them in such enchanting surroundings! But our schedule called for a lovely violin and piano concert on May 29 in a newly built modern hall called Troldsalen in a ravine just below Grieg's house. And this bucolic setting was the end of our very enjoyable Scandinavian tour. The following morning we flew back from Bergen to New York, exhausted but happy.

Our happiness lasted until July 22, when we received the tragic news of the death of our dear friend Martti Talvela. We had attended the 20th anniversary of Martti's Met debut at the Finnish Consulate only a few months before that — a very cordial and typically Finnish event with many affectionate toasts in the celebrant's honor. Caught up in the universal spirit of bonhomie, I found myself joining the parade of celebratory toasters, receiving Martti's bear hug as my reward (a unique experience in itself).

That tower of a man had not been in good health, suffering from diabetes and a weakened heart. Death claimed him while he was dancing at his younger daughter's wedding. On November 2, I presented a tribute to his memory (*Vocal Scene* No. 1088), sending a cassette copy to his wife Annukka and the entire Talvela clan. Kirsi Talvela, the older daughter, who is a stage director and was then assistant to August Everding in Munich, sent us a very touching letter in response and, of course, our friendship with the family has continued to the present day.

We treasure many lasting memories of our great friend. Hedy had given a big party in Martti's honor some years before that, with the Tuohikorpis, the two Jarmilas, Mr. and Mrs. Malcolm Graff, Bill and Francoise Sullivan of the Bagby Foundation, and Bob Jacobson of *Opera News* also in attendance. When the Talvelas arrived, they presented us with an intricately handcrafted wooden wall decoration designed by Martti's late father. He located a fitting place for it, and I had the feeling that if I hadn't immediately supplied the needed hammer, Martti would have used his giant arm to do the job. At dinner, he gave us a hilarious Otto Klemperer imitation, recalling the old maestro's addressing him as "Talfela." At another occasion, we had invited Martti and Annukka to dinner at our favorite Czech restaurant, Vasáta on East 75th Street (a favorite of the two Jarmilas, as well). Before dinner, however, we accompanied the Talvelas to the Finnish Consulate, where the president of Finland and Mr. Arthur O. Sulzberger, publisher of *The New York Times*, sealed a big business deal involving newsprint. Martti, being his country's foremost artistic ambassador, was one of the guests of honor; Hedy and I just tagged along. After the usual toasts and ceremonial niceties, Martti whispered to me: "That's enough, George. Let's go to eat." In the elevator going down, I asked Martti about his opinion of Finland's head of state, President Koivisto. After a moment of pensive silence, his answer was, "He is ... harmless." That comment has become a favorite saying in our household ever since, usually describing a play or movie of no unusual distinction, or an inoffensive but not particularly memorable restaurant.

Hedy and I are in regular contact with Annukka Talvela, and the Tuohikorpi family as well. Tatu went on to become Finland's consul general, first in Hamburg then in Vienna. A few years later, he requested his government to return him to New York, where he continued to render valuable service to Finland's cultural life until his retirement.

Before the year was out, WQXR transferred its location from *The New*

York Times building on West 43rd Street to its present home on 122 Fifth Avenue. It was a welcome change because the station now occupies an entire floor, with studio facilities newly designed for us, all "state of the art," as the saying goes. The only thing I miss about the old building is *The New York Times* Library, because the Times Square area I nostalgically like to recall from my soldiering years is too tumultuous for me now, and certainly not made more attractive by its Disneyfied gentrification.

As my 70th birthday was approaching, I remembered a similar occasion we celebrated in the house of our late friends Edward and Barbara Spevack of Huntington, Long Island, a few years earlier. As the party was gathering in their garden and the time came for giving out the birthday presents, Eddie was commandeered to a central chair to receive a "special surprise." That treat materialized in the shape of a belly dancer hired for the occasion. Eddie happened to be an outgoing and jovial person, but I remember his squirming through the entire act. I know that none of my friends would ever think of subjecting me to such a birthday treat. Nevertheless, I proposed to Hedy that we should take advantage of a special Christmas package offered by British Airways, and off we flew to London for a few days of celebratory siesta — and perhaps some theater. And so we rounded out what Franz Liszt had called *Années de pèlerinage,* our "Years of Travel."

26. Writing a Book — Slowly

Sometime around 1990 I received an invitation from Katherine Gertson, administrator of the Adult Education Division of Juilliard School, to join the faculty for a series of classes in opera history similar to those I had presented at N. Y. U. I accepted partly because at age 70 plus I still wanted to prove to myself that I "still had the goods," and partly because of the extremely cordial and flattering nature of Ms. Gertson's invitation. What I failed to consider was the enormous amount of research needed for the writing of my book, *History Through the Opera Glass*. Just as I had hoped, Hedy was tremendously helpful in searching out obscure data, tracking down microfilms, and other minutiae, but the basic historical research for the unique nature of the book had to be done by me. My Juilliard classes were extremely enjoyable because the students were intelligent, responsive, and kept me on my toes with their probing questions. But, after three semesters, I regretfully resigned, suggesting to Ms. Gertson that Cori Ellison, dramaturg of the New York City Opera and my occasional fellow panelist on the *Texaco Opera Quiz*, would be an outstanding choice to take over my classes. The two ladies got together and Cori smoothly succeeded me, adding a new dimension to the Juilliard curriculum. At the same time, I also recommended Mortimer Frank, a close friend of mine, recently retired as professor of English at the City University. Mort Frank was not an opera man, but a music critic of wide knowledge and experience, a longtime panelist on *First Hearing*, and a natural teacher. He, too, was enthusiastically received at Juilliard, and his classes on Haydn, Mozart, and Beethoven are enjoyed by many students to this day. And I eased myself out of my brief activity as an academic headhunter-godfather with a deep contentment.

Our travels continued, this time on a more moderate scale, as we vis-

Three generations, Amy, Nancy, and Hedy (1985).

ited the Santa Fe Opera for the first time. I found the city a curious place, full of art galleries and Indian American jewelry, with Hispanic-styled buildings laterally spread conforming to the local zoning that limits structures to a certain altitude. Environmentally, the idea is appealing, but with public transportation limited and taxis in short supply, those not owning a car face a problem, at least they did in 1990. The Santa Fe Opera, outside the city proper, is, deservedly, an institution of great local pride. Its efficient modern structure takes maximum advantage of the prairie-like scenery, especially in an opera like *Madama Butterfly*, where the backstage becomes wide open, revealing distant city lights that audiences easily accept for Nagasaki harbor. We attended *La Bohème*, *Così fan tutte*, and *Ariadne auf Naxos*, all imaginatively staged and well performed. A New York colleague, the artist agent Matthew Epstein, had previously called my attention to the young Canadian tenor Ben Heppner, the Bacchus in the Strauss opera, who was earmarked for a major career. Epstein was right: Heppner was more than impressive in that killer role, and his career properly reached its summit soon thereafter.

We found the overall poverty of New Mexico's native population and Indian *pueblos* rather depressing. Too many people were living in primitive huts or trailer parks in contrast to the romantic western sites of Taos and the high mountains surrounding the Rio Grande. It was a great pleasure to have Ava and Charles Turi with us on the trip—with all the affectionate bond between our two families, we rarely traveled together since the earlier years when our children were still young. The tour organizers managed to solve the transportation problems to our satisfaction. Our individual bus even drove us to the opera in the morning, designating the site where we would meet after the evening performance. It wasn't the bus driver's fault that one of our ladies, exiting after *Ariadne auf Naxos*, by which time it was dark and at least a dozen tour buses filled the parking lot, nonchalantly entered one of them, and calmly sat down, absorbed in a novel. Never bothering to look up and notice that she was surrounded by complete strangers, she ended up in Albuquerque. Our exasperated tour guide, after alerting the local and state police, spent a sleepless night until our errant passenger was heard from in the wee hours. Still clueless, she had to learn that she might as well add Albuquerque as an unplanned addition to her tour, and take the first bus to Santa Fe in the morning.

The year 1991 marked the Mozart Bicentennial, with institutions large and small celebrating the event. I devoted two *Vocal Scene* programs to the occasion: "Two Centuries of *Don Giovanni*," and "Arias by Mozart—for Operas by Others," both rather unusual ideas successfully brought off. Anxious to do something on a wider scale, I suggested to Warren Bodow a 13-week series devoted to Mozart's last year. Margaret Mercer, WQXR's music director, enthusiastically applauded the idea and, if I recall, sponsorship was obtained from the Austrian Trade Commission. I had a field day chronicling all those treasures of 1791—chamber music, the Clarinet Concerto, small piano and orchestral pieces, the last operas, the "Ave Verum," and the "Requiem"—and presenting them interspersed with quotations from Mozart's letters and relating various events of his final years.

Along with my wonderful colleague, Edward Downes, I was invited to deliver special bicentennial lectures at the Rockport Chamber Music Festival in Massachusetts in June of that year. Edward talked about Mozart and his contemporaries, while I discussed operatic elements in Mozart's instrumental writing. Lila Deis, a singer and voice teacher, was the festival's artistic director, and, thanks to her, Hedy and I spent a wonderful weekend at Rockport. Later that year, I gave a lighthearted presentation called "Mozart's Angry Women" for Friends of Mozart, a small club of New York musical enthusiasts, and another Mozart-related talk at the Vocal Record Collectors Society, where as a longtime honorary member, I always found a hearty welcome.

But before that summer, on May 16 to be exact, another anniversary was observed, honoring Richard Tauber's 100th birthday. My centennial tribute (*Vocal Scene* No. 1168) was devoted to the tenor's legacy of songs, in German and English. On that very day, Francis Heilbut of the American Landmark Festivals, and a Tauber worshiper, organized a lovely centennial tribute at the Castle Clinton National Monument at The Battery in downtown New York. The guests of honor were Marta Eggerth and Jarmila Novotná, both operetta queens in their day. Both ladies had known Richard Tauber and Franz Lehár personally, and Jarmila Novotná had been Tauber's partner in the Vienna world premiere of Lehár's *Giuditta* in 1934. It was a lovely spring day, and Hedy and I have been treasuring photographs linking us with these forever-glamorous singers to this day, all in the shadow of the still towering World Trade Center.

An eternal association links Richard Tauber with the great Lehár song "Dein ist mein ganzes Herz" (Yours is my heart alone), from *The Land of Smiles.* My own heart, however, insisted on beclouding these festive events in late 1991. With recurrent angina attacks and various stress tests that gave less than satisfactory results, my cardiologist, Dr. Daniel Macken, regarded a second cardiac bypass procedure mandatory. But our 50th wedding anniversary was in the offing, and Hedy and I had planned to celebrate it in St. Louis, the "scene of the crime." Dr. Macken, by then a friend, grudgingly agreed for a postponement until after July 1992.

Anna Moffo lent her glamorous presence to *The Vocal Scene* in the spring of 1992, when I also celebrated the 90th birthday of Bidú Sayão, and the centennial of Ezio Pinza, the embodiment of what is meant by a *basso cantante.* Bidú greeted me in a note full of charm and good spirit from her Maine solitude where she was spending her final years. I sent a copy of my Pinza tribute (No. 1216) to his daughter, Claudia Pinza Bozzola, an active voice teacher in Pittsburgh, whom I had met at one of Licia Albanese's parties, and she, too, acknowledged my praise-laden tribute very graciously.

We celebrated our 50th wedding anniversary with a dinner in Manhattan, followed by attending a new production of *Guys and Dolls* at the Martin Beck Theatre. Then we took off for St. Louis, a city far more attractive than the one that had lived in our memories of half a century ago. The Mississippi river bank, a huge disappointment then, was neatly refurbished, glowing in the triumphal shadow of the Golden Arch, the creation of the Finnish architect Eero Saarinen. Our travel agent booked us at the Hyatt Hotel, which was built into the city's old railroad station in a most ingenious manner. We lovingly remembered the station as it stood in momentous outmodedness in 1942. Fifty years later, the rejuvenated building was surrounded by a verdant moat complete with its own aviary and other delights to attract families with children. Needless to say, only the exterior suggested its venerable railway past; inside the hotel was luxuriously up-to-date.

I rented a car to cross the state line to Belleville, Illinois, where we had spent our wedding night in 1942. Belleville was now considerably enlarged, and so was its once very modest hotel. The little jewelry store where I had bought our wedding rings remained within the family of its original owners but, more imposingly housed, it had become a small-scaled Fortunoff in the interim. We drove out to what was once Scott Field, the location of the Air Corps Radio School where I had learned the Morse Code and the operations of military radio equipment, all rendered obsolete by modern technology. Scott Field is now the Scott Air Force Base, and appropriately vast. Once I introduced myself as a former graduate, the military police kindly offered to guide us around the huge base, but we declined. Too much time had passed to look for sites that had become blurry visions of what was once the center of my universe for a brief period of time.

Returning to New York and real life, I entered Columbia-Presbyterian Hospital and met my new heart surgeon, Dr. George Green, Daniel Macken's choice. (Dr. Bowman, who had restored me to life in 1980, had since retired.) Dr. Green, radiating confidence and optimism, assured me that medical science in cardiac surgery had advanced significantly, and I should look forward to full recovery very soon. Interestingly, what was to follow does not emerge in as much detail as I recall my earlier cardiac adventure, primarily because this time I felt convinced that I would survive the surgery, whereas in 1980, inwardly, I gave myself only a 50–50 chance. Also, my initial surgery had happened quite suddenly, leaving my radio programming plans abruptly incomplete. This time, I was able to prepare the sequencing of *The Vocal Scene*, allowing for my personal absence of three weeks, and my limited duties at the station enabled me to pick up my routine with virtually no interruption.

My return was remembered by two very dear colleagues, June LeBell and Nimet Habachy, who organized an intimate 50th wedding anniversary celebration for Hedy and me. In addition to Lloyd and Ann Moss, three couples—our oldest friends from the 1950s—participated in the warm and joyous get-together at Nimet's cozy apartment on East End Avenue. George Calfo—who has been a close friend since my SESAC days, and an excellent photographer—left endearing souvenirs of that spirited evening.

Another close friend, Gabriel Banat, would have been there, had he been in New York at the time. But, as a violinist member of The New York Philharmonic, Gabi, as I called him, spelling his nickname according to the Hungarian usage, was enjoying his annual vacation in Spain. Gabi and his late first wife Rosette had brought property there many years ago, in the distant past when the dollar was still high. Newly remarried to Diana, a fellow violinist, he invited us for a week to share their vacation home in Begur, north of Barcelona, in what is known as the Costa Brava, not far from the French border. The Banats live on a hilltop overlooking the Mediterranean coast, where, viewed from the terrace on a sunny day—virtually every day of our visit—the sky and the sea formed an unbroken unity, constantly reminding me of the "Cielo e mar" aria from Ponchielli's *La gioconda*. Their Spanish-style house is quite modern and capacious on two levels, with a good-size swimming pool to complete the sybaritic joys of their visitors. The surrounding towns—Pals, Palafrugell—have a medieval air, but the shops are all modern and, luckily for us, baffled by the Catalan billboards, everyone spoke Spanish, as well. The two languages are ethnically related but by no means identical. And, antiquity notwithstanding, Begur had also boasted a kind of semi-nude beach, something of a culture shock given my limited (well, nonexistent) exposure to such things, but decisions on attire, or lack of same, were left to individuals. Gabi drove us into Barcelona for a full day, and we enjoyed the city so much that we resolved to return some day.

The Vocal Scene continued on its merry way, and in 1993, I celebrated the program's 25th anniversary on the air with a tribute to record collecting, my only hobby, a preoccupation without which my broadcast career could not have happened. I paid tribute to the 80th birthday of tenor Ferruccio Tagliavini, whose subtle art must have been a revelation to the younger generation, because my program brought such a floodtide of responses that I quickly created a "Part II" to follow the original within weeks. The 80th birthday of Eleanor Steber, alas, received a posthumous tribute from me, but it was enthusiastically greeted by Marcia Sloat, Steber's biographer. Very much alive, however, was Steber's contemporary, the amazing Licia Albanese, my distinguished fellow trustee at the Bagby Foundation. Licia's recorded legacy is so precious that I preferred using as much of her singing as possible in preference to a "talky" interview. Getting ahead of myself, I cannot resist reminding myself and the reader that five years later, when Licia reached her 85th birthday, I paid a loving tribute to her on the air, along with Risë Stevens, and Marta Eggerth. All three ladies share 1913 as the year when Providence, in a smiling mood, graced our unsuspecting world with their presence.

Paul Plishka, the Met's distinguished basso, also became a Bagby trustee that year, and when he came to the station for an anniversary treat (his 25th at the Met), we spent a considerable amount of time on the air discussing his low-register confrères. He told me that colleagues like Nicolai Ghiaurov and Samuel Ramey were his personal friends and that the kind of rivalry that certain tenors, or their press agents, were cultivating was unknown among bassos. (Actually, Paul Plishka and Sam Ramey were coached by the same teacher at that time.) Regina Resnik also reminisced with me about her wide-ranging career. Our paths would cross later on various panels, including judging for the Richard Tucker Foundation. An artist of great wisdom and experience, she is the kind of guest who makes interviewing intellectually challenging and richly informative at the same time. Thanks to my friend Bill Sullivan, who had introduced us, Hermann Prey visited me for an hour partly spent in discussing his decades of Salzburg memories. He grew quite sentimental recalling a *Così fan tutte* under Karl Böhm, one of those moments the Germans call "Sternstunde" when *everything,* the ensemble, the staging, the weather, was just perfect. As usual, I came well prepared for the program, armed with an early LP of his on the London label, singing songs by Schubert, Brahms, and Strauss. Hermann seemed unimpressed and reminded me of his more current CD, offering similar repertoire, recorded in Japan. WQXR's library had a copy, and Hermann wanted me to play part of it. Two decades separated the two recordings, and he was in fresher and far better voice on the earlier, out of print, London disc. But he was my guest, and I followed his wishes, courtesy overriding my programming preference. Artists, as I repeatedly learned, are not the best judges of their own recorded output. It was an entertaining program, nonetheless, and our mutual friend, Bill Sullivan, had a great time watching the two of us in the studio.

At the end of the Met's 1992-1993 season, Richard Mohr, producer of the Texaco intermission features, and Vinnie Volpe, his longtime associate, retired. Richard was honored by Texaco with a farewell luncheon. All the *Quiz* panelists who were in town attended and contributed brief toasts generally spiced with humor and nostalgia. Richard was a perfect "boss" to us, encouraging us to be ourselves on the air, trying to sound smart, but avoiding needless chatter and self-indulgence. Off the mike, he would deliver hilarious one-liners that contrasted with his phlegmatic, sometimes even icy exterior, never at the expense of those present, but seldom sparing anyone else. Needless to say, a great time was had by us all, and I personally remember Richard Mohr with fondness and gratitude.

Fondness and gratitude were not exactly my sentiments evoked by the *Times* column dealing with the final exit from the broadcast scene of WQXR's *First Hearing*. But what made the commentary of Edward Rothstein, music critic of *The New York Times*, quite remarkable was that it appeared at all, seeing print on September 19, 1993, the day of the show's final broadcast. As far as I can remember, it was the only reference to *First Hearing* in the program's 25-year history in the "newspaper of record." Mr. Rothstein commented that the program's finale "will unite Edward Downes, who has been a regular on the show since it began, with its two godfathers, Robert Sherman and George Jellinek, who has produced the program almost since its debut." The year also signified the death knell of Bob Sherman's popular and important *The Listening Room*, a fact also commented on with regretful sympathy. Mr. Rothstein placed these developments in the proper nationwide context, noting that the absence of sponsor support "is gradually crippling classical radio. Mr. Sherman's shows have helped distinguish WQXR from its New York competitor, WNCN, which has been more aggressive in creating a classical top-100 format." That format, to which I had always been opposed, was ultimately self defeating, because WNCN ceased to be a classical radio station by the end of the year.

Two positive developments enlivened the year 1993 for me. A long-time listener and active patron of the arts, Thea Petschek Iervolino, offered to underwrite *Vocal Gold*, a sister program of *The Vocal Scene*, to be heard on Sunday afternoons. These were rebroadcasts of programs previously heard, but attracted a new group of listeners who had found late evening listening increasingly undesirable. Mrs. Iervolino had contacted several musical groups who couldn't afford commercial advertising, and gave them free airtime within *Vocal Gold*'s allotted three "commercial minutes." This welcome patronage, with minor interruptions, lasted for several years, providing WQXR and me with some additional income and pleasing an enlarged audience. I also began hosting the George London Foundation concerts at the Morgan Library, to be presented by delayed broadcast on Saturday evenings. These were vocal recitals featuring star singers who had begun their careers under the personal tutelage of the late great bass-baritone who had established the foundation in 1971. Years later, with generous outside support, the recitals came into being under the directorship of the late artist's widow, Nora E. London. The programs would begin with a brief interview between myself and one of George London's colleagues. The musical portion would be shared by a former London Foundation winner already established in the operatic forefront (Carol Vaness, Neil Shicoff,

James Morris, among others) and a more recent winner on his or her way to future stardom. Among my interviewees over the years were Licia Albanese, Martina Arroyo, Rosalind Elias, Elaine Malbin, Sherrill Milnes, Roberta Peters, and Theodore Uppman. For the broadcast, the interview portion was placed in the middle of the recital itself—a logical programming sequence I had established from the outset. Nora was always a charming and enthusiastic presence who never failed in encouraging (and praising) my contribution.

In early 1994, J. D. McClatchy, editor of *The Yale Review*, asked me to contribute an article of contemporary musical relevance for the magazine's April issue. I suggested an appraisal of the art and recorded legacy of Nathan Milstein, the great violinist who had recently died. That was my first and only contribution to *The Yale Review*, eagerly accepted because, even at 75, I felt it was never too late to enrich my resume with such a prestigious entry. To make my piece more impressive, I asked for, and received, a very gracious paragraph of collegial admiration from Isaac Stern, completing a brief but altogether pleasant episode in my life.

And, finally, after five years of research, writing, and endless enjoyment despite the long and exhaustive hours, my book, *History Through the Opera Glass*, was published. My publisher, Thomas P. Lewis, who labored with me

With Martina Arroyo and Bob Sherman, ca. 1980.

with patience and dedication through all those years, took it upon himself to provide the substantial index, and added a detailed historical chronology all his own, as a surprise to me. This is the book I always wanted to write. However self-descriptive and accurate as its title was, the book's originality was found confusing by some prospective buyers. Believing it to be just another history of opera, I had to answer such questions as "Were there operas written in ancient Greece or Rome?" Nevertheless, Tom Lewis and I took genuine pride in our achievement. Its hardcover first edition, featuring the beautiful interior of the Teatro Girolamo Magnani of Fidenza (a picture lent to me by Walfredo Toscanini) sold out, and the book is now in soft covers published by Limelight Editions.

Thirty-four years have passed between my first and second books. But at least I was able to catch up with my brilliant and more productive daughter Nancy Berezin, who wrote two volumes, *The Gentle Birth Book* and *After a Loss in Pregnancy*, in the years 1980 and 1981. Their titles are just as descriptive as mine was, but certainly less puzzling.

27. Memorable
Vocal Scene Moments

My *History Through the Opera Glass* was warmly received in several music-oriented journals. Beginning with the Metropolitan Opera Shop, I also did readings, always extremely well attended, at the various New York, New Jersey, and Connecticut branches of the Barnes and Noble and Borders chains and the public library of Hastings-on-Hudson. In the succeeding months, I also visited bookstores in Chicago, Boston, and Seattle, sometimes combined with my other musical activities. At one of our periodic visits to Nancy in Mill Valley, we happily mixed business with pleasure, calling on bookstores in San Francisco and San Rafael. We also flew to Pittsburgh, where WQED-FM, the local radio station, had long been a *Vocal Scene* affiliate. Station manager Jim Cunningham not only treated us to a royal welcome, but also arranged to put me on the air, doing a live broadcast with audience participation from the local Borders branch.

A good (or even bad) appraisal in *The New York Times Book Review* would have helped my cause immensely, but that did not happen. On the other hand, the much-traveled distinguished baritone, Thomas Hampson, stopped by the station one day for a publicity stunt on behalf of the Met, greeted me at my office and told me not only that he had read the book with great admiration, but that he was recommending it to audiences at his various lectures. An even more surprising development occurred several months later when New York's Mayor Rudolph Giuliani, answering a European reporter's inquiry about whatever book the busy mayor was currently reading, he identified my volume in the following manner: "It traces history through operas that were written and that have a historical basis. This is wonderful because it combines the two things I like most: opera and history" (*The International Herald Tribune*, September 19, 1995).

While I am not always a practical person, I had the feeling that since I had frequently entertained artists on radio who were plugging their books, why shouldn't I promote my own within an appropriate context? This resulted in "Opera and the French Revolution," with musical examples from *Le nozze di Figaro, The Dialogues of the Carmelites, Andrea Chénier,* Massenet's *Thérèse,* von Einem's *Dantons Tod,* and Berlioz's luxurious choral arrangement of the *Marseillaise.* All these were rather elegantly enfolded into my *Vocal Scene* No. 1312, with one modest reference to the book that had inspired the program.

Back in early 1971, the third year of *The Vocal Scene,* I had invited Dorothy Kirsten to celebrate the 25th anniversary of her Met debut with me. She was still on stage in 1975, to celebrate her 30th, and again to make her final Met appearance in 1979. According to all the encyclopedias, she was 69 that year, but, when she died in 1992, we learned that she was seven years older. She could have fooled anybody, and probably did. Two years later, I rekindled old memories in a program called "Remembering Dorothy Kirsten," generously quoting Kirsten's sassy and outspoken comments from that early 1971 interview. A remarkable woman, full of energy, she was active in her last years as a spokesperson for the victims of Alzheimer's disease, to which her husband had recently fallen victim. The program, certainly enlivened by Ms. Kirsten's colorful and nostalgic recollections, received an award from an organization called "Excellence in Media," a worthy group that eventually vanished from the scene, reflecting the gradual withdrawal of classical radio from the contemporary culture of our United States.

During my brief tenure at the Juilliard School, Cora Campanella, a vivacious lady and former lyric soprano, attended all my classes and often heard my effusions about Finland's scenic wonders and fascinating musical life. Revealing later that she was the owner of a successful travel agency, she proposed to organize a Scandinavian tour based on my musical recommendations. I placed my fairly generous mailing list at Cora's disposal and, within a few weeks, lively folders went out to advertise a tour centered on the Savonlinna Opera Festival for late July 1994. The minimum attendance of 25 people was easily assembled, and Finnair efficiently deposited our group to Helsinki, with easy airplane transfer to Savonlinna.

Finnish summers are ideal, with flowers blooming under usually blue skies, and Nordic breezes safeguarding the visitors from excessive heat. In all my years visiting that wonderful country, I have never experienced Finland in the winter. Since I don't know any Finnish skiers or skaters, their musical compatriots never really urged us to explore their nation in winter. In fact, on one wintry evening at the Met, I ran into the noted composer Aulis Sallinen. On my greeting: "Are you escaping the Finnish winter?" Sallinen replied, "I started my escape in the fall."

In any case, Savonlinna is in the south of Finland, with ripe strawberries everywhere, giving the town an especially welcoming character. Not far from Savonlinna is the town of Mikkeli, near the Russian border, making it possible for the untiring Russian maestro Valery Gergiev to bring his Kirov Opera Orchestra over for a performance of Beethoven's Ninth Symphony at Mikkeli's cathedral. I introduced myself to maestro Gergiev after the performance. In excellent English, he treated me to an outline of his plans for the Kirov Opera Orchestra and Chorus: "I am planning to do Haydn's oratorio *The Creation*, and Handel's *Messiah*, among other things." When I interrupted his narrative in mild astonishment, observing that the fall of the Soviet Union was still a very recent event, Gergiev replied: "No problem. God is OK in Russia now."

Unacquainted with the art of relaxation, and burning with a messianic fervor to bring Russian orchestral and operatic treasures to the newly approachable West, Gergiev soon became a worldwide celebrity and eventually the Metropolitan Opera's principal guest conductor. There he was mentoring artists of the stature of Galina Gorchakova, Maria Guleghina, Dmitri Hvorostovsky, and several cavernous Russian bassos. The town of Mikkeli launched its own music festival in the following years, with a modern and quite imposing concert hall bearing Martti Talvela's name.

The Talvela home was an important excursion for Hedy, our traveling group, and me. We met little Sofie, the grandchild the tragically deceased Martti never knew, her parents and, of course, our dear friend Annukka Talvela. Also present was our old friend Tatu Tuohikorpi, the man who had started me on my lengthy journeys—actual and musical—through Finnish culture. Annukka guided us through their capacious house, where I recalled that wonderful *hausmusik* Martti had improvised for our delectation in 1985 with baritone Vladimir Chernov. I had my picture taken pretending to be the brooding Russian Tsar, sagged in a plush throne Martti must have bought from an early Finnish production of *Boris Godunov*.

The performances at the Olavinlinna Castle were made, as always, unforgettable by the unique scenic beauty of the place. We heard *Aida* with the excellent Hungarian soprano Ilona Tokody in the title role and the veteran and still impressive Tom Krause as Amonasro. Ms. Tokody and her agent friend Larry Riedermann spent some lively Hungarian moments with Hedy and me at the town's Casino Restaurant. The Finnish-language *Zauberflöte* was old hat for the locals but, on second hearing, still a delightful experience for us. *Tosca* was conducted by Gergiev with his outstanding Kirov cast (Gorchakova, Grigorian, Putilin)—all to become world famous soon thereafter. In *Macbeth*, the title role was mesmerizingly sung by our old friend Jorma Hynninen. With boundless energy and unsparing of voice, he added the mournful aria "Mal per me" for the opera's closing scene—a moment Verdi chose to omit from his final score but few baritones are able to resist.

Jorma, now the artistic director at Savonlinna, used his pull to secure some privacy in a bank office where I taped a brief interview with him. Surrounded by some Hynninen recordings of arias and Sibelius songs, our conversation became the centerpiece of a *Vocal Scene* program called "A Savonlinna Summer," aired on October 6, 1994, by which time the delighted Cora, her happy touring crowd, Hedy, and I were ready to hear the show, revisiting our Finnish memories back home.

The mighty Welsh bass-baritone Bryn Terfel had become an operatic sensation in the interim. I read about him a great deal in the English magazines, discovered his voice through recordings, first in subsidiary roles like Angelotti in *Tosca,* and then in a DG recorded recital of music by Mozart, Mahler, and Wagner. Finally, thanks to Nora London, who had cornered Terfel for one of her foundation concerts in 1995, I was able to enjoy his vivid recital skills, and lost no time to invite him for a radio interview. By then the international press began speculating about Terfel as the "heldenbariton" of the future, surely a Wotan and a Hans Sachs in the making.

Terfel is the kind of guy who makes friends instantly—we were on first-name terms from the outset. His imposing appearance reminded me of my dear late friend Martti Talvela, but without the Finnish giant's innate solemnity. When asked about his response to all that sudden fame and the press frenzy that goes with it, he admitted welcoming the publicity, without allowing it to overwhelm him. "I come from simple Welsh surroundings, and when I visit my family and the folks I grew up with, I want them to recognize me as they once knew me." Terfel dismissed the press-created Wagnerian prophesies: "Wolfram in *Tannhäuser* for now, and we'll see what the future brings." Off the mike, when he asked me what new roles I would suggest to add to his repertoire, I unhesitatingly said "Kaspar. You are perfect for that role physically as well as vocally." Terfel innocently asked, "Who is Kaspar?" The honesty of that reaction astounded me. Another artist in a similar situation would have come up with a diplomatic and evasive answer like "I must look at the music and think about it." When, on mike, I explained that Kaspar is the larger-than-life villain of Weber's *Der Freischütz,* Terfel logically inquired about the opera's box office value in the 1990s, and I hastened to assure him that, should the idea appeal to him, his agent should approach Vienna, Berlin, or Munich. "Considering your current and future standing," I said, "those houses will stage a revival just for you." Our program, ushering in the year 1996, brought Terfel and his engaging personality many new admirers, but he continued choosing his singing activities wisely, usually concentrating on Europe, closer to his family and his Welsh heritage.

Of the dozens of *Vocal Scene* programs dating from these years, several stand out vividly in my memory: a centennial celebration of Kirsten Flagstad, a tribute to Franco Corelli, given poignant meaning for me when I rebroadcast it a number of years later as a memorial tribute, honoring Nicolai Gedda on his 70th birthday, and a tribute to the Teatro Fenice of Venice on its 250th anniversary. An expanded by-product of the Fenice program turned out to be an article for *The Opera Quarterly*. I interviewed Leonie Rysanek on one of the Metropolitan Opera intermissions during her memorable engagement as the Old Countess of Tchaikovsky's *The Queen of Spades*. As it often happens, part of our conversation was edited out due to time restraints, but Michael Bronson, the Texaco producer, gave me permission to use all of the material—with exciting musical illustrations added—for *The Vocal Scene*, so everybody was happy.

In 1995, BMG, the German media giant which had absorbed the once powerful RCA Victor label's entire catalogue (Caruso, Toscanini, Stokowski, Ormandy, Rubinstein, Horowitz, to mention only a few legendary names), released the Heifetz Collection, a monumental edition of 60 CDs embracing the great violinist's comprehensive recorded legacy. The project, under the leadership of Jack Pfeiffer, Heifetz's record producer for decades, took years to complete, and added many titles not included, for reasons of legal conflicts, in the Collection's LP predecessor of two decades earlier. A whole legion of writers annotated the individual discs, among them—posthumously—Irving Kolodin, who had been engaged in RCA's earlier Heifetz project. My friendship with Jack Pfeiffer and his associate Nancy Swift had dated back to the 1960s, when, among other things, I had provided LP annotations for many Heifetz releases. So I wasn't surprised that I was among those selected for the new task, along with Mortimer H. Frank (chief editor), Harris Goldsmith, Richard Freed, Gabriel Banat, and Brooks Smith (Heifetz's longtime accompanist). The happy outcome of the enterprise was that all of us writers, along with producer Jack Pfeiffer, who died of a heart attack in his office soon thereafter, were awarded individual Grammys for our efforts. Mine looks very impressive among the other trophies on my shelves, alongside my father's treasured gold watch, the most valuable souvenir of them all.

In 1995, WQXR celebrated its 60th anniversary on the air with a musical event. In more intimate surroundings, General Manager Warren G. Bodow threw a luncheon party in honor of Lloyd Moss's 40th anniversary with the station. A few weeks prior to the event, Lloyd had published his witty introduction to a child's concert-going, "Zin! Zin! Zin! A Violin."

Following Warren's genial greeting, Lloyd himself set the tone for the lively proceedings with his own characteristically witty, nostalgic and acerbic rhyming commentary, whereupon I rose and greeted him in the following manner:

> He doffs his helmet, parks his bike
> And settles down before his mike,
> Holding forth from three to six
> With talk and music—a lively mix.
> Is he ever flustered? Not a bit
> With his verbal skills and ready wit.
> Just listen with what glee he pounces
> On names he breezily announces
> Like Järvi, Schnittke, and Górecki.
> Rozhdestvensky, Penderecki,
> Ginastera, Georges Enesco,
> Castelnuovo-Tedesco.
> But why go one? The list is long
> And nothing ever comes out wrong
> And, away from pavanes and paso-dobles
> His book is sold at Barnes and Nobles!
> He paints and draws and versifies
> And, as a host, he takes the prize.
> Let us remember, most of all,
> A panel show New Yorkers still recall. [*First Hearing*]
> I ask you: How can you avoid
> Admiring this great colleague, our Lloyd?

It was around this time in 1995 that I received a call from Schuyler G. Chapin, a fellow Bagby trustee, then cultural commissioner of the City of New York under the Giuliani administration. It was Schuyler's job to maintain liaison between the city government and the cultural community, and he felt that Mayor Giuliani, a great lover of opera, should make a brief appearance at our station as an evidence of the mayor's active interest in the city's cultural life. As it often happens in such situations, a spark was instantly lit in my mind. "Qual lampo!" as a Verdi librettist would say, "Schuyler, I have just the right idea. Why don't you ask Mayor Giuliani to appear as my guest on *The Vocal Scene* for a full hour? He doesn't even have to come to us. Set a date and my engineer and I will come to City Hall."

And that is how "*The Vocal Scene* at City Hall" came about. With engineer Phil Ward, we taxied downtown to the historical building and were quickly escorted to a spacious office where Phil quickly set up his compact amplifier, connected to two handy lapel mikes, ready for business. After cordial greetings, the mayor informed us that our interview might be interrupted from time to time, should he be called away on city matters.

With Mayor Rudolph W. Giuliani at City Hall, 1995 (Phil Ward).

Mayor Giuliani is a great opera aficionado, but rarely did he have the pleasure of hearing an entire opera at the Met. As a guest of Joseph Volpe, the general manager, in whose box he would always be welcome, he could depart noiselessly whenever certain emergencies should arise. Unsurprisingly, he favored Italian operas—Scotto, Caballé, Pavarotti, and Domingo being the singers he most admired, but, from his younger years, he recalled nostalgically past performances of Zinka Milanov, Leontyne Price, Franco Corelli, Leonard Warren, and Cesare Siepi. At one point we *were* interrupted by an aide who discreetly whispered something to the mayor's ear, causing him to leave the room for some 10 minutes. On returning, he informed us that there was a serious fire in The Bronx and he stayed in close telephone contact with the fire commissioner on the scene. On being reassured that everything was under control, he returned to complete our taped interview. He was calm, jovial, obviously a public figure accustomed to being interviewed, and not always involving appealing subjects like opera. I expressed my appreciation for having so kindly praised my book earlier in the year in that interview with the European reporter. We shook hands, departed, and in the studio I smoothly inserted excerpts of some of Giuliani's favorite operas and singers as they had come up in our conversation. The program was aired on April 25, 1996 (No. 1426). The gruesome tragedy of September 11, 2001, which elevated Rudolph Giuliani into national fame, was still far in the future.

In late 1995, another favorite of our opera-loving mayor, the great soprano Renata Tebaldi, came to New York to launch a nationwide promotional tour for her authorized biography, *Tebaldi, The Voice of an Angel.* It was the first time in nearly 20 years that she set foot in the city that witnessed some of her greatest triumphs in 17 seasons at the Met. A book signing was arranged for her at the Metropolitan Opera Gift Shop, and she was astounded to watch the line of autograph seekers extending several blocks across Lincoln Center Plaza into Broadway.

By pre-arrangement with the book's translator, Connie de Carlo, the great soprano rushed to my studio soon after the book signing. She was breathless, overwhelmed by the enthusiasm that greeted her everywhere and by the visible signs of public adoration after her long absence from the local

Hedy and I with Renata Tebaldi (center) at WQXR, 1995.

scene. Words were literally gushing from her lips and, while I was absorbing her emotion-laden account, I instantly decided two things. One, that this was going to be two programs, not one. Two, that I would reciprocate Michael Bronson's gesture in a similar situation involving my earlier Met interview with Leonie Rysanek, and make my Tebaldi program available to him. Its partial rebroadcast was shared with the national audience on a Met intermission a few weeks later.

Renata Tebaldi was no stranger to my *Vocal Scene* audiences. I had honored her on her 70th birthday in 1992; years later she became the central figure in my program called "Tebaldi and the Tenors" (Del Monaco, Di Stefano, Bergonzi, Corelli, Tucker), and I featured her in individual arias and Italian songs on innumerable occasions. Now we talked about her youthful years and the roles she then sang—obscure Italian operas, as well as Tchaikovsky's Tatiana and Wagner's Elsa and Eva, all in Italian—before her American associations took wing. Touching on her early career, the bitter Callas-Tebaldi rivalry that had developed in Brazil in 1950 brought no evasions from her. The old wounds were still hurting, but she dealt with them with mature wisdom and *senza rancor.* My two consecutive Tebaldi programs were greeted with an enormous outpouring of affection by the radio audience, and were repeated twice more after 1996. Through Carlo Bergonzi I heard later on that, as a diabetic, she was in declining health and took up an alternate residence in the friendlier climate of San Remo, where that beloved artist died on December 19, 2004, deeply lamented by the entire world. I treasure her memory not only in my countless recordings, but also fondly recalling her absolute mastery of the art of the curtain call, with an all-embracing, galvanizing smile and charming manual gestures that were inimitably her own.

28. Closing the Cycle

The bicentenary of Schubert's birth was in 1997 and, recalling the success I had with my 13-week series honoring the Mozart year of 1991, I proposed a similar Schubertian tribute to WQXR's management. Nowadays a project of this kind is not likely to be aired without commercial sponsorship, and I was hoping for the participation of Austrian Airlines. Apparently, the attempts of our sales department did not produce the desired results, leaving my Schubertian project "unfinished." WQXR honored that great composer with appropriate dignity and splendor throughout the year, with the symphonies, chamber works, and piano sonatas claiming primary representation. Luckily for me, an independent ruler of *The Vocal Scene*, I could forage freely through Schubert's sylvan land of bushes, streams, Erlkings, and moonlit meadows. Five programs were spread through the bicentennial year, exploring the operas (most of which are still unknown to the general public), the masses, the vocal rarities, and two studies exploring some of the greatest Schubert Lieder grouped under the collective titles of "Outdoors with Schubert," and "Schubert and the Four Seasons."

My non–Schubertian programs of the year included a centenary tribute to Rosa Ponselle, a 70th birthday celebration of Leontyne Price, which she graciously acknowledged, a special roundup honoring the visionary orchestral songs of Berlioz, and personal visits with the charming mezzo-soprano Jennifer Larmore, then at the early phase of her career, and the veteran baritone Robert Merrill, who stopped by to reminisce about his Metropolitan memories, coinciding with his 80th birthday. The lustrous voice of the great Rosa reappeared toward the end of the year in one of my fortunate juxtapositions called "Callas and Ponselle," creating parallels between these two contrasting and highly individual divas performing identical arias by Bellini, Ponchielli, and Verdi.

The year had actually begun with an invitation by Stephen Lord, conductor of the Boston Lyric Opera, to lecture to their guild about Massenet's *Werther,* the Lyric Opera's current production. The company had purchased fifty copies of my *History Through the Opera Glass,* which I happily autographed. Since they also took care of our hotel accommodations and treated Hedy and me with kindness and utmost courtesy, it was an altogether delightful visit to a city we very much admire.

With the onset of spring, the time had come for Cora Campanella's devoted band of operaphiles to gather again, this time to join us for an Italian tour centering on three major operatic centers — Milan, Naples, and Palermo. I had learned from Edgar Vincent, Samuel Ramey's press representative, that Sam was going to make his La Scala debut as Méphistophélès in Gounod's *Faust,* coinciding with our schedule. Edgar put me in touch with Sam, who gave me the telephone number of his Milan hotel as well as his promise that he would see his New York fans and me after the performance.

Everything went well. Our hotel was within walking distance from La Scala, which looked as grand as I remembered it, but somewhat on the shabby side, ready for the major reconstruction that would occur within a few years. Sam had a great evening with lengthy ovations for him and his colleagues, particularly tenor Giuseppe Sabbatini, a new name for me in 1997, but securely established among the world's leading lyric tenors in the succeeding years. Conforming to Italian customs, the performance started at 9 P.M. and, with the merciless addition of the *Walpurgis Night* ballet, the evening never seemed to end. But end it did, and Sam Ramey gave me a hug and smilingly welcomed our perseverant group at the appointed place, looking more triumphant than tired.

Unlike the timeworn La Scala, the San Carlo di Napoli glittered in all its 18th-century glory. The city traffic around the bay area had become virtually impassable during the 20 years we had been away, but the theater made up for all relatively insignificant aggravations. Verdi's *Nabucco* was our operatic treat in what appeared to be a new production: imposingly granitic, yet simple in its biblical grandeur. Renato Bruson sang the title role, considerably past his prime, but the Zaccaria of bass Carlo Colombara sounded eloquent and deeply resonant, and the daredevil American soprano Lauren Flanigan brought the house down in the killer role of Abigaille. The grand chorus "Va pensiero sull'ali dorate" has an allegorical significance for Italians and, apparently, it is habitually encored in stage performances. (The new Met production under James Levine adheres to that tradition, also probably mindful of the convenient rest benefiting the solo singers.) Our Naples conductor, Paolo Carignani, dispensed with the traditional repeat, and the local press scolded him for it. Briefly separated from our group, Hedy and I spent a delightful time with our friend, the eminent novelist Shirley Hazzard. She and her late husband, the author-scholar Francis Steegmuller, had established a home in the outskirts of Naples many years ago, and Shirley spends several months there in quietude, usually working on her latest novel.

We flew to Palermo to begin a 3-day Sicilian mini holiday. Our hotel was located on the Viale Mariano Stabile, making me mistakenly believe that it was named after the celebrated baritone favorite of Arturo Toscanini. Later on I found out that Stabile was indeed a Sicilian native, but the man so honored was his grandfather, a hero of the Garibaldian wars. The "modern" Mariano Stabile (1888–1968) was a famous Falstaff in his day, which seemed appropriate, considering that Verdi's last opera was to be the final event on our Italian journey. Interestingly, our performance was staged at the Politeama Garibaldi, because Palermo's famous Teatro Massimo was still under reconstruction. The French baritone Alain Fondary played the earthy-girthy knight with a rough sound but colorful spirit, and Raina Kabaivanska was the charming Alice Ford.

Springtime turned out to be ideal to explore the island and absorb its multi-ethnic traditions. The weather was perfect, the grasses green, and plums and oranges abundant. A tour bus took us to the coastal spa of Mondello for a heavenly lunch, then to Agrigento to admire the ruins of ancient Greek temples. The tour guide, probably a schoolteacher by profession, impressed us with his English, but less so with his blasé personality and unprofessional insistence on setting a quick pace among the ruins, without regard for the advanced age of many of our members, myself included. That forced march made me leave Agrigento with a painful knee condition that stayed with me for nearly a year. A mountain tour to the splendid town of Taormina followed, over scary serpentine roads. Cursed with a lifelong phobia, I had to close my eyes at every turn in preference to enjoying the magnificent vista of the bay below.

Exploring Taormina was an eye-filling experience. Among the ancient houses, we discovered a garden restaurant with a magnificent view of Mount Etna, emitting suspicious rings of white smoke toward the azure skies and placid Mediterranean waters. Knowing that our last day's agenda was a trip to Catania, I suggested to Hedy that we should skip that adventure and spend another day relaxing and exploring Taormina's wonders. Catania is very close to the unruly Etna, and according to other travelers, its air is polluted by floating volcanic ashes. Besides, hitting the road meant another journey down that scary mountain and up again. My strong arguments convinced my nature-loving but otherwise not overly adventurous wife to skip the Catania trip and enjoy the remaining hours gazing at Etna from our choice garden restaurant view. Several fellow travelers followed our example, while the more venturesome friends returned in the evening, moderately enthusiastic about their Catania adventure. The following morning, our bus took us to the Palermo airport and thence, by way of Rome, on the long voyage home.

Soon after our return home, our granddaughter Amy graduated from Middlebury College in Vermont in May 1997 and married her college sweetheart, Matthew Ford, a week later. The wedding took place at the beautiful Lilac Inn in Vermont, a triumphant discovery of our daughter Nancy, who had made the preparations with her customary finicky attention for detail. The wedding party was well attended and — again thanks to Nancy — with a discreet string quartet providing the musical entertainment, very much to my liking, and in contrast to the raucousness that frequently accompanies such events. Amy, looking very pretty, made me happy by choosing me, the only steady father figure in her life, to walk her down the aisle. Our close friends, the Banats and the Calfos, were present, as was Charlie Turi's son, Dr. George Turi, and his wife Sue. Hedy and I spent a relaxing week between the graduation and wedding ceremonies in Burlington, Vermont.

George Turi represented Hedy's side of our family — there were no more living survivors on my side — and he stood in for his younger brother Andy and their father Charles. In less than a month, Charles, Hedy's cousin and very close to me since our Havana years, was also gone. That once high-spirited, ever-optimistic man had suffered a lot during the last five years of his life. It started with a series of strokes that left him paralyzed from the waist down. Then his very attractive wife Ava succumbed to ovarian cancer that ended her life with alarming rapidity. It was heart wrenching to observe our once cheerful Charlie in his wheelchair watching in quiet despair as the casket of his wife was lowered into the ground. I kept remembering our unforgettable wartime meeting at the Brenner Pass in 1945, and other episodes from our young lives with our baby-boomer children playing together as part of an extended, fun-loving family. Having lost my parents, my sister, and Hedy's parents, and haunted by the shadows of an ever-decreasing circle of schoolmates and close friends, at age 77 I felt like a man death had somehow strangely overlooked.

On December 6, 1997, there was an all-day seminar organized by the Smithsonian Associates in Washington, D.C., entitled "Maria Callas Remembered." The panel celebrating the great soprano's life and career consisted of host John Ardoin, authors Nadia Stancioff and myself (three Callas biographers), conductor Will Crutchfield, and Callas colleague Shirley Verrett. We covered various aspects of her remarkable life, with videotapes

Amy and Matt at their wedding in Vermont, 1997.

enriching our discussions, all enthusiastically received by a rather large audience. After an exhausting day, Ardoin, Crutchfield, Stancioff, Hedy and I unwound at a cozy dinner, and raised a toast in Maria's memory, still vibrant 20 years after her passing.

Life went on, and so did my activity at the station. In retrospect, 1998 appears to have been a year of singers' autobiographies. Régine Crespin, Christa Ludwig, and Dame Joan Sutherland had their volumes published, and their agents happily steered these distinguished divas into my studio, one by one. I found Crespin the most entertaining of the three and, not suprisingly, her memoirs, translated by Gladys Bourdin, the most enjoyable, refreshingly candid and outspoken. Talking about the many conductors she had worked with, Crespin admired Karajan, who had persuaded her to add Brünnhilde to her repertoire, even though she didn't think the role was right for her. Her appraisal of Karl Böhm was succinct: "Except for the fact that he didn't like me and I didn't like him, we worked well together." Toward the end of our interview, I couldn't help citing a passage from her memoirs. Answering a San Francisco reporter's indiscreet inquiry as to whether it is advisable to sing after lovemaking, Mme Crespin gave the following succinct advice: "If you do it quickly, yes, but if you do it the French way, I'd say no." Knowing that whatever else would follow our conversation would have been anticlimactic, we ended it right there, leaving her with a bemused smile.

Christa Ludwig, with whom I'd had several very pleasant encounters during her active years, was Crespin's close match in terms of outspokenness and lively anecdotes, especially involving certain outlandish productions in which she had participated "only for the money." Joan Sutherland was more congenial and spirited in her conversation with me than the person revealed in her memoirs, a book rich in information and dutifully enumerated detail, but lacking the warmth and humor of her true personality. Off mike, at her request, she delivered a stinging opinion of the Met's earlier production of *Il trovatore* in which she had participated. (That production did not endure long, and was replaced by one even weirder.) The year also brought out *A Centennial Portrait*, honoring Lily Pons, edited by James A. Drake and Kristin Beall Ludecke. Beverly Sills wrote the foreword to the book, which contained Pons's own recollections as well as André Kostelanetz's nostalgic portrait. Francis Robinson, Andrew Farkas, and Edgar Vincent were among the other contributors. I was responsible for "The Recorded Legacy of Lily Pons," which, in one critic's opinion, was not laudatory enough. I have fond recollections of the great lady, but her voice had certain imperfections which I duly and objectively pointed out in my article. On radio, I did rebroadcast, with great affection, my earlier program with André Kostelanetz, full of André's loving remembrances of his glamorous former wife.

Early in the year, I received an invitation from Indiana University to spend a few days at the campus, interviewing several celebrated singers, all by then professors of the I. U. faculty. This was my second visit to the university, and I am quite sure that my professor friends, János Starker, Imre Palló, and Virginia Zeani (an earlier much admired guest on *The Vocal Scene*) used their local influence to make our visit possible. I chose five distinguished members of the faculty — sopranos Martina Arroyo, Teresa Kubiak, and Virginia Zeani, tenor James King, and bass Giorgio Tozzi — to be interviewed at the studios of radio station WFIU, a longtime syndicated outlet for my program. In between the individual tapings, supervised by WFIU's cordial program director Christina Kuzmych, I delivered a talk to the faculty and students, attended a lovely dinner in our honor hosted by Madame Zeani, and an excellent student performance of Poulenc's *Dialogue of the Carmelites*. The special pertinence of that opera was that Virginia Zeani had been the composer's choice to create the role of Blanche at the opera's world premiere at La Scala in 1957. A portion of that historical performance, a property of Mme Zeani, was part of my interview. Several of my guests contributed rare live recordings, among them Giorgio Tozzi, who brought along an impressive "Eri tu" from his younger years as a lyric baritone. Martina Arroyo, whose engaging liveliness and humor is an interviewer's dream, supplied me with excerpts from live performances on German stages, not otherwise available on commercial recordings. Our all-too-brief Indiana visit ended with dinners with János Starker and Imre Palló, and also Mark Ross Clark, the ever helpful production director of the Indiana University. The five programs emanating from the occasion appeared on five consecutive Thursday evenings on WQXR in October 1998, reaching the 70-odd syndicated stations, including WFIU in Indiana, a month or so later.

I know enough about the sensitive egos, rivalries, and tensions that are concealed beneath the placid surface of academic life, but we experienced none of it during that extremely pleasant week. Returning to WQXR, on the other hand, we found sudden turmoil. Warren G. Bodow, who had succeeded Walter Neiman as president and general manager of the station in 1983, resigned with an abruptness that clearly suggested his resignation was ordained by higher (*New York Times*) authorities. The light-hearted farewell memo that Warren distributed to the staff on May 15 clarified nothing.

Warren's farewell party, held at a Broadway restaurant, a regular WQXR client, was a strange affair. Frank Roberts, head of *The New York Times* Broadcast Group, headquartered in Memphis, and Warren's immediate superior in the *Times* hierarchy, gave a nondescript speech totally lacking in warmth. Warren, known for his quick wit and offbeat humor, chose pointed irony instead, reserving his compliments only for the WQXR staff. We, silent witnesses to this puzzling parade of corporate shenanigans, stood around baffled until a group of jazz musicians broke into some dance music, and the rest of the evening ran its course with a fair degree of normalcy. Warren Bodow, a somewhat aloof and distant personality, always treated me fairly, and we have remained friends to this day. His successor was Thomas Bartunek, former program director, and our music director, Margaret Mercer, was elevated to Tom Bartunek's former position.

Enjoying my relatively carefree existence as a freelance "contractor," in the fall of the year, I delivered a talk at the Casa Italiana of New York University on Schubert and Italy. What made it unusual was that, however far that great composer's fantasy roamed in his brief lifetime, he never set foot in Italy. But he had studied with Antonio Salieri, and composed a celebratory song to the old composer's birthday. He had also written several songs to Italian texts, intended for Luigi Lablache, the noted basso famed for his roles in the operas of Mozart (Leporello), Bellini, and Donizetti. Of course, Schubert, forever in search of operatic glory, also left behind two charming *Overtures in the Italian Style*. It was fun to collect these bits together, and a good-sized audience found the joys of discovery allied with Schubert's gorgeous music an irresistible combination.

To add further praise to the freedom of "freelancing" life, a sudden invitation came my way from a travel organization planning a musical tour down the Danube. In contrast to my proverbial maritime abstinence, I have always loved lakes and rivers and, as a native of that region, I always put the Danube at the top of the list. But, for all my early Danubian memories in Hungary and, to a limited extent, Vienna, the river's northern extension was unexplored terrain for me until 1998. Again, I was engaged as a musical guide for the tour on the ship, the *Mozart*, already a propitious omen. We flew to Munich, where a tour bus transferred our group to Salzburg. While staying at the sumptuous Österreichischer Hof for a couple of days, we visited the child Mozart's erstwhile residence, sauntered around the ancient and crowded Getreidegasse, and attended a performance of *Die Fledermaus* by the unique Salzburg Marionette Theater, elaborately choreographed to one of the Viennese Staatsoper recordings.

Our bus then delivered us to the Bavarian city of Passau by way of the Salzkammergut region, where Hedy and I revisited the famous Im Weissen Rössl (The White Horse Inn). Docked in its Danubian port, the *Mozart* was already waiting for us. The vessel was owned by the Deilmann group, a German shipping company, and on embarking its captain greeted us passengers in two languages (German and English), both tinged with an unmistakable Hungarian flavor. We soon discovered that virtually his entire crew was Hungarian, a circumstance that only added to the enjoyments to follow — an ample cabin, extra-courteous and attentive conversation with the crew in the familiar tongue, and delicious food.

After a walking tour of Passau, we journeyed east on the majestic river, stopping at the medieval town of Dürnstein, remembered in history (so we were told) by the fact that Richard the Lion-Heart was briefly held captive there in the 12th century. Dürnstein is a choice summer resort now, known for its vineyards and many picturesque hostelries. The imposing abbey of Melk, our next Danubian stop, also has an historical significance for this strongly Catholic nation. Given its present luxurious dimensions and state-of-the-art, computerized facilities, the abbey today is a complex many-winged structure of nearly Vatican-like dimensions. There were several tourist groups on the ship, all grouped together for various lectures on Austrian history and culture, with zither solos providing fitting musical interludes. My group then gathered in a smaller room, and I took over with a preparatory talk on Richard Strauss's *Ariadne auf Naxos*, our operatic treat for the evening. As these matters usually happen, friendships are quickly formed on voyages of this kind. So it turned out in our case — music being a mighty bond — by the time we reached Vienna in late afternoon.

The Staatsoper's *Ariadne auf Naxos* was a solid traditional production with Cheryl Studer in the title role. That soprano once enjoyed a meteor-like career in America, and I was glad to hear her still in good form before she faded again from view. The *Mozart* picked up anchor at midnight, with some entertainment to follow but, after a sociable cocktail, we retired for the night. The following morning, after a calorie-laden breakfast, I gave further details on *Ariadne auf Naxos,* an opera barely known to our touring group. Soon we passed Bratislava, our next brief and uneventful stop, and found ourselves in Hungarian waters. On the left bank of the Danube lie the ruins of the ancient castle of Visegrad, destroyed by the Turks in the 15th century, but often excavated since by stubborn archeologists who restored long-forgotten relics from the country's early history. Our ship didn't drop anchor there, but took a sharp turn southward at the Danube bend, and sped toward Esztergom, the site of the ancient Hungarian kings and, eventually, the commanding location of the Basilica, Hungary's most imposing church and the residence of the country's reigning Cardinal.

The rest of the journey was familiar to me from my early past, and the Danubian entry to Budapest was, as always, spectacular. For obvious reasons, we excused ourselves from the obligatory tour of the city, rejoining the group for the evening's concert at the Franz Liszt Academy of Music, guest-conducted by Rudolf Barshai, with cellist Misha Maisky as the featured artist. Hedy's cousins were waiting for us as the *Mozart* entered the port, and joined us on the ship for a lunch of Habsburgian grandeur. We spent a little time with them the following day before our traveling band regrouped again and was taken to the distant Buda hills for a touristy dinner I could have done without. A folk ensemble of singers and dancers did their honorable best, entertaining the appreciative crowds. They responded to the lively rhythms of gypsy music with high spirits but, at that stage of my life, I found no joy in that kind of entertainment, nor did it awaken any childhood memories that might have been sweetened by nostalgic feelings. Something nevertheless stirred in my subconscious, because I told Hedy that I wanted to return once again the following year to celebrate my 80th birthday in Budapest, certainly not for this kind of ethnic revelry, but once more surrounding myself with family members and a few still remaining childhood friends.

We had expected to return home via a direct flight to JFK, but that wasn't to be. Our German tour organizers flew us to Paris's De Gaulle airport (a messy and time-wasting transfer, the reason for which has escaped my unwilling memory), but eventually we came home to land via Lufthansa, with fond memories of the *Mozart*, the beautiful sights along the Danube, and distant Straussian echoes of *Ariadne*. We were also enlivened by the company of new friends, Jude and Patricia Wanniski. Jude, a political economist formerly associated with the *Wall Street Journal*, had acquired a legacy of hundreds of *Vocal Scene* tapes from a deceased uncle. To the present day, he has remained an avid listener, and we are following each other's careers with unceasing interest and involvement.

Possibly inspired by that romantic Danubian journey, Hedy and I decided to celebrate our wedding anniversary (no. 56) with a World Yacht cruise on the Hudson, starting near the Chelsea Piers, circling the Battery and then veering north, taking in the full splendid measure of Manhattan at night, while sipping our drinks and enjoying a pleasant dinner along the way. Our little ship stopped near the illuminated Statue of Liberty, a grandiose view at night, before returning to our customary and more prosaic Manhattan surroundings. My extracurricular activities were modestly but interestingly expanded in the months that followed. The New York Singing Teachers Association, which included many radio listeners among its members, appointed me as a guest speaker and interviewer for their annual meetings. These were intimate, non-ceremonial affairs, and I recall entertaining interviews honoring Grace Bumbry, Jerry Hadley, Judith Blegen, Simon Estes, and Deborah Voigt on the association's behalf in succeeding years.

An entirely different "appointment" materialized shortly thereafter. We met a very friendly Westchester couple, Raymond and Gail Watkins. Ray is a chemical engineer with far-flung international connections, while Gail is a third-grade teacher at Hastings' very highly rated Hillside School. She specializes in music and art, very proud of her success with gifted children, and invited Hedy and me to drop in at one of her classes. Impressed by the eagerness with which the kids responded to Gail's enthusiastic talk on music and musicians, enlivened by video clips of familiar orchestral and operatic favorites, I offered to make annual visits to her class and engage them in music-related conversations. It evolved into a yearly event, attended by several involved parents. For all my experiences as a teacher, I am not sure that I was able to communicate to 9 and 10-year-olds at the appropriate level, but the kids seemed to enjoy my brief talks and musical illustrations on CD and video. The parents certainly responded with keen interest, and so did the local papers. This isolated example shows that in our times, where basic musical appreciation has virtually disappeared from school curricula, the efforts of a lonely but highly motivated teacher like Gail Watkins can make a difference in responsive youngsters' lives.

Although originally not so intended, I have since discovered that, in tracing the circuitous narrative of my life, I have been following what musicians recognize as the "rondo treatment," where the principal theme frequently reappears between other subjects in the musical fabric. My story's rondo theme is *The Vocal Scene*, which had passed its 30th continuous year on the air in 1998. I briefly — very briefly — entertained the thought of retiring from it, but then I decided that round numbers *per se* mean very little in the overall scheme of things. I was still in reasonably good shape physically as well as mentally. Dr. Macken urged me not to reduce my activities, and I remembered the wisdom of the old golfer Sam Snead, who was once asked by a reporter if he considered retirement at age 60. "Listen," Sam replied, "at my stage of life I can do only two things right. I play golf and I fish. Since this is what I am doing now, what am I going to retire to?" Since I don't even fish, I began my 80th year of life and 31st season on the air in the good-natured company of Joe Pearce, the witty secretary of the Vocal Record Collectors Society, with a program called "Odd Couples." The title was naturally inspired by the Neil Simon play, but consisted of unexpected musical pairings of singers. (Tonio's "Prologue" by tenor Mario del Monaco and Canio's "Vesti la giubba" by baritone Lawrence Tibbett, succeeded by Paul Robeson and the great Ukrainian tenor Ivan Kozlovsky singing a duet, were good examples of our jointly conceived zany programming.)

There were a few other surprising ideas among the new year's radio offerings. "Two Baroque Beauties" was among them. The idea was simple in its concept, but required a certain amount of thought in execution. The "Beauties" in question were Handel's "Ombra mai fu" and Giordani's "Caro mio ben," both familiar but irresistible pieces. Hearing the same selections performed by different interpreters has always been a crowd pleaser — my crowd, in any case. My choices for Handel were Caruso (one of his late recordings, from 1920), followed by the rising countertenor David Daniels, Tito Schipa, Jennifer Larmore, Marilyn Horne, and Dmitri Hvorostovsky. All great singers, presenting imperishable music in the tenor, countertenor, mezzo, and baritone alternatives — how could such a sequence sound repetitious or even boring? For "Caro mio ben," the only reason for the immortality of the highly prolific but obscure church composer Giuseppe Giordani, my choices included Elly Ameling, Cecilia Bartoli, Ezio Pinza, Tito Gobbi, Richard Tucker, Carlo Bergonzi, and Luciano Pavarotti. They sang with accompaniments embracing solo keyboard, solo guitar, a Baroque ensemble, and other alternatives, with the characteristic timbres of these great voices adding the needed variety. Again, how could I go wrong?

With *The Vocal Scene* achieving a certain semi-institutional reputation over the years, I became somewhat spoiled as celebrated artists sought me out instead of the other way around. But the case of Cecilia Bartoli, the unique mezzo who had attained huge international success through her videos, recordings, and recitals, was different. Here was an artist on the Marilyn Horne level, with a lighter sound but equally brilliant in florid music, not satisfied with being typecast as a "Rossini singer," but constantly looking for new fields to conquer. Edgar Vincent was her publicist in the 1990s, so I made a contact through him, and Cecilia soon breezed in, a small but full-figured young woman in a black leather jacket and matching pants, all business and ready, almost eager, to talk. Her speech was animated by the agile facial muscles noted from her video appearances. Among other things, she was a true scholar, always eager to discover unfamiliar musical gems from the 18th century by Vivaldi, Gluck, Salieri, and their contemporaries, not to mention the Italian poems of Metastasio, Vittorelli, and the ubiquitous Anonymous, set to music by Beethoven, Mozart, and Schubert. She recorded many of her discoveries because her label, Decca, knew that nothing chosen by Bartoli would be less than a best seller. I was enchanted by her intense and vibrant personality, and not really surprised that the Met's huge interior would not be the right venue for Bartoli's mercurial art. As a matter of fact, her operatic activity has lately been limited to the European theaters.

Soon after being exposed to the whirlwind animation of Bartoli's youth, I met Elisabeth Söderström's worldly wisdom before a live audience at Lincoln Center, organized by the Metropolitan Opera Guild. She was already in her seventies, having progressed from light lyric soprano roles to a sensitive zone where stage characterizations take precedence over vocal allure, and singers are perceived as "singing actresses." She was already making her farewell appearances in Europe when the Met offered her the part of the Old Countess in Tchaikovsky's *Pique Dame*, a powerful stage role previously associated with Regina Resnik and, more recently, with Leonie Rysanek. Initially doubtful about accepting the engagement, she rose to the challenge when told that Plácido Domingo would be the dissolute gambler Gherman, her stage antagonist. Ms Söderström's lively theatrical persona worked extremely well in the intimate surroundings of Lincoln Center's Kaplan Auditorium, and I was delighted when the guild allowed me to share with my radio audience an edited version of our conversation, obviously dominated by my spellbinding guest, in a program that included her exceptional recording of Schubert's "Erlkönig."

Another study of how artists of stature confront the declining stage of a once glorious career was witnessed by me at a rather close range. It involved Sherrill Milnes, whom I had known since his Met debut in 1965 and initially interviewed on the air in 1990, on the occasion of the 25th anniversary of his Met debut. By that time, we were friends and shared a deep appreciation of our respective careers. On that earlier occasion, Sherrill reminisced about the beginning of his career and spoke very touchingly about his parents, whom he had lost in recent years. He brought along two private recordings of songs in which his mother (an accomplished teacher and choral director) acted as his accompanist. Recalling the events, he had tears in his eyes and, haunted by my own childhood memories, I was near tears myself. By 1999, Sherrill's autobiography had come out, and in that second interview he freely discussed his delicate throat operation which forced cancellations of several engagements. These, in turn, brought about a constant diminution of his Met appearances, aggravated by a tense relationship with the Met management and, finally, the break of their 32-year association. Sherrill took this turn of events bitterly, unwilling to accept the fact that singers — all singers — must face a noticeable decline in their vocal resources when they reach their sixties (if not sooner). Having heard his Amonasro during those crucial years prior to his retirement, I knew that he no longer lived up to the standard he himself had set in his prime. As artists age, they are forever challenged by the memories of their younger and widely recorded selves. He is a warm-hearted man, a dear friend, and strong enough to put this bitter episode behind him. But I must completely agree with Sherrill that the Met should have handled the situation with infinitely more understanding and delicacy.

Honoring great singers and great singing had always been one of the principal missions of *The Vocal Scene*, and it was particularly true of the year 1999, when I offered the powerful pair of Birgit Nilsson and Jon Vickers in scenes from *Tristan und Isolde*. I also interviewed Deborah Voigt, a recent winner of the Richard Tucker Award and about to embark on a brilliant international career, which eventually was to encompass some of Nilsson's famous roles. But there were also programs of a certain originality, devised mainly for my own enjoyment, hoping that my audiences would appreciate the thought that went into them. Such an undertaking was "Echoes of *Don Giovanni.*" It displayed the wide-ranging influence that great opera had on the music of Offenbach, Beethoven, Hummel, Chopin, and Liszt. In each case, I presented part of the original Mozart episode that had caught the fancy of a later generation and inspired fantasies, variations, and sometimes brief and passing echoes of *Don Giovanni* that formed the real essence of my program.

In the summer of 1999, we were making plans for our visit to Budapest in conjunction with my approaching 80th birthday. Since I was born in December, not an ideal time to visit Hungary, we decided to travel in September, instead. Budapest's 100-year-old Gundel Restaurant, a local landmark, was partly owned by George Láng, of New York's Café des Artistes. A fellow George Washington Award recipient and an old friend, George and I went over the details involving a special banquet room for about 25 guests, agreed on the finances, and the invitations quickly followed. Our relatives on both sides were contacted by phone, as were my friends Miklós Róna in Switzerland, Joe Marton in Pennsylvania, and George Besnyö-Braun in Budapest.

My memories with the legendary Gundel go back to my childhood. Aside from its culinary reputation, the restaurant, located within the confines of the Budapest Zoo, was naturally a rare treat for my sister and me when our mother took us there in the days before we still lived in suburban Ujpest. Later, during my brief residence in the big city, it served as the locale for opera performances in concert form during the summer, and I still remember an *Aida* with the Hungarian-born American soprano Anne Roselle in the title role. This is the name under which she was internationally recognized and recorded, but in her native surroundings she was known by her original name as "Gyenge Anna."

Now it was my last time to revisit Ujpest, where I was born and educated, where I learned to swim and rabidly rooted for the local soccer team, where I was once a part of a large extended family of aunts and uncles and little cousins. With very few exceptions, they were all to perish in the holocaust, perhaps wistfully remembering that lucky relative who had escaped to America, the land of riches and unimaginable career opportunities. I also said goodbye to my grandfather's old house, and the gymnasium where I learned a lot in preparation for a life entirely different from what destiny had in store for me. Nowhere did I linger long, because I was anxious to confirm that all my guests would be present for my birthday dinner. Miklós Rona was already in town, staying with his sister Ágnes, a lawyer already in retirement and caring for her severely ill husband. Ágnes couldn't come, nor could a former classmate named László Sólyom, a noted playwright who, after having been banned during the communist regime, sank into a deep depression that caused him to avoid contact with everyone, including me, his friend from first grade. George Hivessy was severely ill and under doctor's orders not allowed to leave his house after sundown. But he joined us for breakfast at our hotel, and for a rather emotional final hug.

Hedy's relatives, a large family of four generations headed by Hedy's first cousin Marianne (Marcsi), in her late seventies and already a great-grandmother, were all living either in the same old ancestral house or near to one another in a closeness barely possible in America, except, possibly, in close-knit old-line Italian families. There were Gábor and Zsuzsa, the two children of my own late cousin Bandi, with their spouses and children, Gábor's son Peter being the only blood relative to carry on my family's surname. The enormous oval-shaped table was completed by my childhood friends and George Besnyö's wife Sári. There was no music, but lots of conversation oriented more to the present than the past. Hedy and I were happy to note that all family members pursued good careers, enjoyed good health, and that the young generation had every right to look to a promising future.

My friend George Láng saw to it that the Gundel people took extra-special care of us and, after the giant birthday cake and the traditional apricot brandy, the party gradually dissolved. The following day, Hedy and I walked around the streets of Budapest, taking yet another shot at the Hungarian State Opera House, before George Lendvai, (yet another George, married to Marcsi's daughter and Hedy's namesake) delivered us to the train station. The train rides between Budapest and Vienna is singularly unvaried but at least relaxed, with a tasty *chicken paprikás* on the dining-car table. For people not in a hurry, it was much preferable to a short but tumultuous plane trip that would have landed us in Vienna's outskirts, rather than the heart of the city.

I had never visited Vienna in the fall, and we were lucky to find the city in full autumnal splendor, walking ankle-deep in fallen golden leaves around the Ringstrasse and in the various parks, accompanied by our Swiss friend Elisabeth who had come over from her lakeside home to spend a day with us. The three of us met Einzi Stolz at the Hotel Imperial for lunch, and she imperiously dismissed my attempt to reach for the check. That turned out to be the last time we met that unforgettable lady, who died five years later at age 92, enterprising and energetic to the end. For dinner at one of our favorite Viennese restaurants we were joined by the Steckelhubers, close friends of ours from Harrison, N.Y., native Austrians who were visiting aged parents there.

So this is how the cycle closed, a 19-year-old youngster returning to the place of his birth at age 80, perhaps wiser but most certainly older. "You can't go home again," as the saying goes. You may visit places and recall childhood memories, but your home is elsewhere.

At radio station WQXR, my musical home, as the year's end approached, I was told by Gina Dona, our publicity director, that a special birthday luncheon was being planned in my honor on or near my actual birthday, December 22. In addition to my longtime radio colleagues, the following invitation went out to personalities associated with the Texaco-Metropolitan Opera broadcasts:

Please join us at a very special 80th birthday luncheon for our friend George Jellinek: writer, teacher, opera devotee, and cherished colleague.

The event was held on December 20th at the Belmont Room of the Metropolitan Opera. Tom Bartunek saluted me in glowing terms, followed by warm tributes by Mike Quinn, Texaco's longtime liaison to the Metropolitan Opera, and Lloyd Moss on behalf of my radio colleagues. I received a beautiful Tiffany plaque inscribed as follows:

> To George Jellinek
> In recognition of your devotion to opera and music,
> which you have unselfishly shared with radio listeners
> across the country.   12/22/99
> Affectionately, your friends at Texaco-Metropolitan Opera
> International Radio Network and
> 96.3 FM WQXR

I was pretty emotional in my response, sharing the spotlight with Texaco's Michael Bronson, Elaine Warner, Ellen Godfrey, Ed Beaty, and *Texaco Quiz* associates Bill Livingstone and Martin Bernheimer. Among the WQXR colleagues I am shown individually embracing are Gina Dona, Nimet Habachy, June LeBell, and others too numerous to mention. I specially cherish a letter from my eminent *Quiz* colleague Father M. Owen Lee of Toronto, a true Renaissance man of universal erudition. Aside from his eloquent congratulation, Father Lee revealed that I held the honor of having been most frequently paired with him on the *Texaco Quiz*, an association we mutually treasure.

Since the love of opera has formed such a lasting link in my complex life, I find a certain symbolic significance in being honored at the Metropolitan Opera at that particular time. Within a few days a new century was dawning, and I was still pursuing an active and fulfilling life.

Epilogue

My activities in the new century settled into a relaxed mode. In relatively good health, I continued *The Vocal Scene* with a slight reduction in the number of new productions and a corresponding increase in the rebroadcasts of earlier favorites. My nationwide audience voiced no objections and I recognized that my "easing up" was properly in tune with the life of an octogenarian. There was no decline in my creative urges: I was pursuing new program ideas with the eagerness of old, though a sense of wistfulness and nostalgia continued to darken my mood as the end of *The Vocal Scene* was approaching — by my choice.

In the meantime, I remembered the centenary of Puccini's *Tosca* with a stellar sequence of great interpreters through the decades. I welcomed Renata Scotto after a 20-year absence, and was gratified when she reminded me that it was "about time." Her comments were wise and enlightening. Listening to her recorded rendition of Violetta's farewell aria from *La traviata* ("Addio del passato"), she concentrated on the subtle contrast between the first and second stanzas. Many sopranos and conductors omit this repeat, but the aria is more poignant when the two musically identical but textually and emotionally divergent verses are left intact.

On May 21, 2001, I presented "A Björling-Wunderlich Parallel," a predictably irresistible program in which the two wonderful tenors performed identical musical selections, offering my listeners an unforgettable double treat. Thanks to the courtesy of the Met Opera Guild's Clarie Freeman, I was able to include my highly entertaining "live" discussion with José Van Dam, which had taken place at Lincoln Center's Kaplan Penthouse a few weeks earlier. When I reminded the audience of the great baritone's eminence in his native Belgium, calling him a "virtual king," he modestly demurred: "Not quite, but ... maybe a prince."

The morning of September 11, 2001, started like a routine autumn day.

Hedy and I left our apartment at about 8:30, bound for WQXR's studio, where I had planned to record tenor Rockwell Blake. Ten minutes later, I turned on the radio for the morning news and heard our announcer, Gregg Whiteside, refer to a "horrendous accident" involving the World Trade Center. When we reached the Hudson River toll bridge that separates The Bronx from Manhattan Island, the police urged us to turn around and return home. With the radio on, we gradually became aware of the unthinkable. Nancy was supposed to be in Washington, D.C., that morning and, hearing about the attack on the Pentagon, we could hardly wait to contact her in California. Her flight had been canceled; she was safely at home, sharing the anxieties with us and the rest of America.

I am writing these lines in early March 2006, and feel no need to comment on the calamitous events that propelled the nation toward a tragic war and the fateful entanglement in the Middle East. With no end in sight, our leaders are caught in a quagmire of their own creation. The final chapter of my own life — so insignificant in the context of the circumstances that surround us — will continue without further reference to these events that have brought vulnerability to our nation's existence and have beclouded my thoughts ever since.

Rockwell Blake's visit, canceled during the days immediately following 9/11, was re-scheduled soon thereafter, dazzling the audience with the tenor's familiar high-note wizardry. Then I hosted an array of some of the best of the world's current mezzo-soprano abundance. First, in the twilight of her great career and recently honored by Opera Index, Grace Bumbry breezed in happily, followed a few days later by Susan Graham, who regaled me and my audience with her dazzling Berlioz, to say nothing of her sunny personality that immediately established an entertaining conversational intimacy between us, the kind that rarely happens at first meetings. Soon thereafter, Vivica Genaux — whom I had previously met through Karen Nelson, Vivica's publicist — arrived, causing a furor among our announcing staff, all clamoring for her photos. In the succeeding months, I discovered Vivica as an immensely attractive recitalist, with a physical allure enhancing a vibrant stage persona. For me, her expertise in the Spanish and Latin American repertoire merely added an extra zest to the total charming package.

Resorting to my fondness for alliteration, I also honored "Lotte Lehmann's Lieder Legacy" in 2002 (No. 1729), and soon thereafter, I welcomed Renée Fleming for a return engagement on *The Vocal Scene*, where she had been introduced six years earlier, at the beginning phase of her career. She was at her peak in 2002, a true prima donna of the operatic world, preparing for Bellini's *Il pirata* at the Met. The selections I chose highlighted her versatility: Mozart, Bellini, Dvořák, Massenet, and Richard Strauss. She gave me and my audience valuable personal insights to the arias discussed, explaining, among other things, why "Dove sono" (the Countess's aria from *Le nozze di Figaro*), seeming so simple in the printed score, is so difficult to master for a young soprano. Turning to Massenet's *Thaïs*, I made the observation that Thaïs, a person living in the 3rd century, was as tormented by the idea of fading youth and beauty as was the Marschallin, the sophisticated 18th-century character in Strauss's *Der Rosenkavalier*. Renée musingly added that this particular anxiety affects women in all epochs, including herself. Toward the end of the program, I asked her this question "How are you taking fame?" I meant fame at her own Olympian level, starring in new productions at the world's leading theaters, hugely successful and munificent recording contracts, popular adulation, and so on. Renée's answer was honest but far from simple. "Increased fame brings increased expectations and new challenges. I take a historical view of my career. With a narrowing repertoire, I still have fields to conquer. I cannot end my career without performing Verdi's Violetta. As for fame, I thank my lucky stars." (Her first Violetta, Houston first, then the Met, was to happen in about a year.)

Renée Fleming, ca. 2000.

At the end of 2002, I made the decision to stop creating new programs. I am a long-range planner to a fault. I do everything in advance, try never to miss a deadline, never to work under extreme pressure. This goes with a severe self-discipline, bordering on rigidity, that has always guided me in my work. It is not necessarily a virtue. In any case, I was going to repeat previous *Vocal Scene*s I regarded especially valuable during 2003 and planned to depart from the scene in December 2004. Having made that decision, contrary to Hedy's wishes, I so informed Tom Bartunek and Margaret Mercer. Over the years, I have accumulated a mailing list of about 500 recipients who then would receive forthcoming program titles for the next three months. Toward the end of 2002, I received a call from Jack Mastroianni, manager of several celebrated singers. "George, Mirella Freni is coming to New York next week for a brief period. She will do *Fedora* with Plácido Domingo. I can squeeze in an interview with you, if you can arrange it."

I told Mastroianni that, unfortunately, *The Vocal Scene* is about to fold its tents forever, my advance programs are already printed, and, regretfully,

I must say no. We ended the conversation, I hung up and 10 seconds later I grabbed the receiver again, saying "Jack, I changed my mind. I'll be delighted to see Miss Freni. Call me and we'll set a date."

During those 10 seconds, these thoughts raced through my mind: "Am I crazy being such a slave of *my own schedule*? Why should I pass up an opportunity to interview one our generation's outstanding sopranos? Who would benefit by this omission? Who else but I would later regret it? Mirella Freni came to my studios, and the program aired on November 21, 2002. She was very charming and allowed me to choose the musical selections that represented her at her lyrical prime, at various salient points of her career, from the mid–1960s, conducted by Solti, Abbado, and Karajan, with her appropriate fond recollections. I am happy not to have missed the opportunity, and learned my lesson, but I suppose I was too old by that time to rid myself of such flights of inflexibility.

The year 2003 went by uneventfully, while I was contemplating the radio events leading up to the final program of *The Vocal Scene*. On July 7, 2004, Pavel Lisitsian, the great Russo-Armenian baritone, died at age 92. He was one of my all-time favorites whom I had featured many times in the past. Countless listeners discovered his artistry through my programs and have voiced their enthusiasm for his rich and uniquely bright sound. Instead of rebroadcasting one of my earlier programs, I decided to pay this exceptional artist a newly assembled final tribute that aired on October 7, 2004.

And so it went until the final week of 2004, until *The Vocal Scene* No. 1878, which I had titled "A Farewell to All." It was all about leave-taking, and it began with the operatic counterpart of Shakespeare's "parting is such sweet sorrow" from Gounod's *Roméo et Juliette* with Angela Gheorghiu and Roberto Alagna as the tragic lovers. Manon's farewell to her little table followed, with Bidú Sayão's sweet and tear-provoking sound and, for a lighter touch, Joan Sutherland and Luciano Pavarotti in their endless *Addios* in *Rigoletto,* followed by a similarly prolonged farewell between Mirella Freni and José Carreras in the last scene of *Don Carlo.* Appropriate *Lebwohls* (Schubert), *Adieus* (Bizet), *Addios* (Rossini) eventually led to *Adiós Granada,* Victoria de Los Angeles's favorite encore piece to her own guitar accompaniment.

Finally, under the strains of Haydn's "Farewell" symphony, I began my own, somewhat emotional farewell, the conclusion of which went as follows:

> My close friends and professional associates who know me regard me as a modest person. But my modesty has its limits, and I am not modest enough to deny that I am very proud of what I have accomplished in the

past 36 years. You heard the world's greatest singers on *The Vocal Scene,* many of them previously unknown to you. Every one of my nearly 2000 programs was conceived with a central idea in mind, and your thousands of letters, postcards, and E-mail messages have assured me of your enthusiastic appreciation.... Thank you all for having enjoyed my work and making this great journey possible for me.

I had a very important guest with me to witness my last program on the air, while watching me work and communicate with Juliana Fonda, my sound engineer. She was Janet Malcolm, noted author and longtime contributor to *The New Yorker.* As an occasional listener to *The Vocal Scene,* she became particularly attracted to my program called "Eight ways to sing an aria." She had left a message for me with Gina Dona, WQXR's public relations director, and I called her back and invited her to visit me at the station, exploring the possibility of a *New Yorker* article. That was our first meeting, to be followed by several phone conversations, a visit to our apartment in Hastings, and a desire on Janet's part to sit in on my farewell program. During our first taped conversation at WQXR, I learned that we had a few things in common, notably our Central European heritage. A native of what is now the Czech Republic, Janet had come to the United States as a child with her parents. While I was recording my farewell program, she made copious notes, as a good reporter would, and — as it became gradually evident to me — the prospective article was already taking shape in her mind. "It depends on the approval of my editors," she answered my curious inquiries in a cautionary mood to keep me from taking it all for granted.

The article, called "The Émigré," appeared in the November 24, 2004, issue of *The New Yorker,* four weeks before my final program. Very perceptively, Janet placed my character in the context of the émigré experience with its attendant tendency toward over-achievement. To say that it was complimentary to me was an understatement. The timing of it was propitious, and the relevance of its coinciding with my departure from *The Vocal Scene* was not lost on the industry. Most surprising to me was a very warm-hearted article by Frank L. Prial, wine reporter of *The New York Times,* which appeared on Thursday, December 23, the very day of my farewell broadcast. Prial was a longtime listener, but we never had a personal contact before. We had lunch together at a Hastings bistro before departing for home, where he admired my huge record collection. Commenting later in his article, Prial said, among other nice things, that "Almost unnoticed except among dedicated fans, New York is losing one of the oldest and best loved facets of its opera life: after some 36 years, George Jellinek's weekly radio program, *The Vocal Scene,* is going off the air."

That wasn't all. David Hinkley, columnist of the *New York Daily News,* contributed a warm-hearted article that ran the day before my farewell broadcast, and Iris Hiskey Arno, in *The Rivertowns Enterprise*, my local newspaper, ran an illustrated item honoring this fellow Hastings resident in early January. That kind of sudden and widespread eminence was a rare event for me, but I certainly enjoyed it while it lasted. It lasted well beyond early January 2005 when, at the invitation of the Museum of Television and Radio (25 West 52nd Street, NYC) I was treated to "A Conversation with George Jellinek," hosted by my dear colleague Bob Sherman. A fairly large audience was treated to several segments of *Vocal Scene* episodes chosen by Rebecca Paller, curator of the museum, accompanied by Bob's entertaining commentary while I was basking in all that affection and merriment. Miss Paller and I subsequently selected dozens of my programs assembled over the years, to be stored at the museum ready to be enjoyed by listeners of future generations, assuming that my long activity will have some meaning to those generations.

My connection with radio station WQXR has never really ended. I still have my old desk and files, and I still perform activities useful to the station. When three glorious singers — Renata Tebaldi, Victoria de Los Angeles, and Robert Merrill — left us for a better world within a short period of time, I quickly assembled a "Triple Tribute" honoring all three of them, all once lovingly remembered on *The Vocal Scene*, my private Pantheon.

In June 2005, Hedy and I became great grandparents of an adorable girl named Ava Ewyn Ford, currently a New England resident. And these lines are written in early 2006, when the world of music celebrated the 250th anniversary of Mozart's birth. Radio Station WQXR honored the event with many special tributes originating in New York, Vienna, and Salzburg. One of them was 26 "Mozart Vignettes" spread throughout the broadcast hour, written and narrated by this stubbornly reluctant retiree.

While I was exploring the fascinating events of Mozart's life, I received a call from Ambassador Dr. Gábor Horváth, consul general of the Republic of Hungary, with surprising news. Apparently, Dr. Horváth had submitted my name to the president of Hungary for an award honoring my activities on behalf of Hungarian culture over the years. Once award is granted, he assured me, it would be presented to me at one of the cultural events to be scheduled at the consulate.

It occurred on Wednesday, May 31, 2006, at the miniature concert hall of the Consulate General. The Bartók Quartet performed Mozart's "String Quartet in B flat, K. 458" and Bartók's "String Quartet No. 1." But first, I was called to the podium by Dr. Horváth, who, on behalf of the president of the Republic of Hungary, bestowed upon me the Knight's Cross of the Order of Merit of the Republic of Hungary "in recognition of his activities for enhancing better appreciation and understanding of Hungarian classical music internationally and particularly in the United States."

I accepted the award with an appreciative speech and the concert began. While the quartet was playing, my wandering thoughts first skipped back to 1939, the year I left Hungary as a 19-year-old exile. The image of my father's tearful goodbye at the train station lingered in my consciousness for a long while, leading to cascades of fast-moving but blurry impressions of all that followed in the more than sixty years of anxieties, tensions, challenges, and accomplishments.

The Schiller motto that has guided me through my life makes its first appearance earlier in these pages, when I was still a homeless youngster between youth and adulthood, literally at sea. The poet's lines speak the truth but offer no easy solutions to the mysteries of life. Mine has been worth living.

Index